Inside the Lightning Ball elong

UFO Ex

Irena McCammon Scott, PhD

Published by Flying Disk Press in 2018

Flying Disk Press

4 Saint Michaels Avenue

Pontefract

West Yorksire

England

WF8 4QX

CONTENTS

Acknowledgements

I am greatly indebted to many people who made this work possible: Special thanks to the initial ufologists I met: Paul and Becky Burrell; Bill Jones, J.D., former Senior Contracting Officer for Federal Projects at Battelle Memorial Institute (Battelle) and Ohio director of the Mutual UFO Network; Pete Hartinger, director of the Roundtown UFO Society; and Jennie Zeidman, who worked with Dr. Hynek, at Battelle, in Wright-Patterson AFB's Project Blue Book and in many similar positions. Additional investigators who originally brought me into ufology include members of the Mid-Ohio Research Associates: Frank Reams, pilot; Joe Stets, Battelle scientist; Rebecca Minshall; and Barbara Spellerberg, as did Warren Nicholson, Battelle scientist; Jean and Richard Siefried; and Paul Althouse. Thanks also to Robert Snow and Andrew Watson for proof reading of my manuscript.

Many others helped me in numerous ways including: Phyllis Budinger, MS, former research scientist from BP/Amoco and head of Frontier Analysis, Ltd.; writer, publisher and investigator Rick Hilberg; Budd Hopkins, artist, abduction authority and author of many seminal UFO books; my sister, Sue Postle; and J. Allen Hynek, PhD, noted astronomer, writer, founder the Center for UFO Studies and father of ufology. Many thanks to ufologists Chris Parsons, Aaron Clark, Thomas Wertman, Linda Stephen Sodomire, and the many others from Ohio MUFON, the Cleveland ufology project and Starlight and those interviewers listed in Chapter 1.

Other ufologists have included Walter Andrus, former head of MUFON, with whom I edited a number of MUFON Symposium Proceedings; and Leonard H. Stringfield, who told me about his intensive investigation of the UFO phenomena including Wright Patterson AFB. Julia Shuster, daughter of Walter Haut, who was the Roswell Air Base public information officer who put out its press release about the UFO.

Additional people who were of immense help included William Allen, Ohio State University professor emeritus who had published his own experience; Robert Dixon, PhD, former director of the Ohio State University Radio Observatory "Big Ear," director of the Argus and SETI projects; Kathleen Marden, niece of Betty Hill and abduction expert; and Walt Mitchell, PhD, former Astronomy Department professor at OSU. Also, State of Ohio seismologist Mike Hansen, PhD and Mr. Reams, William Carlisle and Rick Shackelford, with whom I worked at the Defense Intelligence Agency, were very helpful. French ufologist Jean Sider and I wrote several articles and the Cordell Hull family members helped with other stories. Art Sill, PhD; Brian Thompson, PhD; Jan Aldrich; fire chief, Virgil Newell; and many others have provided great help. My family including John and Rosa Scott who tolerated and aided this work, were also very helpful.

Harley D. Rutledge, PhD, in his Project Identification study whose discussions with me greatly aided my understanding of the phenomena. I wish to thank writers Lee Jansen, John and Jan Brinkerhoff and Randall Silvis, who helped me with the writing, Daniel Del Toro for the illustrations and Rick Hilberg, Phyllis Budinger and Jennie Zeidman for the photographs.

Still others who I have met or corresponded with include: Timothy Good, author and investigator; James Spangler; Jerry Ehman, PhD, discoverer of the "Big Ear" telescope 'WOW' signal; Stanton Friedman, nuclear physicist and ufologist; Bruce Maccabee, PhD; and Leo Sprinkle, PhD Others include Beverly Trout, Robert Orndoff, PhD, Linda Wallace, Barb Osborne John Carpenter, Stan Gordon, Diana DeSimone, John Timmerman, Bruce Widaman and Terry Hamilton. Bob Collins, who was operative "Condor" of the Aviary; and Donald Schmitt, Tom Carey and Anthony Bragalia, UFO authors, who have spent a great deal of time exploring the field. Especial thanks also to the many very helpful and insightful witnesses and experiencers that I interviewed.

And many thanks to Bruce Ashcroft, PhD, Wright-Patterson AFB historian and archivist, who invited me to meetings, discussed UFOs with me, showed me around the AFB and helped me to understand much about ufology.

I wish to extend very special thanks to Philip Mantle, director of Flying Disk Press the publisher of this book, whose effort has very greatly improved all aspects of this work.

******

INTRODUCTION

UFO study is legitimate science. I am crawling out of the closet. I am a scientist. The standard method of refuting UFO phenomenon is to claim that no scientists see UFOs, science discredits UFOs, no scientific proof of the phenomenon exists, and there are no studies in the peer-reviewed scientific literature. I am contesting the above ideas about UFOs. And not only that I am showing that study of UFOs is legitimate.

My career has been in scientific work: a PhD from the University of Missouri College of Veterinary Medicine, post-doctoral research at Cornell University, a professorship at St. Bonaventure University, a PhD-level (GS-11) position with the Defense Intelligence Agency, a Physical Scientist/Cartographer position in the DMA Aerospace Center/Aerospace Center in St. Louis, Missouri, and others.

I have worked also in crucial institutions involved in the UFO field–the Defense Intelligence Agency, Battelle Memorial Institute, and Wright-Patterson Air Force Base and I present inside information. And I see UFOs.

These experiences began in early childhood before I had even heard of UFOs and I have had several other experiences as an adult. I would not say a thing about it except that I had other witnesses, which proves to me that I was not just seeing things. I have also had the perhaps one-and-only experience that my sister and I had the early childhood and then an adult sighting together. We belong to a group of people, as described by Jenny Randles, who begin with childhood "bedroom" sightings and then have later adult sightings. This pattern, often called repeater sightings, normally happens to individuals but we had the unique event of seeing ours together.

This work is legitimate. Because I am trained in science and realize that empirical observation is a foundation of science, I am reporting these experiences. I have tried also to scientifically analyze some of the data and have submitted to and had the work accepted by the peer-reviewed scientific literature. Thus it is legitimate science.

Some of these experiences have included close encounters–one so close we thought we were looking into the windows, lengthy sightings, lights shinned into our car, a mysterious man, a car chase in which we might have been killed, and a sighting over an airport.

This book includes discussions with others–including scientists that have also had experiences, and scientific analysis of the events. It shows scientific proof that UFO phenomena exist.

Additional facets that are analyzed include: mass spectrographic examination of a mystery burn, new photographic analysis, technical examination of reports of lights shinned on people before missing time events, laser technology, and lightning ball and electromagnetic phenomena. It also includes new Roswell information, seismographic analysis of a mysterious sound heard throughout a portion of the US during the 1973 international UFO wave, study of lighting that is invisible to humans and associated with UFO phenomena, correlations such as UFO activity and sunspot cycles, and why UFO photography is difficult.

And I present some of the synchronicities that also helped to bring me into the UFO field, such as a spooky–but beautiful–old mansion, where I also had several experiences, including some that caused me to learn and later write a book about my family and its genealogy.

I examine scientific method and explain how many kinds of data can be used–that good studies can be made without such "hard" data as a landing on the White House lawn.

Also, although people say the reason people report UFO sightings is to make money, I have worked my whole life and do not need the extra work or money.

******

CHAPTER ONE: BACKGROUND

Many people think they may have seen a UFO. But they are told they did not because UFOs do not exist. They may be harassed, mocked, considered a kook, or viewed as mentally disturbed. Even people, who question whether there might be other forms of life in the universe, experience this treatment. This is because the UFO phenomenon is unacceptable to science, as expressed in the passage below:

No professional astronomer in his right mind would be caught dead stating publicly that he'd seen a UFO or been abducted by aliens. He would be ostracized by his colleagues. Serious educational institutions and research facilities would treat him as though he had suddenly acquired the Ebola virus. His career would be finished.[1]

The above quote shows the attitude of the scientific establishment and general public about scientists, government officials, pilots and people in similar occupations, who admit to the possibility that they might have had a UFO sighting.

I have a background in science and recently had a book about UFOs published. But I assumed that if I said anything about having sightings of my own, there would be no chance of being taken seriously. During numerous interviews, many questions about this work have come from some of the top UFOlogists all over the world. These have included: Whitley Strieber in Unknown and Country, Shirley MacLaine in shirleymaclaine.com/ieradio (apple.com/us/podcast/oprahs-supersoul-conversations), Ben & Paul Eno in "Behind the Paranormal," Timothy Beckley in Exploring The Bizarre and I have been contacted by Owen Slevin of the History Channel and others listed below.*

About the first question, nearly all have asked is whether I have had sightings. My innocuous answers included my having a childhood interest in astronomy. But this has made me think that people are interested in sightings by those trained in science. And this interest is increasing because of information newly released in 2017 about serious government study of the phenomena.

This has caused me to question giving this answer.

Behind this general interest in UFO phenomena are burning questions, such as: Are UFOs real, are we in communication non-human entities, can we know the future of humanity, are we alone in the universe, is there life after death, do we have alien visitors, have these visitors made advancements far surpassing ours and will they share them with us. And because scientists are presented as logical beings that see the world as it is, people are interested in their perspective.

However the popular impression is that scientists do not see UFOs, which dashes our hope for answers. This impression is:

No serious astronomer gives any credence to any of these stories ... I think most astronomers would dismiss these. I dismiss them because if aliens had made the great effort to traverse interstellar distances to come here, they wouldn't just meet a few well-known cranks, make a few circles in corn fields and go away again....the idea that only kooks see UFOs is prevalent.[2]

Thus we view UFO phenomena as the purview of flakes, the mentally disturbed, liars and hoaxers.

But why do we have this impression and do these representatives of logic, unemotional thinking and rationality really never see UFOs, or do they just not talk about it for the reasons given above.

A corollary to this is the idea that UFO phenomena have not been proven to exist by science. It is commonly reported that there is no peer-reviewed material about UFOs in the scientific realm.

This is what has caused me to rethink my answer. I think people in scientific fields should speak out. For one reason, perhaps hidden in the UFO paradigm are answers to some of our most basic questions and maybe even the most important of all that can provide answers to our very reason for being. Through such scientific acceptance we may develop the knowledge to do such additional exploration.

Thus, rather than writing books on the general UFO subject and giving innocuous answers, maybe I should speak out. Yes, I have a background in science, a PhD, have been a professor in a scientific field, have much published scientific research and have experienced UFO phenomena.

This material includes several sightings and their investigation. It includes reports from other witnesses, scientific examination and peer-reviewed reporting to legitimate scientific organizations. My sister and I have had several sightings together, so that we fortunately have another witness for our very early sightings and we may fit a pattern of people who may have several such UFO events throughout their lives. It includes also the experiences of and discussions with many others, including scientists. These examinations may help others in exploring this mysterious, sometimes impossible, world of UFO phenomenon. One additional reason for my own admission is personal. This is because in several sightings I thought we had been in considerable danger,–for example, during one sighting, about to be murdered. None of the objects on which we reported have been identified.

Our sightings were somewhat odd and dramatic and have been investigated and written about by some of the world's foremost UFO authorities. Jenny Randles included our report in her book, *Star Children: The True Story Of Alien Offspring Among Us*.[3] Budd Hopkins had investigated us and written about using some of the material in his book, *Intruders: The Incredible Visitations at Copley Woods*. [4] The former Dr. J. Allen Hynek discussed these sightings with others and invited me to his home to talk to him. He is an example of a scientist who takes the UFO phenomenon seriously. He was a noted astronomer and chair of the astronomy department at Northwestern University and often called the "Father of UFOlogy."[5] Portions of this information have been published in other publications. And we have been contacted and interviewed by many others. We have also discussed the subject with some of the people who have reported forms of UFO contact such as Budd Hopkins' "Kathie Davis" and Raymond Fowlers,' Betty Andreasson.

Further corroborating evidence includes reports from other witnesses, correspondence about the experiences, photography and further discussions with experts (with a few text updates for clarity and new information from previous write-ups). We reported most to Dr. J. Allen Hynek's Center for UFO Studies (CUFOS) in their sighting forms and saved copies of these and the reports from our additional witnesses. Portions of these events have been published in a number of journals, such as the CUFOS *International UFO Reporter* (*IUR*), the *MUFON JOURNAL*, *FATE* magazine, the *MUFON of Ohio Newsletter*, the Black Vault, my recent book, *UFOs Today: 70 Years of Lies, Misinformation and Government Cover-up*,[6] and a number of additional publications. Detailed write-ups and citations for published information are given.

In addition, although it is the common impression that UFO phenomena are unacceptable to science, I have been able to do something unique. That is to publish some of this research in peer-reviewed scientific journals. From the very beginning the general media, newspapers, TV, scientific societies, Internet, etc., have proclaimed that the UFO phenomenon is not acceptable to science or to any organization, because the material is not subject to scientific peer review. Well portions of this material have been peer reviewed by well-recognized scientific societies. Two of the scientific journals that have accepted my work are the *Ohio Journal of Science* (*OJS*) of the Ohio Academy of Science and publications of the American Association for the Advancement of

Science (AAAS). An example is, "Survey of Unidentified Aerial Phenomenon Reports in Delaware County, Ohio," in the scientific journal, *OJS* (Figure 1).[7] My book, *UFOs Today: 70 Years of Lies, Misinformation and Government Cover-up,* recently won an achievement award from ResearchGate. Some of the photography has been accepted by scientific journals. Thus some of these elements are acceptable to science, validated and published in the scientific literature.

We are not far-out kooks; we lead normal lives. We have had no mental or legal troubles; do not drink, smoke or do drugs; have never been fired or released from a job; have married and reared families that turned out well; do not have wild lifestyles; never had hallucinations; were very poor during our childhood; worked our way through school; and are healthy, educated, honest and have good eyesight. We are not the insane, hallucinating kooks that are presented as UFO observers.

For example, I had one sighting while working for the Defense Intelligence Agency (DIA) in Washington, DC with above top secret security clearances and my sister had a sighting in Brazil with another missionary. We hope such positions will add to our credibility. We are not reporting because we are "believers," but to explore our own empirical observations.

My sister attended The Ohio State University, OSU, then Scarritt /Vanderbilt/Peabody for her 'BS' and later Drew University in New York for post-graduate work. She became a missionary in Brazil for four years, returned to the US, started a family and a business and does a lot of volunteer work. Her husband is a metallurgical engineer, with a BS degree in this field from OSU and a specialization in plating. He has worked for Western Electric, Holberg Electric and Jenn-Air/Maytag.

I have had much training in several scientific fields from some top institutes. I received my PhD from the University of Missouri College of Veterinary Medicine in physiology (a field that is a combination of chemistry and biology) with a specialization in radioisotope techniques (thus I had training in physics also). I did post-doctoral research at Cornell University (an Ivy League university) and have had a professorship at St. Bonaventure University. My MS was from the University of Nevada and my BS was from OSU with majors in biology and astronomy. I have done research and teaching at the University of Nevada and The Ohio State University College of Medicine.

I am well trained also in photographic analysis and aircraft identification. I have been employed by the DIA in PhD-level (GS-11) research in satellite photography with some of the highest security clearances (above top secret) in the government (Figure 2). Such clearances entail a Federal Bureau of Investigation (FBI) investigation and may take years to obtain. I worked in such divisions as Air Order of Battle, which should have been a government monitoring point for UFO activity and I have been stationed at Wright-Patterson AFB (WPAFB). I was employed in MS-level work as a Physical Scientist/Cartographer in the DMA Aerospace Center/Aerospace Center in St. Louis, Missouri, using satellite photography that included six months of training in the physical sciences and I was sent for specialized training at such places as Lowery AFB in Colorado. Through these positions, I had much training in and experience with photointerpretation and photogrammetry.

I have also worked at Battelle Memorial Institute (Battelle). I was a correspondent for *Popular Mechanics* magazine with byline articles and photography in its "Technology Update" and "Science" sections. I was a volunteer astronomer at the Ohio State University Radio Observatory "Big Ear" (noted for the WOW SETI signal that might be humanity's only signal from ET) and am an amateur astronomer. My publications include books, such as *Uncle: My Journey with John Purdue*, the first book in the Founders Series published by the Purdue University Press; and numerous papers in peer-reviewed scientific journals; magazines; and newspapers. My published photography has appeared in magazines, on TV and in newspapers. Because I have always had an interest in astronomy, but could not get a job because the positions were male only then, I have continued to take on-line courses in astronomy, quantum mechanics and relativity from Harvard and other universities.

My husband obtained his BS degree from Mississippi College with majors in chemistry and algebra. He worked at the Nevada Test Site in the famous Area 51 where he had a Q clearance and then at the Nevada Power Company as a computer programmer. He was later Director of Data Processing for Tioga County, New York and after that a systems analyst at Columbia Gas in Ohio.

We now live on our old family farm near six airports and are very familiar with a variety of normal and unusual aircraft–such as ultra-lights, hot air balloons, helicopters, blimps with lighted sides and even TV shows on their sides, military aircraft, Chinese lanterns, all kinds of advertising airplanes–including ones towing signs and ones with lighted signs under the wings, etc. and I have videotaped many. Some have made close passes over and even landed on our family farm (Figure 3). We live by an interstate freeway that blimps often follow from city to city and are very familiar with blimps by a freeway. I have had flying lessons and have flown in helicopters, large and small aircraft, balloons and gliders. We would not be apt to mistake such aircraft for UFOs.

One of the most significant findings from this examination is that scientists do see UFOs. These are not just sightings, but can include complex interactions. And another is that the subject is acceptable to science. Not only that but the amazing but generally unknown work of some scientists clearly shows that within the paradigms of science, UFOs are real and not just misidentifications. And that science has the means to move forward to find out what the UFO phenomenon is, why we experience it, whether it represents communication with the future or with aliens and much more.

Through working in scientific fields, I have numerous publications in peer-reviewed journals, with experience and training in such methodology as statistics, data analysis and experimental design. I have tried to examine the data from each sighting as extensively as possible and to learn all I could from it. I used this material as I would in writing a scientific paper. The material we obtained contains hard data such as photography, trace evidence, spectrographic and seismographic analysis, consultation with experts, is compatible with the methodology of science and has been accepted through the peer review process. Thus it is valid to draw conclusions and speculations from our data.

This data includes several photographs. I had intensive training in photogrammetry and photo interpretation and have used a variety of computer techniques, such as scanning; digitizing; filtering, enhancement; transparencies; brightness, contrast, level, saturation, sharpen and similar adjustments to examine this photography.

This may be the only good photography to have passed scientific peer review that shows several specific anomalies. One such anomaly is our data indicating that UFO phenomena may employ lighting that is invisible to people. This was evident in photography taken during two different occasions. This might suggest that UFO phenomena could have expertise in adjusting emitted radiation such that it is modulated in frequency and intensity. Such abilities could include laser technology–such as the production of images holographically or by volumetric display. Through such methods, UFO images could be created that might be difficult to tell from an actual object and perhaps some sightings are created in this fashion. This leads to a need to develop ways to distinguish such images from real objects. It could also explain why UFO phenomena are so notoriously difficult to photograph. But the laser can even be used to convert light into matter. The material suggests also that new forms of matter might be involved in UFO phenomena. Such processes could explain some observed UFO phenomena and lead to methods to study the phenomena scientifically.

It includes many additional findings, such that the phenomena may be interactive with human thoughts and feelings. It includes discussion of abduction and contact and speculation that such reports might be simply the tip of the iceberg to more complex happenings. It also includes first-hand reports of UFO events from scientists and professionals, including high strangeness episodes, unusual UFO shapes and weird beings. But it also contains many unsolved mysteries, such as a mysterious sound that was heard throughout a portion of the US at the time of an international UFO wave, odd characteristics of the phenomena and its relation to poltergeist activity and much else.

And it includes new Roswell material with more information about a witness that we had reported on earlier and information about a new professional Roswell witness.

We know such reports do not prove that UFO phenomena exist and are not trying to instill belief or disbelief. We simply see this as empirical data to be put together with other data and used for scientific analysis in the future.

This book is unique among UFO books because within the standards of science, parts have passed peer review by established scientific societies and it may be the only one to do so.

And perhaps such activities can help to construct a serious examination of UFO phenomena and a bridge to understanding what might be the final frontier.

Additional interviews that I have had include: Alejandro Rojas of Open Minds tv/radio, Jim Harold of Jim Harold media, Kat Kanavos of katkan@comcast.net, Dave Schrader of Beyond The Darkness and Guest Host for Coast to Coast, Martin Willis Host & Producer of Dark Matter, Rebecca Roberts and Becky Escamilla on a radio show called Sci-Fi-Sci-EarthTM Beacon of Light Radio, Kevin D. Randle in "A Different Perspective," Bryan Bowden with Ronald Murphy of "Inside The Goblin Universe," and Janet Russell of Long Island Internet Radio. Still other interviewers from the US include: Gene Steinberg of Paracast, Jeremy Scott and Ken Pfeifer of "Into the Paranormal," Rodney Shortridge of Within the Chaos, Arizona Tramp, Jim Heater of Paranormal Geeks and Rosanna Schaffer-Shaw and Kate Valentine of Shattered Reality and others.

Interviewers from Hawaii include, Janet Kira and Dr. Sashas Lessin of Sacred Matrix on Revolution Radio KCOR.

Interviews by people in the UK have included: Ben Emyln-Jones of HPANWO, Jonathan Dean of Radio City In The UK and Kevin Moore of the Kevin Moore Show, From Scotland I have been interviewed by Alyson Dunlop of BST/UK and from the Netherlands by Maarten Horst.

Survey of Unidentified Aerial Phenomenon Reports in Delaware County, Ohio[1]

I. Scott, Department of Physiology, The Ohio State University, Columbus, OH 43210

ABSTRACT. People living near the location (Delaware County, Ohio) of a recent, unpublished, possible observation of an unidentified flying object (UFO) were surveyed to examine the frequency of UFO observations, the ratio of reported/unreported observations, and the accounts of the observations. The 62 respondents were well educated and used to being out-of-doors. Thirty-one percent of the respondents reported UFO observations; 17% reported knowing of someone who had made an observation. Thirty-two unit sightings were reported; of these, three could probably be explained as known phenomena and one contained insufficient information for evaluation.

OHIO J. SCI. 87 (1): 24-26, 1987

INTRODUCTION

Numerous surveys have shown the unidentified flying object (UFO) phenomenon to be widespread. National surveys in 1947, 1950, 1966, 1973, and 1978 (Gallup 1935-1978) have shown an increasing awareness of this phenomenon. In 1966, 96% of the people surveyed had read or heard about UFOs; in 1973, 11% of respondents thought they had seen a UFO. Similar results have been found during surveys of the readership of *Industrial Research* (Anon. 1971), the membership of the American Institute of Aeronautics and Astronautics (AIAA) (Sturrock 1974), and the membership of the American Astronomical Society (AAS) (Sturrock 1977). The present survey was conducted to study the frequency of UFO reports, the ratio of reported/unreported observations, and descriptions of reported objects in an area with a recent, unpublished possible UFO sighting.

METHODS

The survey was done on persons who were acquainted with the interviewer, and who lived within approximately 16 km of the location (Bale Kenyon-Powell Road intersection, Delaware County, Ohio) of the UFO observation. The respondents were queried about possible sightings of their own and of associates. The reliability, stability, and intelligence of the respondents were assessed by assign-

[1] Manuscript received 30 June 1986 and in revised form 5 November 1986 (#86-26).

ing one point each for more than 12 years of school, membership in a landowner family in the community for at least five years, being continuously employed (or a responsible housewife) for more than five years, and no evidence of other factors such as psychological problems that could result in hallucinations or being untruthful. Respondents also were queried about any special training in relevant observational techniques. The reports from respondents or associates were either oral accounts or a signed report form from the Center for UFO Studies (CUFOS).

Possible UFO sightings were classified using the conventions developed during a study done for the Air Force (ATIC 1955). A sighting was a report (or reports) of an observed phenomenon that remained unidentified to the observer until reported. A single observation was a single report of a sighting; a unit sighting was a group of reports for each sighting. Sightings were categorized (Table 1) according to ATIC conventions (ATIC 1955, Maccabee 1979) as those containing: 1) too little information for evaluation; 2) sufficient information for an identification as a known phenomenon with an expected probability greater than 50% that the identification was correct; 3) sufficient information so that an identification as a known phenomenon should have been possible, but the characteristics of the phenomenon did not match those of known phenomena; and 4) those characteristics of the phenomenon described in the report that did not conflict with those of known phenomena, but for which there was insufficient information to specify the nature of the phenomenon.

RESULTS AND DISCUSSION

Of 62 people questioned, 19 (31%) reported possible UFO sightings of their own (Table 1). In comparison, 11% of professional astronomers (Condon and Gillmor 1969), 22% of the readers of *Industrial Research* (Anon.

Figure 1: The peer-reviewed scientific literature has accepted important components of this study. This work is unique and these may be the first ever such acceptances into well-established scientific organizations that have been made. Thus, although it is said that UFO phenomena should be ignored because it is not accepted by science, important portions of this study have been accepted and published. This is strong evidence for the reality of UFO phenomena.

NNEL ACTION

(COMPLETE — See General Information on Reverse)

(FOR AGENCY USE)

1. NAME (CAPS) LAST—FIRST—MIDDLE	MR.—MISS—MRS.			
McCAMMON, IRENA C.	MISS			

3. VETERAN PREFERENCE				4. TENURE GROUP
1	1—NO 2—5 PT.	2—10 PT. DISAB. 3—10 PT. COMP.	5—10 PT. OTHER	1

5. FEGLI		10. RETIREMENT		11. (FOR CSC USE)
3	1—COVERED (Regular only—declined Optional) 2—INELIGIBLE 3—WAIVED 4—COVERED (Reg. & Opt.)	1 1—CS 2—FICA	3—FS 4—NONE 5—OTHER	

12. CODE	NATURE OF ACTION
317	Resignation

15. FROM: POSITION TITLE AND NUMBER	16. PAY PLAN AND OCCUPATION CODE	17. (X) GRADE OR LEVEL	(X) STEP OR RATE	18. SALARY
Intelligence Research Specialist (P.I.) (1442-G) CLC:XA	GS-0132	11	01	pa $11,233

19. NAME AND LOCATION OF EMPLOYING OFFICE	
Defense Intelligence Agency	Soviet/East Europe Division
Assistant Director for Intelligence Production	Eastern USSR Branch
Photographic Interpretation Office	Washington, D. C. 20301

20. TO: POSITION TITLE AND NUMBER	21. PAY PLAN AND OCCUPATION CODE	22. (X) GRADE OR LEVEL	(X) STEP OR RATE	23. SALARY

24. NAME AND LOCATION OF EMPLOYING OFFICE

AP9A2

25. DUTY STATION (City—county—State)			26. LOCATION CODE
Washington, D. C.		OTHR	

27. APPROPRIATION		28. POSITION OCCUPIED	29. APPORTIONED POSITION	
953123-A	MC-1	2 1—COMPETITIVE SERVICE 2—EXCEPTED SERVICE	FROM: 1—PRONED-1 2—WAIVED-2	30: STATE

30. REMARKS: A. SUBJECT TO COMPLETION OF :   YEAR PROBATIONARY (OR TRIAL) PERIOD COMMENCING
B. SERVICE COUNTING TOWARD CAREER (OR PERMANENT) TENURE FROM:
SEPARATIONS: SHOW REASONS BELOW, AS REQUIRED. CHECK IF APPLICABLE.   C. DURING PROBATION   D. FROM APPOINTMENT OF 6 MONTHS OR LESS

Reason: To get married and return to college for graduate degree.

Forwarding Address: Route #1
Galena, Ohio 43021

03412			A31,71,81
POINTMENT-AFFIDAVIT (Executive only)	34. SIGNATURE (or other authentication) AND TITLE		
	ELEANOR G. TUNG, Chief		
AINING PERSONNEL FOLDER (If different from employing office)	Admin & Records Branch		
	Civilian Personnel Division		
ING DEPARTMENT OR AGENCY	35. DATE		2086
IA, Arlington, Virginia	10-31-69		

1. EMPLOYEE COPY   ☆ U.S. GOVERNMENT PRINTING OFFICE: 1962—310-306

Figure 2: My position at the Defense Intelligence Agency (DIA). I was a GS-11 working in the Photographic Interpretation Office in Washington, DC.

Figure 3: The family farm is near six airports, along a blimp route between two cities and a large variety of aircraft fly over it. We are familiar with both military and civilian aircraft. The photograph below shows a blimp below treetop level in the author's back yard.

******

CHAPTER TWO: INSIDE A LIGHTNING BALL?

First Event

This happened when I was five years old. I was standing by a north window in my father's cousin's house with her beside me on the other side of the window. It was about a week before Easter and she was telling me all about the Easter bunny. I wanted to know how tall the Easter bunny was and she told me that it was man-sized, so I pictured a big, white, fuzzy, bunny-faced man hopping around delivering Easter eggs and candy.

A fierce thunderstorm was raging outside with loud cracks of thunder. Because of my small size, I could look almost directly up through the window. Suddenly I saw a ball. It was around, basketball-sized and seemed to be the color of lightning. It was near the top of the window frame and about five feet above me.

I reacted as a five-year-old would; I was terrified, began to scream and cry and jumped away from the window. My relative began trying to calm me down. Because she was taller, she probably had not seen the ball, but needed an explanation to make me stop crying.

She told me that this happens when two thunder storms or lightning bolts collide–thus all I had seen was two lightning bolts hitting each other. I am sure she had no idea what I saw, but just came up with something to sooth me.

At the time of this event, I had not heard of lightning balls. Although this happened many years ago, it is definitely not something that a person would forget. But what was it?

In seeking an answer, information about ball lightning should be examined. Although many of today's scientists accept the concept of ball lightning, lightning balls remain a modern day mystery. In general they are glowing spheres that occur near the ground during thunderstorms, in close association with cloud-to-ground lightning. They may be red, orange, yellow, white, or blue in color.

However, another aspect of this examination should include UFO phenomena. Although most scientists would say that the only kind of lightning balls are the prosaic ones, it is not all that clear. There are close similarities between the actual descriptions of ball lightning and UFO phenomena. Both are often reported as generally spherical, glowing objects traveling through our atmosphere.

In fact some papers in the scientific literature explain some or even all UFOs as ball lightning.[8] [9] Thus, in any exploration of UFO phenomena, information about lightning should be examined closely and compared with UFO reports. One similarity between it and UFO phenomena is that scientists, in even the recent the past, did/do not "believe" in either ball lighting or UFOs:

Until the 1960s, most scientists treated reports of ball lightning skeptically, despite numerous accounts from around the world. Laboratory experiments can produce effects that are visually similar to reports of ball lightning, but how these relate to the natural phenomenon remains unclear. [10]

Perhaps two similar ball-like objects, lightning balls and UFOs, exist. One might think there would be ways to distinguish them. It is thought that lightning balls receive their energy from lightning or other electrical sources but it is unknown how they form. It is now thought that lightning strikes may contain nuclear forces and even antimatter, so lightning ball formation is very complex and may involve even the most recent quantum theories. It is also unknown what provides the energy for the UFO/orb type of object or how they are formed. Both objects have been reported to have the ability to levitate or to be unaffected by gravity. Both are very rare, unpredictable and may behave in strange ways.

Although little is known about ball lightning, scientific descriptions exist in the literature and new frontiers of knowledge are being explored all the time, which should also happen with UFO phenomena.[11] [12]

Ball lightning is extremely complex; it may involve nuclear energy, quantum mechanics and even unknown forms of life. Many scientific publications view it as self-organizing phenomena; thus, it could show all sorts of odd properties as discussed in the *Journal of Plasma Physics*: "The ball lightning as a self-organizing phenomenon was considered in Kadomtsev..."[13] Our self-organized microwave bubble can have the same potential to persist for a scale of seconds. Zheng calculated that hundreds of joule microwaves can maintain the plasma shell of the bubble for a few seconds."[14]

A new 2017 paper in the journal *Nature* contains even more amazing information about the mysterious formation of ball lightning. This shows that it can even result in matter-antimatter annihilation in a series of radioactive decays that follow some strikes. The electric fields in thunderstorms are able to accelerate electrons to extremely high energies. This generates a zone that contains unstable isotopes of nitrogen and oxygen. Radioisotopes and even positrons–the antimatter equivalent of electrons–have been formed in the process. Thus, research is needed to examine whether lightning flashes can pose a radiation hazard to people near them.[15]

There have been hundreds of papers written in scientific journals speculating on these issues, variously assigning the energy source of ball lightning to nuclear energy, anti-matter, black holes, masers, microwaves ... you name it. [16]

A description of a green lightning ball seen rolling down a hill after a green fireball had passed over, which was witnessed and photographed by many people, can be found in the *Proceedings of the Royal Society A*, the scientific academy of the UK:

Momentary electrical connections between the ionosphere and ground created by the passage of a meteor are probably very rare and fleeting. However, the observations described in this paper do provide circumstantial evidence for this ....It is of course possible that the observed phenomenon was due to something more exotic such as a mini black hole...anti-matter meteorites...cosmic strings or some physical process as yet unknown. If confirmed, this hypothesis may be able to explain previously unexplainable UFO sightings and the so-called foo fighters and other aerial phenomenon.[17]

So many extremely strange characteristics have been reported that they might suggest it is a new form of matter: "Various conflicting reports: hovers in the air, may float through walls or other solid objects without effect or may melt and burn them. Ball lightning is an unexplained atmospheric electrical phenomenon. ... Scientists have proposed many hypotheses about ball lightning over the centuries. [18]

Several publications have even considered that it might be a kind of life-form: "If not a rational skeptic, your author could suspect that fireballs might be a transient life form with some form of "alien" intelligence...Perhaps DNA-based life is not the only form of life on earth. If so, then are fireballs non-carbon-based life forms?" The above quote remarkably was from Paul Devereux author of *Earth Lights Revelation*. In general, Devereux is a skeptic who has said that small percentage of unexplained aerial phenomena can be flying objects having an unknown nature. He views them as exotic natural phenomena–likely some form of plasma with extraordinary properties. He coined the term "earth lights" to label this kind of phenomena. [19]

Inside a lightning ball

Since that time, I have been close to lightning a number of other times in my life and have been able to explore the phenomena first hand. For example, two trees once stood in front of my house. Each was about 20 feet away from the house. I was at home when both were struck by lightning–at different times. One fell over. I heard the other being stuck. My computer flicked off. I went out and found large splinters all around the tree and many on my porch. The tree was so damaged that I had it taken down later.

But I have been even closer than this. Once I was standing by a kitchen window with my hands on the metal faucets. A bolt of lightning hit right outside the window (3 or 4 feet away) and I felt the electricity. This is called an indirect strike–when the electricity is felt but the person does not experience a direct strike.

Another time I was able to make highly unusual videotape, because lightning struck only a few feet away from me horizontally while my camera was recording. If I had been standing on the ground, my camera and I would likely have been fried, because the bolt appeared to hit very close to me. However, I was standing outside on a dry wooden deck about 8-10 feet high and above the location of the hit. In this case, although I was very close to the hit I was able to get a good and unique video because I was above ground on the deck with dry air and wood for insulation. There are very few photographs or camcordings during such a close lightning strike because the observers would generally be dead and the camera blown to bits. This video if examined in detail might provide much information about close lightning strikes, ball lightning and even UFOs. I posted this video on YouTube as "Incredibly Close Lightning Strike–feet away, Explosion, shorts up guy-wires, volcano."[20]

I was filming an interesting location. It was by a house in Texas near the McDonald observatory complex. This high elevation area is important for astronomy–the McDonald telescope complex includes the Hobby-Eberly Telescope, which is one of the largest optical telescopes in the world, with the second largest mirror in the world. It now ranks as the fourth largest telescope in the world. Glimpses of these telescopes may be seen in the video. And also the house was actually built on top of a wall-like mountain range between two massive ancient extinct volcanoes and I was also filming the large crater and uplift in the center of the north one. Only very large craters have central uplifts and these are called complex craters. This crater is many miles wide. The ground here is generally solid rock–ancient lava–and it is unknown if this volcanic rock had any effect on the electrical transmission.

Suddenly lighting struck. This was so close that I just saw a white flash/whiteout and heard an ear-splitting noise at what seemed to be the same time. I think I saw the bolt before it hit and thought it hit the ground a few feet away from the deck but I am not sure. Immediately when it hit, I could just see white for a while, which blinded me. And afterwards my ears were still ringing half an hour later. The electricity went off.

I ran inside with the video camera as best I could and when I was able to see, was very disappointed when I re-ran the tape, because all it captured was a whiteout. Because I thought I had seen the bolt striking, I was unhappy that this did not photograph. But it did capture the noise of the thunder, which appeared to begin at the time of the strike, thus the strike was very close. It also captured a loud ringing sound in the house.

Later after I returned home, I downloaded the video into the computer and replayed it in slow motion. I was very happy to find out that it had captured more than I thought. Close to me was a high cellular tower with guy wires. I had captured an electrified guy wire and at first thought that the lightning had hit the tower.

After that I realized that only one guy wire was electrified–the one nearest to me. This meant that the lightning bolt had hit very near to me and then shorted up the guy wire to the tower. I made a photograph from this video of the electricity shorting up the tower guy wire over 100 feet away from me (Figure 1). And although at first I had seen the whiteout as disappointing because I did not see anything, I later realized its uniqueness and importance.

One way to tell that the strike was close to me is that the tower was much higher than I was, but it did not hit the tower, it hit right by me.

When it happened I just remember seeing a large blob of white all around–the video just photographed an all-white image. Next, when the whiteout ended, electricity was seen shooting up the guy wire (I made this into a photograph). I assumed the electricity traveled through the ground to the wire, but do not know how the specific type of rock would be affected. It was mostly ancient lava. There were places where the lava flow was quite visible, although very old (hardened lava such as basalt is generally viewed as having high electrical resistivity). I did not think to look at the rocks afterward.

Other evidence that the strike was very close to me is that the lighted wire was seen after the whiteout was over–it took a while longer for the electricity to reach the guy wire. This shows that the electricity was at the distance of the wire, after the whiteout portion that was near me was over and so it was not instantaneous with the strike, but was there a fraction of a second later. It was still very powerful at that distance though.

Still another reason that I thought it struck closer to me than to the wire is that there were trees between the wire and me. I think if it had struck closer to the wire, the trees would have blocked some of the whiteout from my sight and I would have seen it behind the trees. In the video, only the sparking up the top part of the wire is visible; the trees blocked this light at the bottom. It is likely that trees could absorb enough light/radiation to block part of the whiteout.

During the lightning strike, deafeningly loud thunder could be heard. But a loud high-pitched sound came on right after the lightning shorted up the wire. Because the electricity in the house went out, it was not from a device connected to the electricity and must have been a battery smoke alarm. It is unknown why it went off, because I was not aware of any smoke. Perhaps the jolt of electricity had activated it. It was inside the house's second story, maybe 20 feet further away from the lightning than I was and directly behind me from the lightning strike. It went off a fraction of a second after the wire lit up. How lighting strikes can activate smoke detectors/fire alarms is controversial; it is sometimes attributed to Electro Magnetic Pulse or ionization.[21] It would take a very close hit of lightning to set off a battery-operated smoke alarm.[22]

Also, I am not exactly sure what a short is, but light can be seen coming from the guy wire in segments all the way up. So far as I know, the lightning rods on houses do not glow like this when lightning strikes. The wire was quite heavy and strong with a good-sized diameter because it was used to anchor the tower. It must have had much more resistance than lightning rod wires. Because some guy wires have lightning protection and the electricity traveled through basalt, the bolt must have been very powerful. Sometimes such guy wires are coiled and perhaps this caused the segmented appearance of the flash.

The large ball of light I saw (the whiteout) might have been a form of ball lightning–it fits many definitions of ball lightning. If it had been, I would have photographed a lightning ball also. For example, I thought for a split second that I saw a boundary around the whiteout. Of course, there would have been a boundary. Most lightning strikes do not have a ball of whiteout around them, as shown in the many photos of lightning hitting tall buildings.

Thus this whiteout area could have been some type of ball lightning. It that case, since I was in the whiteout area, I would have been inside a lightning ball also.

Ball lighting can be as large as this whiteout appeared to be. There are numerous reports that lightning balls can range in size up to the size of a bus:

A Coast Guard officer reported this enormous ball lighting sighting in 1977. The ball lightning phenomenon was very large and estimated to be about the size of a bus.... Intense light was emitted for about three seconds before flickering out. Severe static was heard on the radio. The object slowly rotated around a horizontal axis and seemed to bounce off projections on the ground.[23]

This is a unique video; because it was so close to a lightning bolt and lighting shorting up a wire is seldom photographed–actually I could not find any photographs on Google of lighting traveling on a wire–so this might be the only one. Electricity going through a wire may be too fast to see. This was a large heavy wire connecting to near the top of the tower to hold it in place and likely had some resistance. The electricity traveled up the nearest guy wire, but did not electrify the tower or other wires.

This video can supply useful information about a number of properties of a lightning strike:

1. It gives an exact time for how long the smoke detector/fire alarm went off after the strike.

2. It shows that the whiteout was instant and real; it was not caused by ground debris. Sometimes ground debris can look like a whiteout, but in this case the whiteout was almost instantaneous and I saw no debris afterward either. This whiteout appeared to have lasted for a time–a tiny fraction of a second.

3. This whiteout might also have been a form of ball lighting (and I may have not only photographed it but been inside it).

4. The electricity was traveling up the wire when the whiteout had ended. Thus it took the electricity some time to reach the wire, from where the whiteout and I were located. It shows approximately how long it took to travel that distance.

5. It shows how quickly the guy wire was electrified after the strike, which was almost instantaneously. No guide wires other than the closest, or the tower, were affected. This was very soon after the strike and strong enough to travel to the top of the wire. This electricity showed as shorts, rather than as a continuous stream. These shorts were maybe a foot or more in size, which indicates a lot of electrical energy. (If the bolt had struck close to the wire, the tower and rest of the wires would likely have also been electrified.) So it shows the distance range of the greatest danger from the current–where the closest guy wire was. The amount of electricity that appeared

to be traveling up the guy wire might have killed a person. This happened much more quickly than the effect on the fire alarm.

6. This bolt was quite powerful, for the guy wire was some distance from location of the strike and it would take a lot of energy to electrify this thick, strong wire.

7. As measured roughly on Google Maps, the guy wire might be about 125 feet or less from my location on the deck and the tower might be about 150 feet.

8. It is very rare to get a video of a lightning strike this close, which includes a whiteout and effects on a guy wire, video camera, fire alarm and others. It gives an exact time (if you can figure out the nanoseconds) for the sound of thunder and fire alarm sound, the exact time and length of time for the whiteout/lightning ball to exist and a good approximate time for the electrification of the wire. The speed can be roughly calculated.

This video is also interesting because it shows the lightning's unbelievable power. One lightning bolt can contain about 1 billion volts of electricity. It can reach temperatures of 50,000° F–much hotter than the sun's surface–that can fuse soil or sand into glass. I have taken numerous videos of cloud to ground lightning from a distance, know what it looks like and have seen its power after it has hit objects.

And one can certainly see its power here. For example, the guy wire was approximately 125 feet from me. Thus a huge circle of 250 feet in diameter around me was extremely electrified (as shown by the short up the thick wire in Figure 1). People standing in this circle could be killed–and maybe ones further away. Figure 2 shows a daytime photo of the tower and telescope complex in the background.

The whiteout in the video is interesting and such whiteout phenomena seem to appear only to those very close to a strike. Others have reported seeing a whiteout during a close lightning strike, when they have been hit, but there are few if any photographs of the effect (the camera might be destroyed if such close photographs were taken):

As I begin to load the car there is an incredible explosion and searing flash of white light. It is as if a bomb has gone off. There is no warning, no thunder and no flashes, just a huge, blinding white explosion. And then it starts. I am being electrocuted. My feet and legs begin to vibrate. My whole body goes rigid. And the sound! A roaring buzz fills my body as the electricity climbs up through me into my chest and arms. I feel completely helpless. The ground is alive with current that is killing me. I can't move... I feel my feet vibrating in my sandals as the lightning comes up out of the street and climbs over the rubber soles into my legs. It is the most excruciating pain I have ever experienced. Every muscle in my body tenses and cramps like thousands of Charlie horses all at once. I am convulsing. They do not know I am dying.[24]

An article about what happens when the body is struck by lightning also describes this white flash and I noticed these effects, "The effects on the body can vary. Eyesight or hearing may be adversely affected, Claypool said, due to the loud clap of the thunder and the bright flash from the lightning. A person could be temporarily blinded or rupture an eardrum."[25] I had these, but no long-term effects because I was not directly struck.

But one might also wonder in the face of such new material, whether this whiteout near a very close lightning strike is totally caused by visible light or by something else. For example, there are many photos of lightning striking the Empire State Building, but such photos taken from a distance do not show a huge blob of whiteout around the place where the lightning bolt hits, as does a close up event (Figure 3). The photos of tall buildings being struck by lightning show a clean clear bolt with no whiteout or ground debris. It is possible that a nuclear reaction is involved rather than just visible light. For example, new reports indicate that a lightning strike can even result in matter-antimatter annihilation with a series of radioactive decays to follow. When a particle meets its antiparticle, they annihilate into gamma rays, which is the highest energy type of light and in accordance with $E = mc2$. Could this energy, rather than just the visible light, also affect the eye and electronic camera to make one very close to the lightning see a large whiteout that would not be visible from a distance?

For example, this whiteout looked more like the whiteout from an atomic bomb explosion rather than a lightning strike. There is always a huge whiteout when atom bombs explode that looks more like the one I saw during the close lightning strike, rather than as seen in videos of more distant strikes. "…found a recording of an American atomic test in 1953, which shows an enormous flash of white, so white it blanks out the entire sky, then thick clouds of ash (or maybe dirt?) tumble up…:"[26] Such a massive amount of energy might affect the eye only if it is very close to the strike and cause a visual whiteout that is much larger than that caused by visible light only. I wondered about this because the videos of lightning hitting tall buildings do not show ground obstructions such as dust flying away, they just show a clean, clear strike and you do not see a whiteout as you see in very close strikes.[27] The atomic test recording also showed that the white flash occurred before the debris tumbled up.

But still other mysteries lie in this strange place. The lightning video was taken from the north deck of this Texas house, overlooking the remains of an enormous volcano (Figure 4).

However, the south deck overlooks an important place in the annals of UFOlogy–the town of Marfa about 20 miles away. It is well-known for its Marfa Lights–mysterious lights that repetitively appear in the area. This area is so well known that a large viewing area for these lights has been built and they have been described in many UFO books (I have watched from the viewing area, but thought the lights I saw were just traffic in the mountains). From this south deck, I once took a video of a large object over Marfa that stayed in the same place and slowly blinked on and off (Figure 5). This was not normal air traffic because it was hours after the local airport closed, the airport knew nothing about it and there is little air traffic in this deserted area. The object was large compared to the normal Marfa lights and very low. I have watched Marfa for many hours from this location and even flown from the Marfa airport, but have not seen anything like this and do not know what it was. It is unknown if similar reported objects/lights could be Marfa lights, UFO phenomena, some form of Earthquake light, or Earth light phenomena.

Although it is mostly unknown, Marfa is a geologic wonder. It is in an enormous volcanic caldera, the Chinati Mountains caldera and the house from which I photographed it is also on the rim of this caldera described as:

The granddad of all gargantuan fire mountains that vulcanized the Trans-Pecos badlands eons ago… This eruption yielded a volume of igneous debris more than 1,000 times greater than Mt. Saint Helens… Fortunately, the world has not experienced an eruption of the Chinatis magnitude in modern times…Visitors to the Trans-Pecos are often surprised by the presence of rugged mountains that encompass a triangle formed by the towns of Fort Davis, Alpine and Marfa, Texas….and the titanic forces that were released by this event caused widespread volcanism stretching from Mexico's Sierra Madre…as far north as Montana!" [28]

Although the Marfa lights are famed with UFOlogists, this geology is mostly unknown. However, such massive tectonic forces are sometimes associated with Earthlight phenomena. As described by Paul Devereux, 'earth lights' seem to be exotic natural phenomena that appear to belong to the same family as earthquake lights and ball lightning but having their own distinctive characteristics. These characteristics include sometimes behaving as if they have a rudimentary intelligence like inquisitive animals and sometimes displaying illogical effects including being visible from one side but not the other.[29] Another type of light that might be associated with such stress is earthquake lights, a luminous aerial phenomenon that is reported to appear in the sky at or near areas of tectonic stress, seismic activity, or volcanic eruptions and is also poorly understood. Although these events occurred many years ago, there might be lingering stresses in the area, which seems to be still be geothermally active.

For example, such lights as those at Marfa; the valley of Hessdalen, Norway; the Boulia region of western Queensland, Australia; and the Pennines of England; have been described as geologically "special" in such respects as the presence of fault lines or mineral deposits.[30] The area experiences some earthquakes.

Thus I might have not only photographed a close lightning strike from this house, but possibly Marfa light/Earthquake/Earthlight phenomena.

This lightning ball described above is not the only one that our family has experienced, however. My mother also had a close encounter with ball lightning. She told us about it a number of times. As I remember (and not too well), she was in a room. Suddenly a lightning ball entered through the window. She said it was basketball sized and orange. She was terrified and stood on her bed. The ball rolled around the room, I think she said it rolled around her bed and then left through the same window. She did not try to see where it went after that.

My sister remembers this differently and maybe better, because she may have questioned Mom in more detail. She thought that this happened to her when she was very young probably in the 1920s in West Virginia. She said that, when Mom was in a house with the lightning ball, she had been terrified and thought she was going to be killed. She said Mom may have experienced something in the form of Post-Traumatic Stress Disorder (PTSD) for the rest of her life. She mentioned that Mom made us stay in the center of the house during electric storms and how people teased her about this fear. I remember this too, but had not paid much attention to it. Sue did not recall her saying how it entered the house and thought it was just in there. She thought it was the color of lightning, whitish and shaped somewhat like a basketball. She thought Mom's PTSD would be somewhat normal because it happened when she was very young and she thought she was going to die. Although it was long ago another relative thinks that she heard this too.[31]

Someone had told me that in the 1920-30s, Mom's sister, Isabel Nuzum, used to see glowing objects floating though their house. This would also have been in West Virginia. There is another story in the family about Isabel, "Aunt Isabel had a fireball from lightening come through her window of her apartment in Columbus once. She may have had a fan near the window, but there was a bad storm and she said a ball of fire came in."[32] We do not know the year. They saw the lightning balls in West Virginia, possibly in the same house, way before anyone had heard about

UFOs, likely did not know much about them and probably did not talk about them much, so we have just heard these stories–everyone is dead now so we cannot ask anyone directly.

In another instance, I was nearly struck with a ball of electricity. I was in my laboratory at the University of Nevada with one of the old gooseneck lamps with a metal shade around the light bulb attached to my desk. Suddenly the old lamp shorted out and a small fireball shot from the area near the bulb. This fireball burned its way right through the metal shade and nearly hit me in the face as it flew by. It left a hole with burn marks beside it in the metal shade (maybe around 0.5 inches) and probably could have damaged me severely. I am not sure what kind of metal the shade was made from, but the one that looks exactly like it on the Internet is described it as, "Fully adjustable….with goose neck arm and rolled rim parabolic steel shade," and further described as a "cold-rolled steel deep bowl shade or parabolic reflector." [33] I cannot find information about fireballs going through steel, but think this was quite a powerful ball of electricity, because it went right through what was probably steel. It was probably made of electricity and much like a lightning ball. There was a burning odor afterwards and my heart was pounding because it nearly hit me. I think the fireball must have just burned out. It happened in about a second.

This fireball might have been quite similar to the ones in a paper published in *The Journal of Physical Chemistry*, reporting that researchers at the:

U.S. Air Force Academy in Colorado last year figured out how to reproduce ball lightning in the lab. They used electrodes partially submerged in electrolyte solution to create the high-power electric sparks. The result was bright white plasmoid balls…

Because of the difficulty in capturing ball lightning, scientists do not know much about it. A popular theory is when lightning hits something; it blasts a cloud of highly energized nanoparticles in to the air. Those nanoparticles emit a ball of light as they wear down.[34]

Such balls of light are considered to be the lightning balls.

This is additional evidence suggesting that because I was inside the ball of light from the lightning strike that I was inside a lightning ball.

Scientists may see forms of lightning balls also. For example, Dr. Harley Rutledge wrote to me, "I have observed many lightning strokes. From my office in daylight, I saw a too close lightning bolt that appeared to form 'liquid light globules' along the surface of the stroke."[35]

Another comparison between UFO and ball lightning phenomena shows that lightning can be dangerous and even deadly, as described by the American Physics Society (APS) and others: [36]

In the spring of 1984, my youngest brother was struck and killed by "a ball of lightning". This happened during the beginning of a thunderstorm in western Lower Michigan. The "ball" made no course changes, just traveled in a straight line about 3 feet off the ground. It struck him square in the chest and blew his shirt off him. The heat from the impact was so fierce that it burned his internal organs.[37]

This supplies some evidence that might be used to compare a lightning ball to UFO phenomena. It appears that the lighting ball phenomena contains more energy and may be more dangerous to come into contact with than UFO phenomena.

There is some evidence that the UFO phenomenon is less dangerous. For example, as will be mentioned in the next chapter, such a ball hit Betty Andreasson right between the eyes but did not harm her. This is unlikely with ball lightning. Perhaps such a difference might exist because ball lightning is thought to need a strong electrical source, such as lightning, to provide its energy.[38] Similar UFO-related objects may have lower energy levels. Ball lightning is made naturally. The UFO phenomena might be made intentionally and thus show different characteristics.[39] It may last longer than ball lightning. Another difference may be in behavior— many reports describe the seemingly intelligent behavior of some lightning balls and maybe these are UFO associated ones.

And my inside the lightning ball experience in the flash/whiteout/lightning ball area, may have given me a flash of insight about UFO phenomena. As mentioned, the inside of a lightning ball is a place where amazing physics, such as quantum phenomena, nuclear reactions, self-organization, positrons, antimatter, mini black hole, cosmic string phenomena, intelligence, etc., is postulated to exist. Or if UFOs are actually lightning balls, the object I saw might be considered a UFO. And perhaps UFOs themselves encompass such strange physics and that is why they are so weird. Perhaps study of ball lightning will help to illuminate understanding of And the *National Geographic* sums up the experience of actually seeing the phenomena:

"It's extraordinary—you're so startled that you remember it for the rest of your life," he said. He describes seeing a glowing, tennis ball-size formation hovering nearby....While some skeptics remain; there is significant observational evidence for ball lightning's existence.[40]

According to *Scientific American*, the American Physical Society and other sources, about 5 percent of the Earth's population has seen ball lighting and close lightning strikes:

"According to statistical investigations...ball lightning has been seen by 5 percent of the population of the earth. This percentage is about the same as the fraction of the population that has seen an ordinary lightning strike at close range—that is, close enough to see the direct point of the lightning impact.[41]

Thus, our family has had an unusual number of experiences with lightning.

So what did I see? I fully view that my sighting of the ball-shaped object when I was five years old was ball lightning and accept prosaic explanations for it and many other occurrences in my life such as close lightning strikes that might have seemed mysterious. My mother was very close to one lightning ball, her sister may have seen more than one and I was close to one or two—maybe even inside one and have been close to four strikes. Our family has experienced close transformer strikes. I may have also photographed some form of Marfa light/Earthlight/Earthquake light phenomena. It is way out on the bell-shaped curve to have this many close encounters with lightning and similar phenomena and very unusual to possibly be inside a lightning ball. But I have some proof such as the before and after photographs of the trees in front of my house (the stumps are still there), the video and memories from several people. It is also quite unusual to photograph a very close lightning strike and possible ball. But I view this as happenstance and do not attribute it to anything supernatural. I simply installed lightning rods atop my house and went about my daily life.

When I had begun thinking about lightning and similar phenomena, I thought that these subjects were evident and clear. Ball lightning, for example, was simply floating spheres that can accompany lightning.

But my experience and study of these events increased my awareness of lightning and similar earthlight phenomena—the fact that it is still unknown to science and that it shares some weird properties with UFO phenomena. And my inside the lightning ball experience made me think that closer examination of the amazing physics—nuclear energy, anti-matter, dark matter, black hole, maser, microwave, quantum interaction, new forms of matter, anything else—and behavior—levitation, passing through walls—of these objects might be important in illuminating some of the mysteries of UFO phenomena.

Although these experiences were generally prosaic, I have had events happen in my life that did not resemble such explainable events. I have had other witnesses who also were mystified. Thus, these lightning events might be used to compare with later ones.

Figure 1: This photograph is from a video of a Texas lightning strike that hit very close to the author. It shows a cellular tower guy wire that was about 120 feet away and was electrified a fraction of a second after the ending of the lightning strike's whiteout that had instantly surrounded the author.

Figure 2: A daytime photograph taken from the same deck shows the tower and its guy wires. This also shows the McDonald Observatory complex in the background. This area is a mecca for astronomers because of its high altitude and clear skies. It is unknown how altitude affects lightning.

Figure 3: Lightning striking the Empire State building. Such photographs taken from a distance do not show whiteouts at the strike site as was instantly experienced in the location of the close Texas lighting strike.

Figure 4: This photograph was taken from the deck of a house built on the rim of a very large extinct volcano. It is from the same deck as the lightning photograph was taken. It shows the large crater and also shows its central uplift in the center of the photograph. Only very large craters have central uplifts and these are called complex craters. This crater is many miles wide. The ground is generally solid rock–ancient lava–and it is unknown how this affects its electrical conductivity.

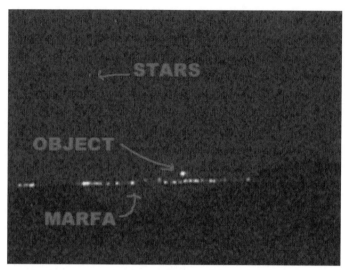

Figure 5: The lightning video was taken from the north deck of this Texas house. The south deck overlooks the town of Marfa about 20 miles away. It is well-known for its Marfa Lights— mysterious lights that repetitively appear in the area. From this deck I once took a video of a large object over Marfa that stayed in the same place and slowly blinked on and off. This was not normal air traffic because it was hours after the local airport closed, the airport knew nothing about it and there is little air traffic in this deserted area. It is unknown if it could be Marfa light phenomena. Marfa is in an enormous extinct volcanic caldera (the house with the deck is also on the rim of this caldera also) and might be subject to unusual tectonic forces.

Figure 6: It is possible to withstand tremendous jolts of electricity when insulated. Here a worker is in contact with a 750,000 volt wire.

******

CHAPTER THREE: CHILDHOOD SIGHTINGS

Bedroom light

This observation took place at 6844 Bale Kenyon Road, Lewis Center, Ohio, after dark with two observers, my sister and me. It was a clear night, my sister was four to five years old and I was two years older.

When I reported this to CUFOS, it was used as the cover story, "Bedroom Light" in the *International UFO REPORTER* (IUR) March/April 1988. [42] CUFOS had an artist design the cover to show the bedroom and the object (Figure 1). [43]

I wrote the CUFOS article in response to an article in the *MUFON UFO Journal* (February 1988), in which Jenny Randles described small balls of light seen by children during bedroom visitations. Randles later published a book in 1995, *Star Children* in which she reported our event and discussed it as a part of a pattern that she called bedroom visitations that happen to young children. [44]

Although this happened a long time ago, it was so unusual and dramatic that not only she and I, but the family and others remembered it. Thus, I have several sources of confirming evidence. My sister and mother also filled out the CUFOS report forms in 1984 about the event. I have a note a cousin, who lived about 100 miles away, who wrote it up for his memory of this event. Several other people also remember it. Also shown are photographs of the room we were in and the chandelier.

This type of sighting is extremely rare, because it normally occurs when there is only one witness. It is then explained as a dream or a made up story. This is especially true because it happens to children. We were very lucky because we each had another witness and saw the same thing. We did not communicate during the sighting, so we did not influence each other. We had heard of neither UFOs nor ball lightning, so the media did not influence us.

My sister and I had beds on opposite sides of an upstairs attic room and normally retired around eight o'clock. Our parents usually remained in the living room reading and sometimes listening to the radio. Because we lived on an isolated family farm and had no TV and our parents carefully selected our exposure to our one radio, we had not heard of UFOs then and I think my parents had not either.

I do not remember that anything unusual happened before the event. It was a clear summer night and I had fallen asleep. Then I slowly awakened to see a small, around 1 inch glow and all, shining object flying around in the room. In color and appearance, it resembled incandescent metal such as one would find in a blacksmith's shop. The part inside the glow looked like solid metal.

The object slowly flew around in the room in a browsing motion. The walls on the east and west sides of the attic room were about three feet high and then slanted toward the ceiling. At the ceiling was an area of about three feet between the two walls.

The object weaved vertically and laterally as it slowly flew through the room. Then I realized that its pattern appeared to show guidance. Although the room was dark, I was familiar with its shape and knew where the walls and furniture were. In the object's meandering as it flew around the room, it never bumped into anything. It always turned (maybe a foot or more) before it got to a wall or other object. I do not recall seeing it reverse and I believe it always moved forward. It flew slowly and, as I remember, it flew around the room several times. At times, it came quite close to us and near our heads. It did not change its shape, brightness, or size. My impression was that its actions showed intelligence–subjectively, it seemed as if it were aware of us and of what was in the room.

I thought that Sue was asleep, so I did not say anything to her. After I had watched it for what seemed to be between around one to five minutes, it flew upward to near the top of the door in the south end of the room. It was close to the ceiling. Then it flew in a straight line from the south end of the room to the chandelier, which was in the center of the ceiling between the two walls and was controlled by a wall switch. Without touching or feeling this lamp or any of the walls, it circled the chandelier in the area between the chandelier and the walls. When it did this it no longer meandered but made a tight circle. Its flight was steady and smooth, but seemed more rapid than when it meandered. It stayed several inches away from the chandelier's periphery and circled in the same place a number of times, perhaps 25-30. Next, it slowly spiraled downward in a perfect geometric fashion with the spiral becoming smaller as its altitude decreased. In other words, if one drew a line from the center of the chandelier straight down, it spiraled around this line, but each spiral was closer to the line. When it was directly below the center of the chandelier, it was about one or two feet off the floor. At that time, I thought I heard a noise and saw lights coming from it, but my sister in the same room and with the same view did not see this.

At this point, I was terrified and ran for the stairs. At the same time, Sue also screamed and ran in terror. We collided, were shrieking, fell down the stairs and then bumped into the closed door at the bottom. We finally managed to open the door and ran screaming to our parents. They did not believe us and I remember that my father threatened to beat us if we did not go back upstairs. We were too terrified to enter the room again and just stood there. My mother sympathized with us and asked my father to look in the room. As far as we remember, he did not find anything and I do not recall anything unusual happening afterwards.

The next morning Sue, my mother and I discussed the incident. I thought I remembered that Sue said she watched the object move around outside the window for a while as if it were looking in and then it came right through the window. When I asked her about it later, she said that she woke up and first saw it in the room. (The window had a screen and glass. I think the glass was open, but the screen was always closed.)

I asked my family about this incident in 1984 and obtained my Mother's recollections from her CUFOS report (Figure 2):

My recollection of this occurrence is quite faint as it happened several years ago. My husband and I were reading after Irena and Sue had gone to bed. All of a sudden, the girls hit the closed stairway door and both of them bolted into the room screaming. They said something came into the window and a light traveled around the room two or three times (as I remember) and then it disappeared. They were scared and watched it until it disappeared. Then they ran downstairs. They were very frightened and we had no explanation for it. My sister's recollections were (Figure 3):

This happened when I was somewhere around six-nine years old....It was summer. My sister and I slept in the same room in different beds. It was probably around 9 - 11 and I had been asleep (or nearly so) when I became aware of a bright little light flying around the room, not at all like a lightning bug—much bigger and moving differently. I watched it, I suppose trying to figure out what it was and then I realized my sister was watching it, too. We became afraid and both ran downstairs to Mom and Dad as fast as we could. They were still awake, as I remember and thought we were nuts.

Years later my mother said Irena had probably been telling scary stories and we just got scared and imagined it, but I'm sure that wasn't true, because I had been asleep and it just wasn't something I imagined, I remember most of all being scared, I saw the object circle the lamp, but did not see it change its appearance or make a noise. It was the color of an ordinary light bulb and as big as a Ping-Pong ball. It was yellowish white.

It was larger than the holes in the window screen. My sister has since then recalled that she was not yet in school, so she was five or younger.

The event must have left quite an impression because several other relatives still remember it. For example, a cousin, now Dr. David Amacher:

June 6, 1987

When I was about 11 or 12 years old, Irena told me about a round bright object ....Both Sue and Irena saw it... I was so impressed by their story at the time that I didn't want to stay in that room by myself...

David Amacher

And people still remember it. I wrote to this same cousin, who lives in Connecticut in March 2018 and he remembered it:

It made quite an impression on me at my age then. We were visiting your family in Galena (or is it Lewis Center?) back then and staying overnight. I was put in the second floor bedroom furthest from the stairs and you and Sue stayed in the first room. One or both of you told me about ball lightning and how it could or did come into the room I was staying in through the window. After a while I became so scared that I left that room and went downstairs to sleep. I think there was a thunderstorm there that same night...I definitely remember the talk about ball lightning when we visited you folks way back then. I'm not sure if Sue said it came through that bedroom window but at that age and the T-storm that night, I was scared. Guess that's why I remember it so many years later![45]

At that time we did not know about bedroom visitations or small UFOs and thought it was a lightning ball, but we always thought it was something unnatural and when we found about small UFOs we thought that is what it was.

My mother described something coming in the window. She was older and may have remembered more than we did when we described the event to her. Because of the Budd Hopkins "Missing Time" theory, it is also possible that something in our minds might have repressed a part of the event. For example, there was no energy source in the room that would have had the power to create the object, so we do not know how it formed.

Because my parents still lived in this house, I was able to investigate further. I still do not know how the object entered the room. The room had one window, which was screened and two doors. The door to the downstairs was closed and the other one, which I think was closed, just opened into another room with a screened window. There were no holes or burn marks in the screens.

In comparison to a firefly, the object was on continuously for some time, had a color different from a firefly's and it did not move up and down in the manner of a lightning bug. There are no swamps in the vicinity, so there would be no reason to suspect it was swamp gas. It may have been shaped more like a capsule, than a sphere.

One inorganic source is ball lightning. As I recall, however, the night was clear. There are two reasons that I think that this was the case. For one reason, we all remember that it was and for another, we had old trees near the house and if my mother even thought it might storm, she kept us downstairs in case an old tree fell on the house. Since my parents made us return to the room, I am sure the weather was clear. Thus, I do not believe that this object was associated with an electrical storm.

It showed a complex, guided trajectory. It responded to its surroundings at a distance without touching them and it acted as if it were aware of the size and the shape of the room. It did not guide itself along electric wires or walls. There were wires at the top of the ceiling going from a wall switch to the chandelier and then to another chandelier in the next room (under wallpaper and plaster). The chandelier in our room was turned off at the wall switch. The object did not follow these wires. Also, there were wires along the wall for wall sockets and the object did not follow any of these wires. It seemed as if the trajectory it followed was intentional, rather than random. For example, when it flew toward something it turned some distance away and did not continue forward. Subjectively it seemed as if it were browsing around, rather than flying mechanically. In some reports, lightning balls are said to bump into things and disappear, but this carefully avoided all obstacles. It did not just fly in the center of the room, but around the periphery. It did not bump into the walls, even though they were slanted.

This is not the way a standard, prosaic lightning ball would behave. It might have sped up when it flew to the chandelier and I think when it circled it was traveling faster than when it meandered around the room. But it circled for some time traveling along the same exact pathway (Figure 4 shows the room and the chandelier).

It would seem as if it would require some type of energy to make it rise and speed up, however the air in the room was still with no breezes, so it is unknown where the energy would come from. This increase in speed did not appear to come from an external source because it flew in a circle–thus the air was not causing its increase in speed.

It flew near us and near our heads, as if it were inspecting us. Normally this would have scared me, but it did not at that time. It came very close to both of us and might have been extremely dangerous if it came into contact with us.

The object meandered while avoiding the walls and the furniture and it did not guide itself along anything. Even taking into account new theories such as fifth and sixth forces and antimatter, there is no basis that I know of that will hypothesize that the objects in the room would produce an effect (the object's deflection), because the object moved close to or away from the walls, furniture and us as it moved around, but it did not collide with anything.

There were no electrical problems in the room and have never been any in the many years since. The object gave no evidence of a propulsive system, such as when it flew to the chandelier, seemed to increase its speed and circled. It did not leave a trail or odor and made no noise as it flew.

We have no idea how long it was there. I could have watched the object for several minutes. Sue became aware of my watching it and thus may have watched it for a longer period of time than I did. However, we have no way of knowing how long it had been in the room before we awakened.

We also cannot explain why we awoke at the same time, or watched it without being scared, or suddenly became terrified and ran from the room at the same time.

We also do not know how it was powered to emit light and fly around, or how it guided itself so that it did not bump into anything, or how it entered our room. Ball lightning is said to leave a changed area when it travels through a screen, but these windows have always been in the room and there is no trace of any type of damage.

This may have happened around the 4th of July. We had not gone to see fireworks and none of the neighbors had set out any. The neighboring farmhouses were so far apart that we could not see them.

Discussion and confirming evidence:

Jenny Randles in *Star Children*, as mentioned previously, described "the presence of small balls of light, often seen in the bedroom whilst the abductee is a child," as a recurrent feature in British abductions.[146] However, she wrote that this happens to Americans also such as to Betty Andreasson, who was studied by Ray Fowler and experienced small balls of light as a child in Massachusetts. [47] [48] She then described our experiences.

Such experiences are often attributed to sleep paralysis. This might be true if it happened to one of us, only. But we were independently watching the light flying around the room for some time and did not know each other was awake. Then we both became terrified at the same time and ran out of the room screaming. We both remembered the same thing. Thus, it was not a dream or example of sleep paralysis, because we each had another witness.

The object's motion had some geometric properties, such as when it circled the chandelier. It seemed to know where objects were and did not bump into anything. When it flew to the chandelier, it very smoothly began to circle. It did not hesitate or feel its way around. It knew where both the chandelier and the wall were and began to circle keeping its distance from both even though it began circling quite rapidly. It seemed like it circled the chandelier quite a few times–maybe twenty to thirty. It made the exact same circle each time and seemed to fly quite rapidly when it did this.

Then it made a spiral of decreasing distance from a line drawn straight down from the center of the chandelier to the floor. When the spiral went exactly into this line, it appeared to me to emit flashes of light. Although my sister did not see this, we both suddenly became terrified and ran from the room at the same time.

The media did not influence us, because we had not heard of UFOs or even such a concept. We were on an isolated family farm with one radio and our parents played only certain programs on it. In addition, even if we had heard of UFOs, they were thought of as airplane-like craft, not objects in people's houses.

There might have been some form of mind control, or missing time, because we both woke up at nearly the same time and then became scared at the same time. This was probably the most terrified I ever was in my life and I still have effects from it. I do not know why we were so terrified because it was just a little object and we had never heard of UFOs, or aliens, or anything like that. My first reaction of curiosity seemed normal.

I have had some sort of aftereffects ever since it happened. For one thing, I am very nervous around north-facing windows at dark. Even now, I immediately close blinds and curtains in north-facing windows at dark. If I cannot, sometimes I crawl under the window so my profile does not show up. I think this began with the sighting. Possibly this has something to do with the window in our room. It was north-facing and my mother in her report gave a recollection of something coming in through the window. I think my sister said something about it at first and then forgot. Also I have always had a fear of looking out a window in the dark. I still have a nervous feeling if I open a blind to see out a window after dark. In addition, I have always felt nervous around chandeliers. I used to avoid standing under one and still am aware of it. Perhaps this has something to do with the object's circling the one in our room.[49]

Although this probably has nothing to do with anything, perhaps I should mention several additional elements that might relate to such childhood experiences. For one, around the time we saw the object, I disappeared. I am just relating this because sometimes disappearances are reported in association with UFO sightings–such as Travis Walton. I do not remember anything about it, but my relatives used to talk about it. In April 1948, just before my brother was born, a traveling magazine salesman came to visit my mother and visiting aunt. When they did not buy anything, he became furious. After he left, they discovered that I was missing and they thought he might have kidnapped me in retaliation. They searched all over the farm and finally found me in a pasture field. This would have been difficult for a young child to get to, because I needed to climb over two five-foot tall wire fences that had barbed wire on top. My mother had become hysterical and they wondered how this might have affected her childbirth. I wrote it up as we remembered it; my mother checked it over and then signed it. So at least I have a record of it. I think our bedroom sighting happened several months later.

This is probably totally irrelevant, but sometimes UFO sightings have been reported as associated with injuries. I will mention it just because I also have a record of it. I also had a bad concussion before this when I was five years old. There were barn owls in my aunt and uncle's barn. I was fascinated and climbed around trying to get closer to see them better. I recall falling through the first story, but nothing else. My father and uncle in the field heard a crash in the barn and came to see what happened. I had gone through the first floor and then crashed into a hayrack hard enough to break it apart. They carried me out and I was unconscious for some time.

I have a video of my aunt describing this. However, this would not have affected my sister, so it should not be relevant.

I tried to understand this experience over the years because it always seemed as if the object were animating, rather than just a physical object. When our observation happened, we had heard of neither lightning balls nor UFOs and were completely bereft of any explanation. Later when we had heard of UFOs, they were presented as space ships and as large vehicles that could carry people.

Years after this, I read Randles' publications about bedroom visitations. She described the bedroom sightings of children of small objects as "psychic toys," and said they "are very specific in appearance and behavior. They are balls of light – between tennis-ball and basketball in size – which enter the bedroom of the youngster…"

She further described them as "these appearances happened between the ages of about three and eight years old…They very rarely persisted into the teenage years or adulthood…"

She added that their purpose might be, "helping to prepare the youngster for the more traumatic things to come in later life. Indeed that may well be another part of their purpose." And, "There is undoubtedly an affinity between children and close encounter UFO sightings, of which these bedroom lights are merely a part. They seem to start the conditioning process that leads the youngster into a lifetime pattern of events where they share their lives with this alien presence".

She later gave my birth year and said that both she and Budd Hopkins noted that abductees were often born that year or began to have their experiences between that year and the next year.

She also mentioned that children, who have such bedroom visitations, often continue to have sightings later in their lives (people who have more than one sighting are sometimes called repeaters). Such people seem to fit a pattern.

She found that often there was some form of interaction between the child and the balls of light. We might have experienced something like this also, for example because we awakened at the same time.

Her description matches the profile of what we saw better than ball lightning does, thus perhaps this is what we saw.

There are a number of reasons to think that this object might be UFO-related, rather than prosaic:

1.*There was no electrical storm or any other kind of disturbance.*

2. The object's guidance seemed directional and intentional, rather than random. For example, it knew the room and furniture and avoided any contact. It appeared to first have a random browsing direction (including up and down and back and forth) that went around the room several times, rather than a mechanical pattern. In addition, it changed its flight pattern–this went from the browsing pattern that wound up in the south part of the room. Then it flew up to a place over the door near the ceiling, but did not touch the ceiling. It next made a straight-line course from the south end of the room along the ceiling to the chandelier. It knew where the chandelier and walls were and instantly began to circle exactly between them. It may have speeded up and it circled a number of times. Then it again changed its course to a spiral and still seemed aware of the chandelier. This spiral had geometric properties. In addition, subjectively it seemed as if it had been observing us during its browsing pattern.

3. There was no evidence for how it entered the room.

4. It appeared to have existed much longer than any typical lightning ball. We consciously remember it as lasting for longer than a minute and it seemed like several minutes. However, it actually lasted longer than this, because we both awakened with it in the room. Hence, we have no idea how long it actually lasted.

5. The object's lifetime exceeded many technical reports showing what it should have been for its size. For example, "Ball lightning is spheroidal, with a diameter between 20 and 50 cm. It is observed for between 2 and 5 s....Log-normal distributions have been described for diameter, lifetime, energy density and luminosity of ball lightning and have also been reported for its velocity and its closest distance from the observer." [50] [51] And, "The typical lifetime of ball lightning is 1–5 seconds. ...Experiments show that fireballs in air produced by a 5 kW, 2.45 GHz microwave can last for ~0.5 s after the source is turned off."[52] Thus, it appeared to last much longer than the calculations would indicate, "By calculating the heat and light that those wispy, charge-laden balls would generate, the team determined that a plausible ball roughly the size of a basketball would last 3 to 30 seconds."[53]

6. We both saw the same thing–showing that it was not a dream or form of sleep paralysis.

7. We do not know why we both awakened at about the same time, even though there appeared to have been no disturbance that would have aroused us.

8. We both ran from the room at the same time.

9. Our emotions at the same time suddenly changed from interest to terror.

10. Other people have reported similar phenomena such as in Randles' Star Children.

11.My sister did not see any type of activity before she ran out of the room. I thought it emitted light, but many UFO reports show this same ability to emit light or objects. There have been a number of UFO reports where two witnesses looking at the same thing, saw something different.

12.It may have changed shape or taken another form. Our mother said that she recalled us saying that something came in through the window and then the object began to travel around the room.

13.We have no idea how it formed. Normally ball lightning is explained as occurring after a lightning strike. The lightning provides it with energy–so far as I know, it cannot just form out of thin air. However there was no lightning and no power source in our room. Possibly my mother's recollection of something coming in the window relates to this.

14.It is strange that we did not say anything to each other. It would be natural to call another person's attention to something in the room with us because it might be something dangerous. I just watched it and saw it come close to her, but did not even think of saying anything.

15.It might have been very dangerous if it had come into contact with us. It obviously had energy but we do not know what kind or energy or how much.

16.Lightning balls often cease to exist because they come into contact with something. The object in our room seemed to know where things were and did not at any time come into contact with anything. When it disappeared, it was in midair and directly below the chandelier.

17.We were not influenced by the press, because we had never heard of UFOs.

18.This was smaller than most lightning balls are reported to be.

19.We experienced extreme terror, even though there appeared to be no reason for this.

20.We felt no electricity, but might have, because we were within feet of the object, "For the first time, we reveal that ball lightning is an alarm signal of the existence of ultra strong microwaves and abundantly hazardous electrons near the ground or aircraft. This result is of great significance for lightning protection and aviation safety. Moreover, it is hoped that our work will stimulate research activities in relativistic microwave physics and technology, an unexplored area before." [54] [55] We also felt no heat.

21.I did not have any after effects or long-term feelings about the lightning ball or any of the lightning experiences, but I had many after the bedroom light sighting.

22.It could increase its elevation and speed, which would take power. But there were no air currents or anything else to supply energy for this.

We had not heard about UFOs until several years later. When I first heard of them, it was in an article in the November 1952 *Coronet* magazine that a relative subscribed to. This instantly interested me, but my parents did not allow us to talk about it. I asked this relative to write a letter to the magazine for more information. (She lived in the house and was a witness of two events–the one where I saw the lightning ball and later had a purple object appear above my head). We had not heard about Mom's lightning ball experience.

In general in comparison to ball lightning, this event appeared to fit the characteristics of the small glowing bedroom objects such as described by Randles, more than those of a lightning ball.

Large orange object with barking dogs

My second sighting took place, when I was in grade or high school, at the same house at 6844 Bale Kenyon Road, Lewis Center, Ohio, as our bedroom light sighting (Figure 5). It was on a hot, clear night in the summer during the 1950s I was sleeping out-of-doors on my back on our porch, which was a large flat rock about 20 feet by 10 feet (Figure 6). I awakened and looked north to spot a soundless object having the appearance of orange incandescent metal and close to the angular diameter of the full moon. It slowly traveled north to south and passed directly over me. Unlike a meteor, it was large, slow moving and did not change its appearance. When it was directly overhead, I heard the dogs in the neighborhood (a farm community) suddenly begin to bark. Our dog, in the kitchen where she could not have seen it, began to bark and sound as if she were jumping, or knocking things over. I listened for our other animals–sheep, cows, etc., but did not hear anything unusual; however, all except the chickens may have been in the pasture. I wondered if it had turned on some type of sound when it was directly overhead. Perhaps it was something that the dogs, but not me, could hear.

The object was soundless to me and not an airplane. It continued south in a straight course. For some reason I do not remember exactly how it disappeared.

The object looked like glowing metal all over, not just in the front like bright airplane landing lights. I saw no other lights, except its glowing. It had the same appearance as it approached me, when it was overhead and as it left. It seemed at about the same altitude and size as a passenger airplane. I was extremely terrified and did not move until morning. After the observation, I heard and saw an airplane pass over.

My mother was sleeping inside, but I did not call her. Probably this was because I was afraid to make a sound or go inside because I thought my parents would say I was lying and beat me up. I told no one about it until many years later.

This was nothing like airplane landing lights. When you see airplane landing lights, the airplane is traveling toward you. With this, the object looked the same throughout the sighting. I sent my orange ball report with my CUFOS report (also published in the *Ohio UFO Notebook* May 1992).

Purple sphere

I had one other experience, but do not know what it was. I was in a neighbor's house–the same one where I saw the lightning ball. The sighting occurred in the 1950s. My parents and the same father's cousin that I had been with in the lightning ball sighting were there. We were talking and I was in a chair. Suddenly a basketball sized purple ball of light appeared above my head and then exploded. A lamp was off to the side of the chair (not where the ball had been) and my father took it apart looking for a short circuit. He did not find anything. I think this was in summer or fall, maybe around the 4th of July. It happened in the daytime and no one knew what it was.

A number of additional strange events happened to me in relation to the family farm and this house, such as my finding out about John Purdue, the founder of Purdue University–that I am related to him and possibly influencing me to write a book about him–discussed in Appendix 1.

People who have these events happen to them are often criticized for such reasons as being weird, or as a mindless believer out looking for UFOs or aliens, or as hoaxers taking advantage of people's gullibility. However, we were not out looking for UFOs, nor mindless believers. This is because we had not even heard of UFOs or any concept related to them when our experience happened. And we did not know anything about hoaxing either. And why would we lie about something we did not know anything about?

The events began when we were very young. They are very similar to the events such as described in *The Andreasson Affair: The Documented Investigation of a Woman's Abduction Aboard a UFO* [56] and other books about her experiences. They are also much like the events that have been described by Jenny Randles and Budd Hopkins.

With this, I am very fortunate to have another witness for the initial event and others who remembered it. In general most such happenings occur when the witness is alone–and therefore they are discounted and especially ignored because they happen to children.

I am also fortunate to have something to compare them to, such as the lightning experiences I had earlier and at different times later in life. These possible UFO experiences seem much different from the lightning experiences.

In addition, they fit into the repeater pattern described by a number of UFO investigators such as Randles. However, there is little if any explanation about what it means.

Several authors had suggested that people who fit such a pattern might be some sort of human-alien hybrids. These authors include Randles and Brad Steiger, in such books as, *The Seed*, *The Star People*, which tells about how thousands of people are discovering that they are descendants of visitors from the stars and *Revelation: The Divine Fire*, which tells how the gifts of prophecy and divination are manifestations of humankind's developing "star consciousness." However, we have had DNA tests and are fully human, so that does not apply to us–not unless the entire human race is hybridized.

Others have looked for specific physical attributes that these people may have in common, such as Kathleen Marden. Marden is now making a statistical study of her data.

So far, there are no definite results and no rigorous statistical study, such as even comparing such witnesses to a control group, has been made. However, I think the subject should be studied and hope Marden's study turns out well.

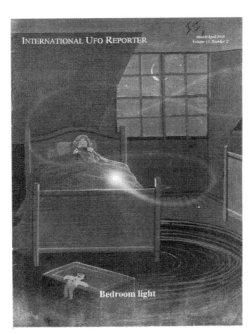

Figure 1: The cover of the International UFO Reporter in which our bedroom light experience was reported. This was drawn by a Center for UFO Studies (CUFOS) artist.

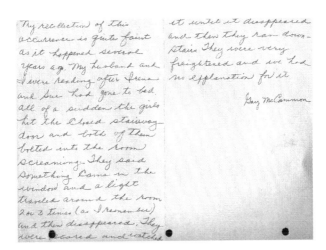

Figure 2: My mother's write-up of the bedroom light event done in 1984 and turned in as a report to CUFOS.

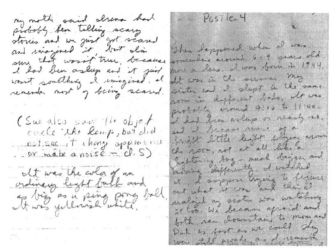

Figure 3: My sister's write-up of the bedroom light event done in 1984 and turned in as a report to CUFOS also. She has remembered since then that she was not yet in school, thus, she was 4 or 5 years old.

Figure 4: The room where our bedroom light sighting took place, showing the chandelier that the object circled, the room that it flew around in, the north window, the walls that were close together at the ceiling and the stairway we fell down (it looked different in 1948). The object had been flying around the room in a browsing manner, then flew up to one side of the ceiling, then straight across to the chandelier and then began to circle it between it and the wall. It knew the location of the chandelier (which was turned off) and the wall. It did not hesitate or feel its way around, but did this quickly and smoothly. It circled in same path a number of times. It circled at about the level of the upper rim of the green chandelier.

Scott 4

This sighting was in the 50's, and, unfortunatly, I don't have other witnesses. On a hot summer night, when I was sleeping outside on a flat open porch of my parent's house (6844 Bale Kenyon, Galena), I woke up and looking north spotted a bright orange object about the size of the full moon, that looked like incadescent metal. I had seen meteors before and this was nothing like a meteor. It was large, slow, kept the same altitude and didn't change appearance like meteors do when they burn up. It was completely soundless. Slowly it traveled straight south. When it was directly overhead, our dog, locked in the kitchen where it couldn't see the object, began to bark and make a commotion. At this time, I heard all the dogs in the neighborhood (this is a farm community and the houses are about 1/4 mile apart) suddenly begin to bark. It was as if it had just then turned something on that caused the dogs to bark; I hadn't noticed the dogs to the north barking before that. I remember listening for the other animals (sheep, chickens, cows) but don't recall hearing anything unusual. The sheep and cows may have been in the fields, too far away to hear. The object was soundless and not an airplane. It continued south in a straight course. After the sighting, I heard a jet plane and then saw one pass over. I wondered if it's pilot saw the object. I was terrified from the instant I saw it and for hours afterwards. I wasn't thinking anything, when I first saw it, which I believe was immediatly after I woke up. Afterwards, I was scared to stay there on the porch, but I knew my parents would be mad if I made noise comming back in, so I just stayed there under its path, terrified for several hours. I didn't write or tell anyone about this because my parents disaproved of UFO's. Also, although my mother was sleeping in the room next to me, I did not think of calling her and have no idea why. My family lives north of Columbus, Ohio, near two airfields-Port Columbus and Don Scott airfield. All of us could identify airplanes and we frequently flew with a neighbor, who had an airplane and a landing strip immediatly west of our farm. We also used to visit airports to watch planes land and to fly with our neighbor. I was familiar with landing lights, meteors, search lights, balloons and that sort of thing.

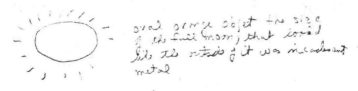

oval orange object the size
of the full moon; that looked
like the metal of it was incadescent
metal

1

Figure 5: *My description of the orange object that flew over our porch in the 1950s. This was sent to CUFOS in 1984.*

Figure 6: The author on the rock porch upon which the orange disc sighting took place and at roughly the age when it occurred. The room above the porch was where the bedroom light sighting occurred.

******

CHAPTER FOUR: ADULT SIGHTINGS: THE DIA, CAR CHASE AND A STRANGE MAN

Massachusetts sighting, 1968

One of the first of our adult sightings was unique because it took place while I was working for a government intelligence agency, the DIA. It is unknown how many government workers, if any, in such agencies have UFO sightings and weird ones at that, while under actual employment in government work that involves high security clearances or work in what might be a related field.

This event had many unique and confusing elements: a near-death encounter, possible missing time and additional events. The photography could even supply proof that UFOs carry lighting that is not in the visible range and might supply information that would help to explain a number of the seemingly unexplainable aspects of the phenomena. In addition, the photographed image might have shown the inside of a UFO, rather than the normal exterior lighting. The objects we saw have remained unidentified.

We also experienced an unusual man whose actions might have killed us. Having a being attempt to possibly murder a witness during a sighting is highly unusual and suggests that UFO phenomena could be more dangerous than previously presented. This man also prevented me from possibly taking a photograph of the inside of a UFO, he appeared to call me crazy and he caused my sister and me to split apart. These events are very rare or maybe never reported before. He also asked what we were watching when we watched the object and then turned in the opposite direction and said he did not see anything.

In addition, a comparison to similar sightings in the area was made, quite a number of additional unusual, common characteristics were shown by these objects and this will be covered in more detail in the following, "A comparison to similar events," section.

I have quite a bit of confirming evidence. Shown are further corroborating reports: the CUFOS report and three write-ups by Sue Postle, as described above. My CUFOS report included a detailed write-up that I had made from the initial notes I took on July 15 below and a photograph I took of the object. It also includes a letter my mother wrote to her sister-in-law about a week after our experience in which she describes it. I also have letters, discussions about this, other people's ideas, other witnesses and much more as confirmation. I think I took my photograph to work that week and using our photographic equipment, made an enlarged copy. I labeled and dated this copy.

Further confirmation is that my photography was accepted into the scientific peer reviewed literature, "Photogrammetric Analysis of a Photograph of an Aerial Anomaly," by an AAAS publication (Figure 2).[57] Both the photograph and the scientific acceptance provide hard evidence of this event. A number of logical inferences can be made from this material and these might provide explanations some of the mystery aspects of UFO phenomenon and show some of its elements.

Information about this encounter was published elsewhere. It was so long and complex that it was published in two parts: "Fear and ambiguity in Massachusetts," in *IUR*: 7/8 1988 and "A Photograph and its aftermath," in *IUR*: 9/10 1990.[58] [59] [60] The first part was the sighting and the second part showed an analysis of the photograph and the account of my poltergeist experience. Dr. Bruce Maccabee had looked at the photography and sent a letter, but he did not have the complete information. I took photographs with both color film and black and white high-speed film.

When we finally reported it in 1984, our sighting was investigated by a number of the world's foremost UFO authorities, such as Dr. Hynek (the father of UFOlogy, the founder of the Center for UFO Studies and author of many important books), who discussed the sighting with Budd Hopkins. Budd Hopkins (maybe the world's best-known abduction expert who has written several books such as *Missing Time* and Intruders, *The Incredible Visitations at Copley Woods*) interviewed my sister and her family. He interviewed her with "Kathie Davis" (Deb White Kauble) in Indianapolis on November 11, 1984. I have been in contact her and she still remembers this interview,[61] Deb "Kathie Davis" was the featured person in Hopkins' next book, *Intruders: The Incredible Visitations at Copley Woods*.[62] No one identified the objects.

Hopkins tried several times to hypnotize me on October 27, 1985. This was taped during unsuccessful hypnosis sessions. In the future, we had planned again try ways to enhance our recall. Mr. Hopkins did this because he thought that I had been abducted. Hypnosis has no effect on me at all. I tried with some medical doctors, but I do not even very slightly go into a trance.

There were also a number of similarities between Kauble's events and ours. Hopkins wanted to use some of our information and photographs in his book as shown in his letters.[63]

We also have contacted the witnesses to similar events such as Raymond Fowler's, Betty Andreasson.

Other investigators included Leo Sprinkle (author of numerous books), Kathleen Marden (niece of Betty Hill, who studies abduction and has published a number of books) and a number of others. I also talked to John Timmerman, Michelle Baumeister and Jennie Zeidman of CUFOS, Joe Nyman of Massachusetts and Walt Andrus of MUFON.

My sister may have and I reported this experience immediately afterward, but I made no formal report, so that there likely is no record of this. I knew next to nothing about UFOs, just looked in the phone book for UFO and found the National Investigations Committee On Aerial Phenomena (NICAP). Also because I knew little about UFOs, I did not report the green light, odd person, car chase, rotating ball and other events, I just reported the shape of the object. To hide my identity, I called them from a pay phone and gave a description and time. I provided no information at all about myself. I was very nervous about doing this because of my DIA position. I also wondered if the government would monitor UFO reports from within that organization (and found out years later that they had been infiltrated by the government and might be doing just that). I worried that they might find out who I was and where I was employed. I also vaguely wondered if the sighting could in some way relate to my work, or that the DIA might know something about it (and later discovered that the DIA was investigating UFOs at that time).

My notes say:

Because of my security clearance, I did not report the observation...On July 15, 1968, I reported the observation by phone to NICAP in Wash. DC. I did not give my name or fill out a report form. I do not believe that I mentioned any of the other odd events, such as the green light in the car. The NICAP woman sounded very bored and remarked that this wasn't much of a sighting. When I asked if there had been other reports, she said to find out from Boston (which I did not do) and mentioned a power failure in Baltimore...Sue thought that there had been a newspaper article about the UFOs near Boston in a Boston newspaper around the time of our observation. She thought that it was possible that she made a report to project Blue Book, but there is no record of this....We both filled out formal reports to CUFOS in 1984.

The Massachusetts Sighting:

After high school, my sister and I left the farm and eventually lived all over the US and in different countries. In the 1960s, we were both living along the eastern coast. She was attending Drew University in New Jersey and the general New York area and I was working for the DIA in Washington, DC.

Because we wanted to see more of the Eastern US while we were there, we decided to make a trip to Boston and the New England states.

The very last thing we were thinking about was UFOs, we had barely spoken at all about the topic since right after the bedroom event and we had not associated this with UFOs but merely thought it a mystery.

But instead of our nice planned vacation, something else happened. We were almost murdered. This happened in our journey when we made an observation outside of Boston of two soundless, mysterious objects: one flying and one on or near the ground. The flying one was large with brightly lit square windows along its sides and the other was spherical and changed colors through a spectrum.

On July 13, 1968, we made a planned holiday trip to the New England states. I picked up two DIA coworkers and left Washington, D.C., at 6:00 am and, after a traffic delay, arrived at her dormitory at Drew University, Madison, New Jersey, at around 10:30 am (I took a photo of them talking to us in front of Sue's dorm and photographs of many other portions of the trip, Figure 1.)

We both forgot our watches and the car clock was not working, so our times are estimates. At around 1:00 pm or before, Sue and I left New Jersey, taking Route 95 north. Around 3:00-4:00 P.M., we stopped in Connecticut (around one hour) and then arrived at Boston around 5:00-6:00 P.M. Since it was still daylight we decided to travel from 128 up Route 3 into New Hampshire. (I took photos in NH, but do not know where–one showed a lake.)

During this drive we had accidentally driven in the area of the Betty and Barney Hill abduction described in John G. Fuller's 1966, *The Interrupted Journey: Two Lost Hours aboard a Flying Saucer*. At the time, we were not thinking about UFOs and did not know even which state the Hill abduction happened. But after realizing this later, we had definitely traveled the route where portions of their abduction occurred, for example, they were 17 miles north of Concord, New Hampshire, when their full awareness returned, they heard the second beeping sound about 20 miles north of that and the abduction was about five miles north of that.

Around 9:00–10:00 P.M., we returned to Boston. We drove from Rt. 3 to 128 and from there entered Boston on Route 9: something slightly odd happened at a filling station here, but I do not remember what it was now. Then, unable to find a motel room in Boston, we decided to search the Boston outer belt. At about 10:00-11:00 P.M., we were traveling west on Route 9 and noticed an unusual object to our south. We hadn't been thinking about UFOs and had previously paid little attention to this subject.

As we traveled on Route 9 and then south on Route 128, we watched the object intermittently. The object was as bright as or brighter than airplane landing lights, but moving in an erratic pattern and blinking. Sue said she thought it might be a UFO. I told her that it was a helicopter blinking its landing lights–although I had never seen anything like this.

A while later Sue told me that she once had a sighting of a possible UFO over our cousin's house. I was surprised because our parents were negative on the subject of UFOs and hadn't permitted us to talk about it during our childhood. I told her that I might have had a previous sighting over our parent's house and I also mentioned the object we had seen in our bedroom when we were children (our Bedroom Light article in the *IUR*).

As we continued on 128, we could still see the object to the south in front of us. It was impossible not to notice it. I was logical and informed Sue that if it were a UFO, the radio and TV stations would announce its presence and the police, newspapers, fire department, public and all else would come out to look at it. Since no crowd was watching it, it could not be a UFO.

It was very easy to distinguish from any other aircraft, it was a very white shade of white, it had no other lights, it was low and bright and it had a regular blinking pattern that was slower than and nothing like an airplane's strobe lights.

To our south we could see airplanes coming in from the east and traveling to the west, some with their landing lights on. Some of them may have been landing at the Norwood Memorial Airport on Route 1. The object differed greatly from the airplanes because it took a meandering path, its light was blinking all the time and it was lower, showing less angular displacement from the ground than airplanes the same distance away. It appeared to be traveling south along Route 95. The airplanes generally appeared to be small single-engine airplanes.

Because I was driving, I did not watch the object as closely as Sue did. I was put out because she was paying attention to the object instead of watching for a motel. Years later, in 1984, after we had submitted our reports to CUFOS, Sue told me that she thought the object was unusual because it would hover and then flit to another place at an incredible speed. Since I did not watch it closely (its unusual appearance was so obvious that I did not even consider that it could be anything abnormal), I noticed only its odd lighting and meandering trajectory.

Traveling south on Route 95, we noticed what appeared to be a basketball-sized object around 20-50 feet away from us. On or near the ground, it constantly changed colors and was in thick woods on the west side of the road. As I remember, the colors varied from red to blue and changed so that they gradually blended into each other. For example, they would change from red to bright pink, dark pink and then to more of a bluish color. The object appeared to be a transparent globe encompassing the changing light and there seemed to have a thin dark strip that slowly rotated around it. It showed one color at a time, not a spectrum like a prism. At that time, I did not know where the airports in the area were and assumed that the light belonged to an airport. Since then, I have learned that the nearest airport— Norwood—was not in that location. And I have never seen an airport light that like that either.

As we passed the object, the inside of the car lit up for a minute or more in green, as if several green Christmas tree lights were shining inside the car. I remember looking for the source of the green light and not seeing anything–I saw no beam. The object by the road wasn't green. I also remember discussing the green light with Sue while the car was lit up. I think we decided it must have been an airport light (although now I do not know what it was). I do not recall that I saw green light on the outside of the car. I do not know if the possible UFO was in sight at that time, because I wasn't watching it. Sue now says that she remembers nothing, or has only a very vague memory, about the ball of light or the light in the car. But I had it in my notes that we discussed it at the time, so I think she forgot.

She had continued to insist that the object was unusual and this irritated me, because I thought a UFO could not be that close to a city and that obvious without attracting attention. I had been bitten by mosquitoes and wanted to find a motel as soon as possible. I remember shouting, "It's a helicopter!"

I had a camera and film in the car and if I even slightly thought it was a UFO, I would have taken a photo.

Further south, Sue said that it was going to pass over the road and insisted that I stop. I pulled to the west side of 95, grumbled and pointed my hand out the window, so that I could immediately say, "See, stupid, a helicopter," as soon as I saw the object. Just as l did this, I saw a distant meteor's brief flash (subtending a small degree of arc) and remarked on it. Immediately, in approximately the same place, several degrees north of east, the low blinking object appeared flying over the trees. I do not know the degree of arc that its long axis subtended, but I was able to easily see and count seven distinct, brightly lit square areas in a horizontal row along its length. These looked like windows. The object resembled a football with seven windows along its midsection. We thought we were viewing the inside of the object (Figure 6). At the time, this seemed so obvious that I did not think of figuring out why we thought the squares were windows instead of panels.

I think one reason was that there was the effect of depth that we were stereoscopically seeing inside the object. It seemed as if we were looking through a transparent layer and into the objects interior.

We have seen advertising airplanes and this object looked nothing like one of them. The squares were on the side of this object. Each of the seven was square; their sides made exact right angles and they were in a row. The object crossed the road slowly so we had plenty of time to view it from different angles and its appearance had nothing in common with an advertising airplane. The lit areas were definite squares with distinct spaces between them. The corners of the windows were not rounded as are aircraft windows (to prevent fatigue cracks) and they subtended approximately ¼ of the object's width.

We had a whole lot of time to compare the object with airplanes. We first saw it when we headed west on Route 9 and continued to see it when we were on Routes 128 and 95. It did not resemble airplane landing lights, because you see them when the plane is heading toward you. In this case we were following it. As we drove south, the object was in front of us also going south. The airplanes were coming in from the east and traveling west. It appeared that many were landing in the airport.

In her CUFOS report Sue said that when we first saw the object, "a light seemed to shine down from it and shined in our car,'' and added in a letter (1984) to me that the inside of the car lit up in blue. I do not remember this. Perhaps only Sue saw this because she had to look across the car, whereas I was looking out the window. I immediately turned off the car, got my camera out, removed my film from the car trunk and watched the object over my shoulder as I loaded my camera by placing it on the car trunk and feeling it. Sue was standing to my west behind the car. The object traveled from east to west.

The object was soundless and much lower than the airplanes. We had seen this as we approached it and thus had been able to compare its altitude with that of airplanes from several angles and distances. The object's inside was evenly lit by a very high intensity white light, which resembled mercury vapor or fluorescent light. The light wasn't concentrated anywhere, almost as if the walls were glowing or even the atmosphere inside the object were glowing. We were also surprised by the light's brightness. We had watched the object all the way from Boston and the light was as bright or brighter than airplane landing lights. The light was nothing like the dimmer yellowish interior lights of airplanes. I thought it might have been bright enough to hurt the eyes of anyone inside of it. It resembled the whiteout light I had seen in the Texas lightning strike.

We could also hear the airplanes when we were close to the object, but could not hear it. We expected to see something like the inside of an airplane with furniture, or pilots, but did not see any features. We discussed the fact that we could not see the operators and were puzzled. I hoped to take a photograph of the inside of the object with operators. Since the windows took up a fair portion of the object's area, we speculated about whether it might be empty or have operators (if human-sized) under the windows or in the front or back, where there weren't any windows.

Sue said that its silhouette occluded stars. I did not notice this because I paid attention to loading my camera. I think, however, that I also saw a silhouette. The object was fairly low and there may have been enough light diffusing from Boston, the freeway and its own lighting to have enabled us to see its dark portion. It passed very slowly over the highway giving us a lot of time to view it from different angles.

As we watched it, we repeatedly asked each other detailed questions, such as: "How many windows do you count?" to determine whether we saw the same thing. The sky was clear. We would have been able to determine whether it had wings. If a wing had been above the windows, their light would have reflected from it and if a wing had been below the windows, it would have blocked our view of the windows. We saw no indication of wings. We heard no sound from it, although we could hear nearby airplanes that were higher than the object during the time we watched it. It had a small unblinking red light on one end and a small unblinking green light on the other end. Neither of us remembers which light was on which end. However, my sister said that it did not matter which light was on which end because the object could have any orientation–it did not go straight forward as an airplane would and it also traveled in all directions including circling. We did not see any blimp above it; thus, we did not believe it to be the undercarriage of a blimp.

We were calm, scientific and methodical and continually checked our observations by asking each other questions. We were not hysterical or emotional. We did not anticipate the observation, had no "Oz-factor" experience and did not experience the events as dream-like. Our environment seemed normal except for the object. Neither of us recall having had a hallucination. We were used to being out of doors and have excellent night and color vision. I had extensive training in photo interpretation and in aircraft identification from my work.

The blinking pattern was complicated. Although I cannot recall the pattern exactly when the object crossed the road, I think that its three front squares would blink on and off twice; then all seven would blink on and off once and the last four squares would blink on and off. Its squares would then be off for a while. Afterwards they would repeat the sequence.

We thought there might have been two compartments in the interior such that the lights in one area could he turned on separately from the others. Sue does not now recall that the lights had any pattern during the rest of the observation. She also thought that the blinking pattern would have depended on the object's orientation. I would estimate that when a group of windows were lit, they stayed on for around a second. I think that possibly when the three windows were lit this blink was of the shortest duration and there was a difference also in the duration of four versus seven squares being lit. Also, during the observation, Sue kept referring to the blinking pattern as a signal. I did not understand why she kept saying this and asked her several times. She seemed to think that the object was signaling someone. When I asked her in 2016, she said she thought that there was some kind of signal that she was supposed to understand but she could not figure it out.

As we watched I had loaded my camera. I had the camera in the trunk and the film in the back of the car. I found both in the dark. When you take a picture with the Polaroid, you pull the film and a coating through rollers. This squeezes a substance that hardens on the rollers. So before you do anything, you clean the rollers. Then you put in the film cartridge and then pull a black thing (that blocks the light from the film) through rollers.

When I finished loading my camera, I believed that the object was still close enough for the separate windows to be visually resolved. I was really impressed because I thought I might be able to take maybe the world's only photo of the inside of a UFO.

By this time, however, a tractor truck with a trailer pulled over in front of us. I assumed that the driver had stopped to watch the object and was glad that we had another observer. The driver came back and asked what we were doing, acting as if he thought we were having car trouble. We knew that it is dangerous to take up with strange men at night and so we just pointed to the object and asked him what it was, acting as if we thought it was an unusual airplane.

I was standing behind the driver's rear tire of our car. Sue stood behind the passenger rear tire to my west and the truck driver was standing east of me about one or two feet away. I pointed to the object's position in the northwest. When I pointed to it, he rotated his whole body 180 degrees, so that he was facing the exact opposite direction–to the southeast–and looked to about the same azimuth as the object and said that he did not see anything. Then he rotated back to face northeast. Then he asked the same question a second time (in a sincere manner). I gave the same reply and he then went through the same set of motions. Then after he had rotated back to face the northwest, he gave us the cuckoo sign (pointed to his forehead and shook his head) and returned to his truck, where he sat watching us through his side mirror. My notes say that he acted as if he thought we were watching a UFO but we did not say this to him.

He never looked in the object's direction and I did not press the issue because I was afraid of him. I have no idea why he asked me twice. Maybe he was emphasizing that he did not see it or something. I think I recall that the UFO had been directly over his truck as the object slowly passed over the freeway and, thus, thought it quite odd that he did not see it when he drove his truck under it.

I do not remember much about his appearance. He was a little taller than I am. He must have been average in appearance, because I did not notice anything in particular about him. To me, he did not have any accent, although we were in Massachusetts. He acted like a normal person and not like anyone on alcohol or drugs; it was just what he did that was strange. Sue doesn't recall talking with him at all; however, she does remember the truck's passing us, parking in front of us and following us later. She vaguely remembered that the driver did not see the object. By the time the truck driver left (I was afraid to take my eyes off him when he was there, so I did not take a picture), the object was farther away and probably too far away to photograph the separate squares. I did not consider flagging down another witness because I was trying very hard to take a picture and I was hesitant to confront strangers at night.

Another thing I just thought about and should have noticed back then was that he just stayed there watching us. If this were just a normal happening, for example if he just stopped to see what we were doing, I think he would have driven away. Instead he continued to watch us for the rest of the sighting. This was somewhat intimidating and why Sue and I argued and split apart.

The object must have been to my northwest when I started talking with the truck driver. When I was finished, it should have been further northwest. At that point, I did not want to take a photograph while standing by the freeway, because I was afraid of getting traffic lights or lens flares in my photograph. I had photographed stars before with this camera and knew that I needed a time exposure. There was a tree-covered hill to the west, so I asked Sue to guard the car while I ran over the hill to try to take photographs. This was a slightly odd thing to do because I did not know what was on the other side of the trees and hill.

Sue began to argue with me, insisting that she come with me. She said later that she thought the object was close and did not want me to run toward it.

But I was afraid that the truck driver would take over the car if we both left. We continued to argue and finally Sue stayed by the car. When I talked with her in 1987, however, she insisted that she remembered nothing about talking with the man and did not understand what I was talking about when I wanted her to guard the car. This was odd because she remembered seeing the truck approach and leave and also recalls knowing that he did not see the UFO. I ran up the hill to the west, through a group of trees and came out on the other side of the hill. There was a freeway fence and an area with no trees. The UFO should have been to the northwest but I'm not sure where it was. If it had been to the northwest, there wouldn't have been any reason for me to go up over the hill.

It is possible that the object changed its trajectory from traveling from the east toward the west to traveling from the west toward the north or northeast, while I was speaking with the truck driver or going through the grove of trees. I looked around this area in 1987 and there is a fence on the other side of the hill, which follows along the freeway.

I was extremely interested in taking the photograph, because I thought that we were viewing the inside of the object and I did not know any other instance when anyone had the opportunity to photograph this. At the time I worked in photography for the DIA and realized that I could not get good photographs, such as a 3-D stereo pair, to "prove" my case, but I wanted a souvenir anyway. I was very careful in taking these photographs. I had run up the hill and could see the object from the hilltop. It was easily distinguishable because it was bright, low and blinking. I carefully looked at it by eye and then also very carefully viewed it through the viewfinder each time I took a photo. I definitely saw and photographed the object. I pulled each photo out through the rollers. I think I took five photographs.

I made sure the object was in view, in focus and its lights were on. However after this, one needs to peel the photography off a backing. I did not do this on the hilltop; I ran back over the hill with my photographs held in order between my fingers and then pulled off the backing and coated them while viewing them with the inside car light. After this a person needs to coat each photograph with a protective coating, which I did. Only one photo came out, number two. I saved it and number one, but cannot find the others. The photo had the number two and K70474 on the back. I need to find out if this could be used for definite identification and dating.

Perhaps only one photograph showed the object because of the difficult conditions in which I took the pictures. It was dark, I needed to take a time exposure but was uncertain how long this should take so I guessed and I had nothing on which to stabilize the camera. I am very sure that I photographed the object.

After I made my CUFOS report and read Sue's report, there were parts of hers that I did not understand. So I asked for her recollections (Figure 3):

We realized that the object was going to go directly over the road in front of us or just over the trees (about 70 feet up). Irena pulled the car over to stop so we could get out to see it better. We both rapidly got out. Irena climbed a small hill to get closer. I stayed near the car. I was watching to see if could see people or beings inside. I could not even see a shadow. Then Irena decided to take a picture of it and hurried down the hill and got her camera out. The film was out in the camera and it seemed to take a long time for her to get new film in. She seemed to have a problem getting the film in. Then she was ready to take the picture, but the object was quite a ways off then. It immediately left the area where we were as soon as it crossed the freeway. There was no sound when it left. It just seemed to suddenly get into another place. In this write up she saw me run up the hill at least twice.

Sue once recalled that when I was over the hill she could hear me talking. (I do not recall talking when I was there and there was no one to talk to.) Also once, she said that she remembered my running back over the hill twice and that I seemed excited and was shouting once. She also said once that when I was on the hill she thought the UFO was right over me. That is why she said in her CUFOS report, "It could be right over you and completely disappear." She reported hovering. This surprised me because I did not recall watching it hover. She thought I was close to it when she thought that it hovered over my head. She also said that she thought it made several passes over the car. It must have made more than one, because it was in the wrong direction when I was on the other side of the hill ready to take pictures. I do vaguely recall another pass, but the memory is discontinuous with the rest of my memory. I do not recall any of this and found out when I asked her after I read her report in July 1987.

Although our recall of the possible UFO's appearance and of most of the observation is generally the same, our recall of certain particular events during the time we were stopped is different. Several events that we remember differently are: (1) The number of times I ran over the hill and whether or not I was talking; (2) speaking with the truck driver; (3) the object's blinking pattern; (4) its trajectory, distance from us (Sue seems to remember that when she first saw it, it made a low close pass over us) and whether or not it was directly over me; (5) its zooming away. These differences seemed to occur when we were separated, not when we were together.

I believe that my recollections are accurate because I made notes on the 15th and kept them; Sue also made notes. She believes that she sent them to Project Bluebook. I have checked and her report is not there – however, it has been reported that a number of reports are missing from Project Bluebook files. These differences may have occurred because (1) We paid attention to different things, (2) her recall over time may not be as good as mine because she lost her notes (3) her recall of the UFO itself and its trajectory might be better than mine because she watched it while I was doing other things, or (4) the possible UFO did something to our minds. In several instances, her memory seemed better than mine, as in her recollection of the object's blinking pattern. The only blinking pattern that I recall had to do with seven, four and three squares blinking. Sue recalls this pattern but in general she thinks the pattern was random and depended on the object's orientation. Perhaps this is because she watched it for a longer time than I did.

Also, three of Sue's accounts say that she saw the object speed away around the time that I took my photographs. I do not remember seeing it do this (Figures 4 and 5). I did not even think about it until 1987, when I wondered why the object wasn't in the location (in the northwest) where I thought it should have been, when I took my photographs. (If it had been to the west, I wouldn't have needed to leave the freeway.) Sue appeared to have watched it "suddenly get into another place" at around the time I was talking with the truck driver. Moreover, although we were parked in public freeway traffic, we seemed to be confused right here and not later, when we followed the object along an isolated road.

The object was now perhaps one to three miles west or northwest of us. It began to circle. The diameter of the circle was perhaps one mile and it appeared to make a perfect geometrical counterclockwise circle each time in exactly the same place. It was too distant for us to see individual squares. Its circling followed a regular pattern that it repeated over and over. When it moved in the south to north semicircle, it started at 180 degrees with its lights off, then it blinked its lights on at approximately 150 to 120 degrees, then turned them off, turned them on at 60 to 30 degrees, turned them off until it reached 360 directly north. When it appeared to be at the northernmost part of each circle (360 degrees), it would turn on its lights and travel in a 360- to 180-degree semicircle incomprehensibly fast. It was almost too fast to see and I vaguely remember each time afterward that it had flashed past (Figure 9). I was afraid each time it made this fast pass because it could have just gone anywhere in a fraction of a second. I have never seen such speed.

Its lights seemed more intense when it made this fast pass, but it might have looked this way because the object was moving toward me and, thus, would have subtended a larger angular displacement as it was approaching me (from 360 to 180 degrees) and also there might have been a Doppler effect. I wondered if the object's increased speed had anything to do with the power to the lights that might make them brighter or their light higher in frequency. The object may have been circling something. At that time, we thought it was circling the airport. We stood watching it and comparing observations. During the time we watched it, we had not heard sounds from it, although we heard the airplanes in the area. As it circled, several times we heard loud booming sounds like a jet engine revving, or like a sonic boom.

We discussed this and decided that the noise might have been from a jet preparing to leave the airport. (In 1987, Joe Nyman of Massachusetts told me, that there were no jet airplanes at Norwood Airport.) The noise frightened me. I cannot recall whether or not I heard the booms each time the object traveled fast, but the sounds occurred while it was circling. I wondered if the sounds might have been associated with the circling, in other words, if it had been making sonic booms during the rapid part of its circular flight pattern, but the sounds did not seem to correlate. It was certainly going more rapidly than the speed of sound.

As we had watched the object, we also watched other aircraft flying in the area. The object stayed lower than the other aircraft. It seemed that airplanes were not landing there, while the object circled. We could see several airplanes as they circled high above the, airport.

We did not know which direction we should take, when we returned to the car. Our car was heading south. We were unfamiliar with the roads in the area and had no idea which direction the object might take when it stopped circling. We decided to turn our car around at the next intersection. When we pulled on to the freeway, the truck driver we had seen earlier pulled in right behind us. He rode our bumper (it seemed like three to ten feet behind us) and seemed to beam his bright lights into my rear view mirror. Because truck headlights are higher than normal headlights, I was blinded—could barely see the road. At first I thought he was trying to signal us and almost started to pull over to ask what he was doing, but I changed my mind. For some reason I thought of the green lights that had been in the car and looked back to see if our car was lit up again. I thought he might have seen the light and decided to look more closely or was looking for something in our car. Then I got scared and floored it. I was going about 80 mph. Whenever I switched lanes, he switched lanes. I thought he might run us off the road or get us killed in an accident. I do not know what intersection it was but we agreed to swerve off the road at the next intersection from the left hand lane so he would not suspect that we were leaving he freeway. This was a very hazardous thing to do, because we could not see behind us, thus, it would have caused an accident if a car in the right lane had been traveling more rapidly than we were. I asked Sue to look, but she could not tell if anyone was coming. I was still blinded by his headlights. I said a final goodbye to Sue, swerved and luckily survived.

The truck trailer might have been gray or silver and about the size and shape of a large U-Haul. I did not notice any identifying marks on the truck. We did not pay attention to the truck or take its license number and when he began following us, it was too late to do anything but get away.

When he had first talked to us, he acted friendly and concerned as if he thought we were having car trouble. He began to act strange after he asked us what we were doing.

We returned to Route 95 traveling north, while the object was still circling. My notes say that I thought the object circled for around 20 minutes. Then the object began to travel approximately northwest.

I just thought of this in 2017, but at the approximate time when we had parked, the object had changed directions. It had been traveling south. When we were traveling south, it was ahead of us going south. Then it passed the road near us and then began to circle the airport. I do not know why we thought it would change directions, but that is why we drove the car south so that we could change our direction to go north. When we returned, it was still circling the airport. When the object left, it traveled to the northwest, so that as we traveled north, it was still ahead of us as it was when we traveled south.

Moreover while it circled, we were undergoing the car chase. This could make me slightly wonder if it were watching us and waiting for us to return. It could even make me wonder if it were watching to see the effects of the car chase and whether we stayed alive. When we returned heading north, it took off to the northwest. We do not know why we thought it would change directions because it had been traveling south.

For some reason I have a very disjointed memory of standing by the road with Sue watching it leave and saying we were so happy that it did not see us. But I do not think this happened because when it left, we were in the car. I do recall that once Sue said that it had passed over the road several times. It seems odd that I would forget something like this because I had made my notes soon after the sighting.

We then traveled past the place where we saw the object that changed colors. It seemed as if it was in a similar position. The inside of the car lit up in green, again. The light seemed to be a hazy, diffused green and, as before, stayed in the car for a while as we drove along. I did not see a source for the light. I believe that the flying object was in view this time, when the car lit up in green. I did not see the green when we were near the possible UFO, only when we were near the object that changed colors. But I saw this object only when the possible UFO was near. I saw it when we first approached the possible UFO and when we were leaving the area with the object in sight. I did not see it the next time we passed the area on our way back south. We did not have time to stop and look at the light; the object was low and we needed to keep right up with it to follow it.

I have asked a physics professor about what might make our car turn green inside. He gave me a generalized answer saying that the metal of a car might be affected by an electrical discharge. He mentioned St. Elmo's fire, a luminous glow sometimes seen around objects during storms. He said this could appear greenish because the electric discharge excites oxygen atoms, which gives rise to a green light as electrons change orbits.

Descriptions of St. Elmo's Fire include,

St. Elmo's Fire...is a sort of weather phenomenon that has collected much attention for years. The phenomenon comes alive in weather, like electrical storms, that generate electrically charged fields. It creates glowing blue and green lights around things, like the masts of ships, or lightning rods.[64]

When the voltage difference between the air and any charged object becomes sufficiently high, around 30,000 volts per cm of space, the object discharges its electrical energy tearing apart air molecules. Light is emitted in the process...Pointed objects facilitate St. Elmo's Fire since these surfaces can discharge at lower voltage levels. For instance, the mast of a ship, tip of an airplane wing or that of a church steeple.

The constant glow lasts for several minutes in some cases. Different gases will glow with different colors. However, since the atmosphere of the Earth has an abundance of nitrogen and oxygen, the emission is mainly of blue or violet color. Nevertheless, it can also have shades of green or pink in rarer occasions.[65]

Another description of such a green color can be found in the "Proceedings of the Royal Society A" in a description of a green lightning ball seen rolling down a hill after a green fireball had passed over:

The green colour is thought to be due to ionized oxygen and has been reported as being similar in colour to green aurora owing to 557.7 nm emissions from metastable neutral oxygen (Halliday 1960).[66]

Another description shows how the green color in an aurora (e.g., northern lights) is produced:

The auroral emissions are the result of processes where neutral atoms or molecules are excited by collisions with precipitating electrons and fall back into their ground state by emitting photons. Often, this excitation is accompanied by ionization. The commonly observed green colour in the aurora is due to the auroral green line of atomic oxygen at 557.7 nm...both lines represent so-called forbidden lines...The excited energy states are relatively long-lived (metastable) ...[67]

It adds that molecular nitrogen produces some weaker violet or blue auroral emission lines. Sometimes this phenomenon resembles a fog or mist. Although I do not remember exactly, the green color in the car resembled that of atomic oxygen's 557.7 nm color.

Thus this green color might have been produced by something other than light and perhaps this is why we did not see a beam. Lasers can produce photons with well-defined frequencies. The frequency of one laser can be adjusted to the right energy to excite atoms from their ground states to some particular excited state.[68] Light that behaves in strange ways might result from electrical forces, with visible light being only a by-product.

My sister also saw a light in the car when we first stopped. This could be done by laser in the same way. Perhaps both effects were done some way by laser.

Also some have questioned me and asked whether we had a windshield tint and whether this might have made the car light up in green. However, I do not recall whether we had a windshield tint, but if one had made the car light up in green, this would happen every time we passed under a street lamp or passed a car, so I think this is not an explanation. Moreover most of the time the car was lit up the object was on the side of us and thus if a beam had come from it, it would have generally come through the side windows, not from above. However I did not see any beam at all.

And the object on the ground was not green, but rotated through other colors of the spectrum in shades of red and blue. This spectrum was not complete. I do not recall seeing either green or yellow. It was as if the central portion of a spectrum was not there. It seemed strange that the inside of the car appeared green, but the object's spectrum did not include this color. Although it appeared to show a spectrum as it rotated, it showed each individual shade one at a time. However although it showed shades, it was not really an emission spectrum because this would show certain fixed wavelengths not a series of blending shades one at a time. Perhaps this might be done with beam-addressable static volume displays using beams of high-powered light to induce a specialized static volume to emit light at spatially defined points in 3D space, voxels, or done by similar means.

Also, the color we saw of shades of red and blue, resembles those of an aurora, which depends on the wavelength of the light emitted. This is from the main components of atmospheric gas:

This is determined by the specific atmospheric gas and its electrical state and the energy of the particle that hits the atmospheric gas. The atmosphere consists mainly of nitrogen and oxygen, which emit the characteristic colors of their respective line spectra. Atomic oxygen is responsible for the two main colors of green (wavelength of 557.7 nm) and red (630.0 nm). Nitrogen causes blue and deep red hues.[69]

We continued to follow the object, which was heading northwest. It was clearly distinguishable from everything else because it was low, bright and blinking. We traveled up Route 95, then northwest on Route 128. Next, we took a highway west; I believe this was Route 9, but it may have been Route 20. We wanted to get a good look at the object. Since it was traveling northwest, we then needed to head north. By this time it was always too distant to see the separate lighted squares. We turned north on the next road, a pothole-filled gravel road, with houses far apart and hidden by trees. I tried to keep us at around 30 to 40 mph with the object, but felt that I was tearing up my car trying to travel over the bumps. Unable to get any closer, we quit following it. We turned around and decided to look for motels again. We drove just off the freeway two or three times but did not stop because there were no-vacancy signs at the motels.

On the way back, we were apprehensive and kept looking for the object. Sue thought that possibly the object was visible only to us and seemed surprised that no one else noticed it. In fact, I had paid attention to it only at her insistence. We do not know exactly how long the sighting lasted, but we may have started back to New York around 12:00 midnight. There was little traffic and we stopped once for a very brief time on the way back north of New York to take a photo of Sue with the city in the background. We breezed through New York without stopping on Sunday morning. I am not sure when we arrived at Drew; it may have been 6:00 am or later. I had also made notes about our feelings:

Although they are subjective, I should probably mention our feelings...Neither of us was afraid of the UFO. We watched it with objective, scientific interest. I believe we discussed this and were both surprised at this. Possible reasons why we were not afraid were: we felt we were in a protected environment–near a freeway by a large city, we had both had previous possible UFO sightings and also the possible UFO did not appear to notice us...I felt that the object did not notice us. It (subjectively) seemed to be following the freeways and did not seem to pay attention to our stopped car. ...I was scared of the truck driver, when I talked to him and when he chased us. I was also slightly frightened when the object circled fast and when we heard the noise as it circled rapidly. When we lost sight of the object, we were following it up a real bad gravel road with lots of holes and not very many houses. I was cautious here because if it had stopped, the road would have been too narrow for us to have turned around in and the houses were off the road, a long ways apart and at the end of long secluded driveways. This made me apprehensive. At the time this happened, I was not even slightly familiar with the subject of UFOs and had not thought of the possibility that the light by the road, the light inside the car, etc., might be associated with the UFO sighting. I just thought they were coincidental and that I should report the appearance of the larger object only. Now that I know more about the subject, my opinion is very much different because the other events can accompany a UFO sighting, so I am certainly glad I made the detailed notes whether I understood anything or not.

Discussion and confirmation:

Our confirmation included our CUFOS reports, three write-ups by Sue and my CUFOS report that included a detailed write-up I had made from the initial notes I took on July 15. We may have had missing time as will be discussed later. Although several people have made the comment that Sue and I were probably watching an advertising airplane, because the writing under the wings of an advertising airplane when viewed from an angle can look somewhat like this. This is not what we saw. These panels were very square, very well defined and very bright. There are numerous examples of fuzzy or roundish windows on UFOs, but few examples of very definite squares. I have seen flying advertising airplanes from many angles and they look nothing like this. I have also seen and filmed many blimps including ones with lighting on the sides and over freeways. This was nothing like a blimp.

Also it seemed strange that when I had stopped the car and saw it close-up, that I first saw a meteor right before I saw it and in the same place. I have since read about other sightings in that area and it seemed that some others saw this type of thing too, to be discussed later.

I checked the wind direction, but then realized this did not apply because the larger object had traveled in many directions and the smaller one stayed in one place.

We noticed that there were times during the sighting that airplanes circled the airport, but did not land. I also had contacted the airport later, but they said that they no longer had records from that far back. If I had been a UFO investigator, or even known much about UFOs, I would have contacted the airport sooner, but I do not know if they would have given me any information about this at any time.

Massachusetts photograph (continuation of Massachusetts sighting)

The following is from my description of the photography during our sighting in the *IUR* 9/10 1990, article, "A Photograph and its aftermath." [70]

As mentioned, the AAAS accepted an analysis of the photography, thus, it was examined under scientific peer review and accepted (Figure 2 of Chapter 4).

I had two cameras, one box type (I think it was a type of Brownie Starmite), with color film and a Polaroid with black and white film. The Polaroid black and white film was high speed. I had already taken nighttime and star photographs with it and was quite familiar with how to do this. A physicist working for McDonnell Aircraft Corporation and Washington University, Dr. David Sloop, had given me the Polaroid film, which I think they were using at that time to capture high speed particle collisions and I had it in my trunk.

The following write-up referrers to the photograph that I took of the object. Both the photograph and a diagram of it are labeled as Figure 10 and this figure was taken from page 13 of my IUR article. Part 3 of Figure 10 shows the actual photograph of the UFO during two blinks. An enlarged and labeled diagram of one blink is shown in Figure 11.

John Timmerman had sent this photograph to Bruce Maccabee for his analysis. Maccabee wrote back and asked about the undulations. This is because John had not given him the complete information, such as that my camera was hand held when I took the photograph. I obviously did not find any way to stabilize the camera in the dark and I took the photographs immediately after I had run up the hill. Below is the write-up (with small updates and clarifications) I made for the portion of the *IUR* article about the photography, using the illustration of page 13 of this article:

During the time when my sister and I observed the unidentified object, I took one photograph of the object (Figure 10 part 3). The camera was a Polaroid model 250, with a 3-element, 114 mm, f/8.8 lens and a shutter speed controlled by an electronic eye. The film was 3000 ASA black and white film. I took five photographs of the object, but only one (#2) showed it. (I do not know why only one photograph came out; perhaps I did not focus the camera properly in the dark.)

When I took the photograph, we were watching an object lighted with blinking squares having the appearance shown in part 1 of Figure 10. Its blinking pattern was such that some or all of the squares would be lighted for a period of time and then for another period of time none of the squares would be lighted, making a blinking pattern. At the time I took the photograph, the object was at such a distance that the individual squares were beyond our visual resolution. Therefore, as the object moved and blinked, it should have presented the appearance shown in part 2, of Figure 10, which shows one light source moving from right to left (East to West) and blinking twice. However, the photographic trace (which is enlarged here) appeared as in part 3 of Figure 10 (parts 4 a and b are enlargements).

I am quite sure this photograph was of the object, because I took pictures only when the object was the only thing I saw. Also, the two blinks on the photograph were approximately where I expected them to be vertically and horizontally. I believe that I controlled the shutter time manually, rather than use the camera's electronic eye. (I had experience using this camera with nighttime star photography and could roughly estimate the time needed for a time exposure, which I made by holding the shutter down rather than releasing it. Although the light from the moving object was brighter than that of stars, I did not believe it was bright enough that my camera would be able take normal shutter-controlled photographs, but I might have tried.)

Part 3, the actual photograph of the two blinks, did not look like part 2, the appearance that I expected the photograph to have. One reason for this is that part 3 shows a vertical undulating movement during the two blinks; whereas, the trace in part 2 is straight. This difference is easy to explain: when I made the photograph, I did not have time to stabilize the camera and, thus, made hand held time exposures. The vertical oscillating motion in fig. 3 is the result of small hand movements during a time exposure. The object did not move up and down.

However, another difference appears between part 2 and part 3. That is each of the two blinks in part 3 is composed of a double trace; whereas, the blinks in part 2 are single lines. This difference is more difficult to understand, because we only saw one light, not two (as shown in the photograph). The vertical oscillation in each blink provides information about these double traces in that the oscillation pattern of the dimmer trace in each blink is moved a little to the right of the brighter one. For example in the fourth blink the brighter blink starts on the right and then makes a dip and a rise, followed by a second dip with a slower rise and finishing with a very rapid dip and rise (a bright spot showed up at the end of a brief period of being turned off at the end). This pattern is repeated in the dimmer blink, which (although to the right) turns on at approximately the beginning of the second rise, then follows the sharp dip and rise and then extends in a very shallow dip and rise (where the first light has turned off). What this means is that although we could see only one light source blinking off and on, the camera had photographed the light from two blinking sources, a bright one and a dimmer one (the trace), which appeared to be connected.

In order to investigate why I had photographed a light source that neither of us had seen, I questioned the Polaroid Company. They said that my camera system is sensitive to a 230 nanometer, nm, wavelength in the ultraviolet, UV, spectrum. The lowest light frequency that the human eye can detect, however, is around 400 nms. Thus if there had been a light source on the object emitting light at a frequency between 400 nm and 230 nm, the camera would photograph it, but we would not have seen it. Therefore, a light source radiating in the UV spectrum below the range of sensitivity of the human eye, would explain why there were the two traces on the photograph: the object apparently had a light that was not in the visible spectrum. I obtained the information that airplane lights are all supposed to be within the visible range, except for military aircraft with lasers. I do not know whether military aircraft were equipped with lasers in 1968 (or even today).

The brighter photographic trace, such as part 4 a, seemed to blink on and off suddenly each time; whereas, the dimmer one appeared to come on gradually and then go off gradually. The traces were not in phase with each other because, if the object were traveling to the left, the dimmer light came on after the brighter, but stayed on for a while when the brighter one went off.

Since the blinking pattern that we observed was one of a light blinking on and off suddenly, the brighter photographic trace probably represents the visible light. The dimmer one was probably the emission that was out of our visual range. In addition, the object was at a distance where we were unable to visually resolve the separate squares. However, the dimmer light appeared to be to the right (behind) what we thought was the body of the object. Thus, the dimmer light may have been on an extension behind the object. It may have been quite a long distance behind the object, because the width of the bright trace may represent the width of the number of windows on the object that were lit. The dim light trace is approximately nine times this width. (Also because I saw the globe that changed colors in somewhat the same direction as the UFO, I wondered if there were any more of these globes and whether one might be following the UFO at a distance. This object had been emitting various colors of light that might photograph as dimmer or brighter, but I saw only one object when I took the photograph).

Other inferences can be drawn from the photograph: 1. The lights were bright; because they appeared bright visually and because my camera system would take a little time to make time exposures of first magnitude stars. 2. The blinking pattern of the bright light during the two blinks was different, because (even after taking into account that the oscillations of part 4 a are deeper than those in 4 b) it appears that b is longer than a. Also, at the far left of a, the light appears to have turned off and then quickly flashed on and off again, because of the small spot to the left of the long trace. Perhaps one blink is longer than the other because some of blinks were longer. For example, it seemed as if when all seven widows were lit they stayed on longer than when three were lit, thus each blink may have represented a different number of windows being lit. 3. The object continued in the same direction and probably did not rotate, because the two light sources are the same distance apart during both blinks, 4. The blinking pattern of the bright light differed from that of the dimmer trace, because the dimmer trace switched on and off later than did the brighter light. It also appeared to gradually increase and then decrease in intensity, in 4a.

Also in 4a, the two ends (beginning and end) of the bright trace seem to be wider than the rest of the trace, as if the light had brightened when it came on and while it was turning off. I did not understand this and asked an aeronautical engineer about the amount of time that it takes for airplane lights to come on and off. It takes milliseconds for airplane landing lights and strobe lights and femtoseconds for lasers. The man knew of no light that would brighten when it came on and when it turned off. There is no change in the brightness of strobe lights during blinking.

It is interesting also that the bright light, especially in 4a, seemed to turn on and off at the top of an oscillation. The oscillation pattern of the dimmer light flattens out at the end of both blinks.

In 4a, there is a suggestion that the bright light came on again very briefly after it shut off, because there is a small blip there that would be in the correct relative position for a light when comparing the oscillation pattern with that of the dim light, which was still lit.

This pattern of switching on, remaining at somewhat the same brightness and then turning off, was not apparent in the dimmer light (although the left half of the bright light in 4a appears somewhat brighter than the right half–perhaps more squares were lit here). The object appears to be descending in 4b. The dim light, however, appears to be at the same elevation as the bright. Thus, the object descended with both ends at the same elevation, rather than lowering its front section during the descent (as aircraft and blimps generally do). Also because the object was moving, it would not photograph as well as a still object of the same brightness

Since the dim trace appeared to be able to smoothly increase in brightness, this variation might result from 1. An increase in intensity, such as in a light controlled by a rheostat or 2. Perhaps have resulted from a gradual change into a photographable frequency, such as might happen with a laser changing a variable wavelength emission. I do not know if blinking lasers are ever used–or any lasers are on airplanes.

My sister reported that when we first sighted the object (from our parked car), a light shown down on us, which lit up the interior of the car. Although she was uncertain, she thought that the light came from an end of the object. Perhaps her observation was of the light source that I photographed. In one place, she said this light was blue and if the light were in the 400 nm and 230 nm range, this is closest to the blue range.

The fact that the photo shows two blinks is in line with what I saw because the object was blinking. I am very certain that I saw only one light when I took the photo, so one of the double traces had been invisible to me.

Discussion and Confirmation

This photograph provides hard evidence of the event and the acceptance of it under peer-review by a well-known scientific society shows that it is acceptable to science.

The above was the general write-up I made for the *IUR* article. I am sure the included photo is of the object because I went to a lot of trouble to make sure that nothing except the object was in view by my eye and in the camera viewfinder.

My photograph showed two blinks (4a and 4b) and this was consistent with what I saw when I took the photograph. However, both blinks were composed of two traces. I did not see two lights, thus, one of these traces was not in a visible frequency.

Because the brighter trace appeared to be more consistent in brightness, it is likely the one that I visually saw.

Because the dimmer trace in both blinks seemed more variable in brightness–it appeared to gradually come on, reach a peak and then go off–it appeared that it was the one in the invisible range.

Thus it appears that this object was shining a light that was not in the visible range. Maybe this is the first evidence that UFOs can have lighting that is not in the range that the human eye sees.

Because the dimmer trace showed more variation in brightness, it might have come from a laser; lasers can emit variable wavelengths and can also be used to make holograms and to create the newer volumetric display platforms.

I assumed the object was traveling from the right of the photograph to the left because this had been its path (east to west) when I last looked at it when I ran up the hill. However my sister said that it had immediately got to a different place in the sky about the time I ran up the hill. I did not realize this until after I read my sister's report that it was in a different part of the sky than it had been before I ran up the hill. Thus, I am not totally sure that it was going from east to west when I took the photograph.

Several other portions of the photographs are interesting. For example, the brighter trace in both blinks appeared to be brightest when it came on and when it turned off. I have found no information on why that would happen. It does not appear to be reported in standard lighting. This might be something unique to the object's lighting system.

I went to great trouble to take this photograph, but I think it was well worth it because it could supply much information about the UFO phenomenon and also provide hard evidence.

Massachusetts possible poltergeist (continuation of Massachusetts sighting)

This is the continuation of my IUR write-up and describes the poltergeist after effect:

I wish also to mention another incident that might be of interest in comparison with other observations of this nature. Within approximately 30 hours after our observation several other unusual events occurred, however, as with the rest of this account, I do not know whether the events were unusual, or just an odd combination of normal circumstances. We arrived at my sister's dorm at around 6:00 am or later on July 14 and slept until noon. Right after we got up, we called our parents and told them about the sighting. We also told my sister's friends in the dorm. They joked and did not believe us. Whenever we left the room, we asked her roommates to listen for the phone, so I would not miss the co-workers' call. I wanted to leave then to get an early start for the drive back to Washington D.C., but waited to hear from my coworkers who were expecting a ride back. I left at around 6:00 pm and arrived at my Washington D.C. apartment around 11:00 pm. As I unpacked, I noticed that my toothbrush was missing. I scoured the apartment and car searching for it–I did not have much furniture. I thought about buying a new one, but did not.

I retired around midnight. Before I went to sleep, I began to hear sounds as if someone were walking in my bedroom. The sounds would start, go a few steps and then stop. They sounded like a man with shoes on just took two or three steps. They would start somewhere, stop and then start somewhere else. A street lamp lit my apartment and I saw nothing in it. Several times when I heard the sound, I would try to quickly jump into the area where they came from but I was unable to feel anything. I was used to hearing neighbors and heard the usual apartment noises. Later, I checked and nothing unusual had happened that night.

It is surprising that although I was afraid, I soon went to sleep. My alarm (which had been set at around 0600) rang. I got up and began to cook breakfast, but I noticed that it was dark. The clock said 01:30. I reset it for morning. I believe that I continued to hear walking sounds, but went back to sleep. My alarm roused me again and I got up. It had been set at 02:30. I checked that the windows were locked and put my chair against the door. The alarm rang again at 0330, 04:30 and possibly at 05:30. I could not understand this, because if I were setting the alarm, I would need to turn on a light. The light was a 100-watt bulb, by my mattress. This much light should have awakened me. Also, the knob used for setting the alarm was broken off. I normally set it with pliers. I was surprised that each time it had been set at exactly 30 minutes after the hour. I thought my fingers should have been sore from twisting the broken knob with sufficient pressure to set the clock precisely. I did not set it precisely when I reset it each time.

It sounds impossible, but although I was extremely frightened, I went to sleep each time after the alarm had rung.

When I got up that morning, I was frightened and also worried about losing my job if I had just gone crazy. I was sitting on the edge of the mattress rehearsing ways to avoid talking to other people at work so that I could disguise insanity. I had high security clearances and would expect to lose the position immediately if I had a mental disorder. (I was unaware of possible UFO after effect phenomena.) At around 0600 (daylight), my toothbrush suddenly flew across the room and hit the wall in front of me about 4 ft. up. It came from behind, but only a wall was behind me. I was not even moving at the time this happened.

I wanted to see a doctor, but was afraid to because of my security clearances. Nothing else like this happened for the rest of my life.

The following Monday, the coworkers who had traveled with me, were put out. They had tried to call me many times Sunday for the return trip, but been unable to reach me. They knew our names, the college and dorm name and location and the telephone number. I had taken a picture of them standing in front of Sue's dorm talking to us. They finally took a train and cabs back, which was quite expensive. So, I have no idea why they could not reach us.

Joe Nyman said that the airport closes at 11:00. We did not see the object land; it continued traveling to the Northeast. Since we watched this after 11:00 p.m., we saw no evidence that the object was from that airport. Walter Web said that an advertising airplane used to use Norwood Airport. We were unable to confirm that one was flown on that date. However, we had seen ad planes previously and had watched this object closely. It had nothing in common with an ad airplane. For example when an ad plane is mistaken for a UFO people see the lit-up message swinging under the wings. This gives the appearance of the rotation/movement of indistinct lights. In this case, the lit areas on this object were on the sides and were in the form of distinct squares with right angle corners during the entire time we observed it when it was close. The lights showed no evidence of rotation. In addition at that time, it traveled toward the front of the squares. If it had been an ad plane, it would have been going perpendicular to the message board i.e., forward (toward us) if one were located straight in front of the wings.

We did not talk about this until about five years later. After this event, my sister moved to Brazil, where she was a missionary and teacher for the next four years. Soon after she returned, she married and she and her husband lived in several different states. About the same time, I married and moved to Nevada, where my husband had a job.

Discussion and confirmation

As additional information, I again interviewed Sue on November 30, 2017, wrote down what she said and also videotaped the session. She signed this write-up. She said that she remembers it as in her previous reports. She said that it had gone right over us very slowly, when we parked. She recalled the red and green lights, the seven windows and the blinking pattern. She again recalled that it had been right over us and then disappeared. It would be in one part of the sky and then it would be somewhere else. I also recalled this fast motion when I had watched it circle the airport. She recalled the airplanes circling above us and that it was soundless, although we could hear the airplanes. She very vaguely remembered the truck driver talking to me and afterwards chasing us. At this time, she remembered my climbing the hill only once.

She kept saying something about it signaling when we were watching it, so I asked her about this. She said that she thought the blinking of the windows was some kind of signal that she should have understood. She thought it should have had a pattern, but she could not figure out what the pattern was.

Also I think her memory of the object was better than mine, because I was driving, paying attention to the roads, looking for open motels and when we stopped, I paid a lot of attention to getting photos. She just spent all her time totally concentrating on the object and paid little attention to anything else.

One thing that really stands out about this event is the car chase. I thought I was about to be murdered when this happened, but I have no idea why the person chased us, who he was, what he was doing there, or anything else.

Another reason for my concern about the truck driver is that if we had had an accident, it would just look like my fault that I was a reckless, speeding driver. No one would ever believe anything about a UFO. But this caused me to wonder if something like UFO phenomena could sometimes be associated with other unexplainable actions and accidents, or even missing planes, suicidal pilots and that sort of thing. It, of course, made me wonder if UFO phenomenon can be dangerous.

Not only the large object with windows was mysterious, but so was the object that changed colors that appeared to be on the ground.

The inside of our car lighting up was another perplexing event. We both saw the inside of the car light up, but at different times. I think I finally figured out something about this. I think my sister and I discussed the green light while it was happening and have that in my notes, but she does not recall this now. It may have impressed me more than her, because she was by the window near the object that changed colors. Thus, she might not have had the view I had because I could see the rest of the car and the green inside it. She reported a blue light when we first saw the larger object and I recall nothing about this. However, the object was on the driver's side of the car this time and my view was to the east. She was the passenger and thus would have seen the inside of the car light up, when I would not have. We both have good eyesight and color vision.

I also think she likely saw the blue light in the car at about the same time that I saw the distant meteor. Such lights shining into a vehicle have been reported previously. For example, in the 1973 Coyne helicopter case in Ohio, the object shined a green light into the helicopter cockpit. Both the helicopter crew and the ground witnesses saw the light and the crew associated it with magnetic anomalies in the helicopter.[71]

Walter Webb once said that beams of light focused on UFO witnesses often precede impressions of missing time and abduction scenarios and perhaps there is an association to our event also.[72]

And several cases have had a strange light appear in a car, or cockpit, or people see a beam. In one case, that of a Soviet Aeroflot airliner flying over Minsk, in an effect somewhat like the Coyne case, it shot out a blob-like object that cast a greenish tint over the landscape. When one of the beams projected into the cabin, it caused weird effects including multiple lights of different colors and fiery zigzags. The beams outside changed shape to mimic the plane. Perhaps there was some relationship between my sister's observation of the blue light and my observation of the meteor and then the sudden close appearance of the object over the treetops.

Years later this event seemed even more mysterious, because after my sister wrote up her account I realized that she seemed to be aware of things that I did not recall and vice versa–this was principally during the time when we were separated.

I think my sister was not too aware of the danger we were in during the truck chase because I did not have time to explain to her that I was going as fast as the car could go, but I was blinded and unable to see.

I had made very detailed notes on the Monday after the sighting and kept them and also have been adding a little more over the years for clarification and detail. So I did not have to rely on my memory, which can misremember things over a period of time. So far I remember everything exactly as I had written it down, but have realized here and there that I did not write everything down.

In addition, Budd Hopkins thought that I had been abducted, but thought that Sue might have been put in some form of suspended animation. Perhaps something like this could have caused the differences in our observations when we had been separated.

The main difference in our memories is from the time we were separated. When we were together, we constantly asked each other questions to make sure we were seeing the same thing.

There were many complexities in this event and I have worked it over in my mind many times trying to figure it out.

For one thing, since I wrote the previous description, I have read more about UFO phenomena. Several people have suggested that the strange man might have been a Man-in-Black. It has been reported that the Men-in-Black MIB are often interested in confiscating UFO photographs (*The Complete Book of UFOs*) or other material evidence. In this case, the man prevented me from taking the picture when the object was close.

I also wondered if he might have been some sort of alien. For one thing, he asked me twice what I was looking at. When I pointed to it, he turned the other way and then said he did not see anything. Could he have been telling me that people would think we were crazy if we said anything? Then he made a motion suggesting that I was crazy. Could this have been the same message?

I also wonder why he asked exactly the same question twice and turned in the opposite direction both times. Could he have been emphasizing something by repeating this behavior?

Also I remember we saw his truck directly under the UFO when it crossed the road. It is strange that we saw it then and then he stopped.

The car chase was definitely real, but I wondered about its elements. For example, Betty Andreasson Luca told that during her abduction, that she was given a bizarre object lesson that caused her to undergo a painful but ecstatic religious-like experience. I wondered here if something like that might have occurred, because I certainly thought that we were about to be killed.

The truck driver had also caused us to split apart. I am now not sure why I ran up the hill. I wanted Sue to stay by the car because I was afraid that he might try to take it over. From that time until I returned to the car, our memories differ.

Also about the next day's events, I had not known about the idea that psychic phenomena might accompany UFO events, so I worried for many years that I might have gone crazy for a while, but now know psychic phenomena have been reported in other cases.

We may have had missing time. We likely stopped seeing the UFO at around 12:00 midnight. When I wrote the CUFOS report I thought we had arrived at the dormitory at around 6:00 AM. However now I am not sure of when we arrived. I checked a photograph of Sue that I had taken as we approached New York and it was full daylight then, thus, we may have arrived later than this.

Google shows the driving distance between Madison New Jersey and Boston, Massachusetts as 298 miles and the driving time as four hours and 37 minutes. Because it was early Sunday morning and there was little traffic and we probably made better time than that.

It appears that we might have had some missing time, because we should have arrived at around 4:30 am, but instead arrived around 6:00 or later. I also noted on the way back from Boston that the motels were closed and wondered why they had closed so early, so that possibly we started later than 12:00 midnight, but I do not know why we would have started later.[73]

Another way I think I can get an estimate of the time is from our memory of the airport. The airport was reported to close at 11:00 pm. Thus, as we watched the airplanes on our way south we saw airplanes landing. When we were stopped, we watched airplanes circling above. But I do not recall seeing airplanes around the airport after this. Thus, it might have been around 11:00 pm when the truck driver had chased us.

This observation had many confusing elements, such as a near-death encounter, missing time and additional events. When we finally reported it in 1984, we were investigated by a number of the world's top UFO authorities as mentioned above.

In addition, there might have been some discrepancy between this UFO sighting and this UFO experience. The sighting ended at around 11-12:00 on the 13th, but the experience may not have ended until the morning of the 15th. This was because there seemed to be some kind of effect afterward. This could make one wonder if a sighting is simply the tip of an iceberg for some underlying event that is more prolonged than the sighting itself.

We also have the correspondence from others who investigated our event including Budd Hopkins and Leo Sprinkle (as shown in the figures). I have also corresponded with witnesses to similar events such as Budd Hopkins' "Kathie Davis" and Raymond Fowler's, Betty Andreasson.

I had not paid attention to UFOs since 1968. Suddenly for no reason at all in late 1983 I became terrified of the subject-so terrified I did not even want to go outside. This caused me to decide to report our observations. In December 1983, I first reported our sightings to Warren Nicholson, who I knew because we both worked at Battelle. I started reading about the subject and found Budd Hopkins' book. Because the reports in his book, *Missing Time*, seemed similar to what Sue and I had experienced, I reported all of our sightings to Hopkins in January 1984. Then in February 1984, I reported them to CUFOS. Something weird happened because on the day I began to fill out the CUFOS form, I had a long sighting at OSU with other witnesses.

My first correspondence was with Budd Hopkins. He is one of the founders of modern-day UFOlogy and has been dubbed "father of the abduction movement" by some. Hopkins was interested in the sightings my sister and I had together. And because he thought I had been abducted, he also tried to hypnotize me. With "Kathie Davis" (Debbie White Kauble, the featured person in Hopkins' next books *Intruders: The Incredible Visitations at Copley Woods)*, he interviewed my sister and her family in Indianapolis. He was also interested in additional UFO events in our family, because he was studying UFO experiences that happened to entire families. He also wanted to know more about a large burn that was discovered on our family farm in about the same time frame as the one featured in *Intruders*.

Hopkins is also a noted artist-he was awarded a Guggenheim Fellowship for painting. His work was included in American Painters, a film documentary of American artists and styles. In 1969, the San Francisco Museum of Modern Art acquired some of Hopkins's works and described him as "a leading American painter who has successfully brought together the vocabularies of painterly abstraction and hard edge painting." He has exhibited his paintings and sculptures in museums, galleries and universities throughout the United States-the Provincetown Art Association and Museum, Whitney Museum, Washington Gallery of Modern Art, Metropolitan Museum of Art, Museum of Modern Art, Corcoran Gallery of Art, the British Museum and others.[74]

In Hopkins' February 7, 1984, letter he asked a number of questions and one was about our timetable, which I described above. I had not thought about possible missing time until then, but it appeared we could have had some.

I had also sent him a photograph of a scar on my calf that I found when I looked after reading his book. He had noted that in some of the abductions he reported in *Missing Time* and in

Intruders: The Incredible Visitations at Copley Woods that the abductees had scars on their calves. I do not know where mine came from, but I had one also.

In Budd Hopkins's letter of August 8, 1984, he said that he had discussed our UFO reports with Dr. Hynek. He wanted information about my sister (Figure 8).

On November 11, 1984, with "Kathie Davis" (Debbie White Kauble), he interviewed my sister and her family in Indianapolis. Both Debbie and Sue then lived fairly close to each other in Indiana and there were a number of similarities between the events that happened in her family and in ours. For one, one of the chief events mentioned in the book was a large burn mark. However, a similar mark had appeared on our farm in the same rough time frame. He was also interested in this mark

In his next letter, October 16, 1985, he sets up a time to try hypnosis with me and confirmed that he would be coming.

We tried the hypnosis. But I simply did not go into any form of trance and remembered nothing else other than what I consciously recalled.

In his September 4, 1986, letter he asked about using photographs of the scars and indentations on my calf in his book, which he titled *Intruders: The Incredible Visitations at Copley Woods* (Figure 7).

Another investigator, Dr. Leo Sprinkle, has a PhD and is an Emeritus Professor of Counseling Services at the University of Wyoming. He is considered Dean of Research on ET Contact Research since his initial study in this arena in 1961. He has conducted several studies, including a survey of the members of the National Investigations Committee on Aerial Phenomena and an initial study of people who have experienced extraterrestrial encounters–both contactees and abductees. He served as a psychological consultant for the Condon Report (1969) on UFOs, which led to further work on several abduction cases through the 1970s.

He gave me a series of tests that he uses to determine the general mental health of UFO experiencers.

In page one of his February 11, 1985, letter, he said I was normal and had the general profile of someone in scientific research. In page two, he says that my results suggest that I might have experienced unusual events in my life. In page three, he said that after thirty years of investigation, his opinion/speculation was that I might be a UFO contactee.

He says that abductees might experience "check-ups" over the years in page four. This might be what causes some people to have repeat sightings.

On page five he offers an explanation for the "crazy" man that I talked to and that chased our car. He said that this might be a part of the total UFO experience, to assist us to look at the psychological as well as the physical aspects of the phenomenon. Maybe so, the man seemed to me to give me the crazy sign anyway. This is the first explanation of what might have been happening with him. He mentioned Dr. Kenneth Ring, who has been investigating near-death experiences. On the sixth page, he says that there might be a connection between UFO experiences and poltergeist activity. I wondered about this because of the after effects of our Massachusetts sighting. He said that there was a good possibility of an abduction because I seemed to have the characteristics of UFO contactees including childhood experiences.

He added that one hypothesis is that "...there is good evidence of a connection of UFO experiences & psychic experiences (including poltergeist activity). One hypothesis: 'invisible' UFOLK could create unusual events in the lives of UFO contactees, bringing attention to their experiences." This was almost exactly the same thing that Betty Andreasson said about her experiences. For example, "A number of people afterwards described having some pretty interesting and unusual experiences, though the one who really stands out in my memory was Betty Andreasson Luca."[75]

In a January 9, 1985 letter, he mentioned:
My speculation is that UFOLKS are providing Humankind with instructional events (UFO sightings), in a gradual manner, so that we can discover the relationships between physical, biological, psychosocial and psychic levels of reality. Then we can build flying saucers & become UFO occupants for another planet, etc., etc.

A comparison to similar events

This Massachusetts sighting seemed very mysterious. In trying to understand it, I looked for similar sightings and compared them. This in some ways helped me to understand the one we had.

The following is a comparison with sightings in the Massachusetts area at around the same time as our July 13, 1968 sighting. It was published in the *MUFON of Ohio Newsletter*, "Uncommon Commonalities: A Personal Experience Comparison to Buff Ledge and Other Events," July, 2016, p. 6-9, by Scott, Irena and Phyllis Budinger.[76]

At the time, I was working for the DIA in Washington DC on satellite information with clearances that were above top secret. Thus, I did not report it, but made notes with every detail I remembered about it on the 15th.

This sighting was probably the closest in time and place to Walter Webb's *Encounter at Buff Ledge* event.[77] He spent considerable time searching for sightings in that time and place and recently has been contacted by me. Also immediately prior to the sighting, we had been in the area where the Betty and Barney Hill event occurred and there were commonalities between their object and ours.

Webb's book also reported that there had been a UFO wave in 1968. He said that abduction accounts reached a climax in 1968 and that the 19 abduction claims listed in the Ted Bloecher-David Webb Humanoid Catalog for that year represented the highest total up to then. He compiled 220 global close-encounter cases for 1968. He found that globally, the year's total number of close encounters of all types crested in August.

Some of the reports included satellite objects ejected or absorbed by UFOs, unidentified objects seen entering and/or exiting bodies of water, animal reactions, objects with spectral rim colors, light beams projected from UFOs and entities, which is interesting because they are similar to our observations. In terms of Close Encounters of the Third Kind, 1968 was noteworthy as the fourth-highest year in history for entity reports. There had been a number of sightings in the general area where these took place.

The write-up below shows a comparison with our sighting and other similar ones it was "Uncommon Commonalities: A Personal Experience Comparison to Buff Ledge and Other Events," by myself and Phyllis Budinger, published in *MUFON of Ohio Newsletter:*

Uncommon Commonalities: A Personal Experience Comparison to Buff Ledge and Other Events

UFOs may be the world's most important mystery, because, although they might represent interaction with alien life, no one really knows what they are. Many have sought answers, such as Walter Webb, who in his 1994 book *Encounter at Buff Ledge* described a UFO event that occurred in early August 1968. He spent an enormous amount of time seeking comparison UFO events with unique characteristics that had occurred within 300 miles of Buff Ledge, Vermont, during the July and August 1968 period. Like Webb, I have also spent much time looking for comparisons to an earlier event experienced by my sister and me. It occurred close to the time and location of the Buff Ledge incident. Two other events are also compared. Their atypical commonalities may provide some insight into this mystery.

The Events:

The Buff Ledge event, 8/7/1968, involved two witnesses who saw what they described as a larger, cigar-shaped, mother ship and emerging from it three smaller, circular, satellite objects, with bands of energy rotating and changing color across the spectrum. The witnesses reported a complex abduction and additional strange events such as extraordinary sounds and maneuvers.

For comparison, our sighting was about a month earlier (7/13/1968), near Boston and around 160 miles from Buff Ledge. I wrote down everything I remembered immediately afterward and kept the notes. We sent in reports (written independently) to the CUFOS in 1984 and I first published the information in two parts—the IUR 7/8 1988 and 9/19 1990. Webb published his book later and I discovered it several years afterwards, but comparison is finally possible.

Our sighting was of two soundless objects. The larger, cigar-shaped one had seven brightly lit square windows along its sides that blinked in different patterns (we've seen blimps with lighted sides and ad airplanes). The smaller resembled the Buff Ledge satellite objects. It was on or near the ground, around 20-50 feet away, globular and changed colors. We drove near it twice and both times the interior of our car lit up in green. During our sighting, we experienced a weird truck driver who parked by us and then engaged us in an extremely dangerous high-speed car chase that I thought would kill us. During the chase, he stayed about a foot or more behind our car beaming his bright lights into my mirror, blinding me. And, there were other elements. We were on vacation, had paid little attention to UFOs and we had little contact or discussion afterwards.

Also, because of the location, our sighting might be compared to two other sightings, such as the well-known Betty and Barney Hill abduction, 9/19/1961, because we were driving in the area of that event (not deliberately—we knew very little about the Hill sighting) just prior to our experience and because there were similarities between this and our account. This classic account of an abduction aboard a UFO by extraterrestrials was the first widely publicized report of an alien abduction in the US.

It also might be compared with the Sharon UFO, 4/18/1966, reported in Raymond Fowler's *UFOs: Interplanetary Visitors*, which occurred near the town of Sharon, Massachusetts, within a few miles of our sighting. This event included close sightings of a larger cigar-shaped and three satellite-like objects by multiple witnesses including police officers. Many other witnesses reported close encounters in this vicinity and timeframe. (Diana DeSimone told me about this one after she read about ours. She said it took place a few hours after the Ravenna, Ohio, UFO Chase, 4/17/66, when officers had chased an object across a multi-state area, while in radio contact with government authorities. She thought that the Sharon UFO might have been the same Ravenna object because it was seen right afterward and in the direction it was headed. The Ravenna event became well known for a number of reasons. Several police officers and others participated in a close interactive, extended chase and jets may have been scrambled. Evidence existed of government knowledge of and cover-up of the Ravenna and Sharon objects.)

The Commonalities:

The comparisons of these events present valuable information because of their many atypical commonalities.

Star-Like Object Initially Sighted:

All the close encounters began with the sighting of a star-like object, which quickly became very close. In our sighting, I saw a distant "falling star's" brief flash and remarked about it. Immediately, in the same place to the east, the low, close, larger object appeared over the trees. At approximately the same time that I saw this "falling star," my sister saw a light shine down on us from this larger object. In the Buff Ledge observation, one witness first saw what he thought was a star, then decided was Venus and then he shouted, "Venus is falling." The other witness reported a falling star appearance. This was followed by a close-up observation of the larger object. Webb described the experience of another Buff Ledge couple, who were watching an object looking like a star. They were dumbfounded when a huge object abruptly arrived and the interviewed witness could not recall watching it come. In the Sharon sighting that was much like ours, the witnesses saw a falling star at a great distance. Within two or three seconds, the close, cigar-shaped object appeared over the trees on the easterly side. The Hills' sighting began when the couple saw a star-like object in motion.

'Possible' Metamorphosis to a Very Close Larger Object:

In all five sightings, witnesses interpreted the objects as star-like, rather than aircraft-like and, instead of the normal pattern of objects gradually drawing nearer, the scene seemed to abruptly shift from the sighting of a distant star or meteor, to a close view of a larger object, as if the object moved at a tremendous speed, or a portion of the approach was removed from the memory.

Close Encounters with the Craft:

Three additional unique attributes of all the observations were that right after the 'metamorphosis' the witnesses had a close encounter. And, these were so close that all thought they saw the UFO's inside and this was through what appeared to be windows. Our main object as viewed through the seven windows seemed to have glowing walls, was filled with an intense, extremely bright white light, showed a blinking pattern and appeared empty. The Buff Ledge witnesses described a transparent dome that allowed them to see inside and curved metallic glowing walls in the main object. The Hills' original sketching done immediately after the sighting showed a row of seven windows, through which they thought they saw the object's brilliant, white inside. The inside of the Sharon main craft was described as having white glowing walls and lit by a very intense white light. On the night before (4/18/66), they thought they observed the same object and sketched a cigar-shape with six windows.

Our object was so close that I tried to take a photograph through the windows, because I thought that no one had ever photographed the inside of a possible UFO. But just when it was closest, the truck driver started talking to us. However, I still think I took a picture of light from its inside, but from farther away (I still have the picture). While all witnesses thought they saw inside the various crafts, no entities were seen in our own or the Sharon sightings; the objects appeared empty. However, in the Buff Ledge and Hill observations, entities were seen inside and these later were reported to abduct witnesses.

Similar Appearance of the Craft:

The initial witness sketches of the close encounters with the larger cigar-shaped crafts were remarkably similar. Seven windows were noted in our own and the Hill encounters and six in the Sharon. While no windows were reported for the Buff Ledge craft, one witness did describe a row of square plates on a side. Because all of these events happened after dark, the exact silhouette of the objects was difficult to discern, but the drawings of the general cigar shape and the windows looked much the same. (The original Hill sketch that both Barney and Betty agreed on below, was done on 9/20/1961 a few hours after the sighting. It resembled the sketch I submitted to CUFOS in 1984 and published in the second IUR article. Kathleen Marden published this original in 2013 *"Betty and Barney Hill: Where the Debunkers went Wrong."* A modified version of this Hill sketch that he did after his hypnosis is shown in *The Interrupted Journey*)

Figure 12 of Chapter 4 shows the original sketches and features of the UFOs described in the text. It includes sketches of the 1968 MA object by my sister (Sue Postle) and me (from our IUR 9/19/1990 and our 1984 CUFOS reports). It also includes the Hills' original two sketches (September 20, 1961), the sketch of a Buff Ledge witness showing the cigar-shaped object releasing three satellite objects (from *Encounter at Buff Ledge*) and the Sharon witnesses' two sketches.[78] All look very similar.

Also unique was that more than one object was reported in the Buff Ledge, Sharon, our own and possibly the Hill accounts. And even more unusual, these satellite objects in general appeared to be rounded, have a neon-like color that changed across the spectrum and rotated (Webb said this in itself is rare). We saw one such object–a neon-like light changing colors across the spectrum (except green) that appeared to be inside a glass globe with a C-shaped bar rotating around it. The three Buff Ledge satellite objects seemed to have a rotating energy band of light held in by something transparent–a glass like chamber encircled the rim. The Sharon witnesses also described three satellite objects that appeared to rotate and change colors. The Hills at one point reported an odd-shaped object with flashing multi-colored lights rotating around it (they thought they saw only one object, but were confused by the appearance change). None of the witnesses reported standard aircraft lighting of bright red and green wingtip lights and a strobe light, nor were wings or airplane sounds observed.

Beams from Secondary Objects Shot at Witnesses:

Still another uncommon attribute of the Bluff Ledge and our sighting was that one of the satellite objects appeared to shoot a beam at the witnesses. Mr. Webb reported that beams of light focused on UFO witnesses often precede impressions of missing time and abduction scenarios. In our experience as we passed near the smaller (satellite) object twice, the car's interior lit up in green. When one of the Buff Ledge satellite objects shined a light on the witnesses, the abduction began. In both the Buff Ledge and ours, witnesses reported an object hovering above a witness. These satellite objects could be within feet of the witnesses.

Entities Seen:

Strange beings/aliens were also reported. Under hypnosis, the Buff Ledge and Hill witnesses reported very complex abductions into the craft, examination and philosophical discussions with aliens. My sister and I are among the minority that cannot be hypnotized, so we were unable to use this technique to explore any possible alien interaction. However, we did consciously meet a highly unusual person/entity. The truck driver was very strange–he asked twice what we were watching and when we pointed (we did not say UFO and pretended like it was an airplane) he would rotate 180 degrees to the opposite direction, look to the same azimuth, then turn back and say he did not see anything. After the second time, he pointed to his head (which I interpreted as the crazy sign), returned to his truck and watched us. He seemed to tell me I was crazy (possibly suggesting the object wasn't really there, or that no one would believe me) and later seemed to try to kill us in a dangerous car chase. Attempted murder is a very rare characteristic, as is having a possible alien call a witness crazy.

Aerodynamic Laws Defied, Interaction, Geometric Patterns and Sounds:

Other extremely unique attributes of the Buff Ledge, Hill, Sharon (and Ravenna) and our own sightings, were that the objects appeared to be interactive, displayed geometric patterns and even put on a show. In ours, the larger object circled an airport and altered its blinking regime and speed to form a geometric pattern. It may have made booming sounds. Aircraft did not appear to land while this went on. The Buff Ledge object's behavior was described as antics and as stalking. When one object plunged into water, instantly a tree bending gale with white-capped waves, dogs and cats howling and other effects occurred that they described as unreal and unearthly. They also heard sounds–such as a complex one like thousands of different tuning forks. Their objects also formed geometric patterns. The Hills felt their object was playing games with them. The Sharon witnesses said that their object hovered while a plane went over and then moved off afterwards (the Ravenna object had been very interactive). The Sharon object had hovered near the same airport that our UFO circled over and when we first saw our object we watched airplanes traveling over the Sharon area. Parts of these astounding aerial displays were erratic–defying the laws of aerodynamics.

Abduction, Missing Time:

Abduction and/or missing time were reported in the Buff Ledge, Hill and our own accounts, along with feelings of fear and of being stalked. The conscious portion of the missing time experiences, appeared to last around an hour, but the actual events may have lasted several hours or even days (for example, some unusual events happened to me the next night). Two main witnesses were involved in each of these events and they did not remember exactly the same thing, or one may have had a more "complete" experience. In both the Hills' and our reports, the driver of the car initially insisted that the object was a helicopter. Another extremely strange characteristic of some, was that when objects were close enough that windows were visible, witnesses saw small unblinking lights at each end of the row of windows, both were red in the Hill and Sharon objects and one of ours was red and the other green. At the beginning of their abduction, the Hills reported that the red lights appeared and then began to extend away from the windows as the object drew nearer. A Sharon witness saw an object with red lights at each end of the windows–these began to blink as the object moved away. Perhaps these lights were too dim to see at a distance, or the UFOs turned them on when near people.

Conclusion:

An important finding is that the attributes of just one of these sightings is extremely atypical, but a combination of them in several completely independent sightings is extraordinary. Webb ended his book by wondering if the Buff Ledge events were real. Because of these unique resemblances, our experience (and the similar sightings) suggests that something real happened. And because these events occurred in a similar time and place, the comparison might even suggest some sort of linkage. Such positive findings could help to advance scientific investigation of the phenomena and suggest the usefulness of more statistical examination, such as possibly cluster analysis.

This information may have helped me to understand the events a little better because some of the same things appeared to happen in these other sightings. For example, the rotating, color-changing round object by the ground mystified me. I could not even imagine what it was. But similar rotating, color-changing round objects were seen in these similar sightings. The fact that I saw a meteor immediately before our close encounter, also seemed like quite a coincidence, but this was also similar to the other sightings, as was the object's sudden appearance close to us and the big windows. The light inside our car likewise resembled parts of the other observations.

One thing, I certainly wondered was the small, unblinking lights on the sides of the sets of windows, because I had not heard of anything like this. The government officers that the Hills had reported their sighting to had also been intrigued by them, as Barney described in *Interrupted Journey*. Barney thought that "they were intensely interested…and that they were intrigued by the fins with red lights. To the Air Force officers this was a new slant in the many UFO reports they had screened."

Apparently such lights were not something the officers were familiar with.

Such lights have not been reported in other sightings. Why did this happen? Kathleen Marden described the sighting of the lights in detail, "The red lights on each side of the craft were observed by the Hills after it swooped down, but before Barney followed it into the field. Betty did not see fins at a later time. She saw only the red lights on each side before Barney walked into the field. From the field, Barney saw lights on the ends of fin-like structures that slid out of the sides of the craft. Then something started to drop down from the bottom of it and Barney fled back to the car.[79]

What Barney had seen as described in *Interrupted Journey*, was an, "enormous disc…raked on an angle toward him. Two fin-like projections on either side were now sliding out further, each with a red light on it. The windows curved around the craft, around the perimeter of the thick, pancake-like disc, glowing with brilliant white light." The projections looked like wings and made a V-shape when extended. The object had continued to descend until it appeared to be only hundreds of feet away. Barney jumped into the car and fled, but they encountered the object again shortly afterwards and this was when it abducted them.

Could these red lights have any purpose? One might wonder, in view of our findings, if these were some type of laser or similar instrumentation that could act together in such a way as to aid in abduction or maybe even to produce an abduction scenario.

Barney had also seen beings in the windows of the object and they seemed to have a strange reaction when these fins began to spread out. This action did not appear as humans operating a machine, it seemed as if it might have been a somewhat robotic action in consort with the extension of the fins and the ramp:

Then, on some invisible, inaudible signal, every member of the crew stepped back from the window toward a large panel a few feet behind the window line…Slowly the craft descended lower, a few feet at a time. As the fins bearing the two red lights spread out further on the sides of the craft, an extension lowered from the underside, perhaps a ladder…

During our observation when the object drew close to us, my sister saw a light shine down on us. She said the light shinned into our car and its inside lit up with a strange light.

Similarly the Hills had remarked also about a light that might have been shinned on the ground during their abduction. In *The Interrupted Journey*, Barney described seeing red lights on the ground near the highway as he approached the object the second time (as described during his hypnosis sessions recounting his drive to the abduction area and what he saw right before the abduction occurred), "you spoke of some lights down the highway. Red lights, I believe. Does that ring any bells? Lights down the highway-as if some men were working down there?"

And as the Hills then drove closer to the object, Barney again described the area as lit up by a strange light:

What was it you saw down the highway'? I saw a group of men and they were standing in the highway. And it was brightly lit up, as if it were almost daylight, but not really day. It was not the kind of light of day, but it was brightly lighted….

And as Barney next emerged from the car, he again described the area around him as lit up, "What light was there? Headlights? BARNEY: It was just an orange light. DOCTOR: An orange light. BARNEY: And I could see this orange glow. And I started to put-to get out of my car and put one foot on the ground. And two men were standing beside…"

And Barney under hypnoses described a red glow at the scene of the abduction yet again and in more detail:

I could remember a red glow in the highway and I always thought someone was doing something like that flagging me down. DOCTOR: You mean like swinging a lantern? BARNEY: No. No. Well-yes-if he had had a lantern in his hand. DOCTOR: Well, that would have given a red glow, wouldn't it? BARNEY: No-the glow wasn't coming from an object in his hand. DOCTOR: I see from somewhere else? BARNEY: The glow was just a large glow. I-I thought, oh, my God, it can't be in the daytime. DOCTOR You had a pretty large moon that night didn't you? BARNEY: Oh, I thought about the moon. But the thing was right there on the highway.... 'Now, how can the moon be on the highway in that kind of position?'

Where did this lighting, in both instances, come from? Could it have been from the lights on the objects side?

Because its color was red, could it have been produced by the red lights on the sides of the Hill object's windows?

Such beams and strange lights seem to be a commonality in many abductions. Could they represent scenes created by laser or some kind of similar methods? As mentioned, Webb reported that beams of light focused on UFO witnesses often precede impressions of missing time and abduction scenarios. A form of this may have happened in these three events. In the Buff Ledge, a beam of light preceded the abduction. In the Hill sighting the area of the abduction was lit by a strange light and in ours my sister saw a strange light as the object made a close approach. In all three events, an emotional event followed: in the Buff Ledge and Hill experiences it was long complex abductions and in ours a strange man and dangerous car chase.

But many other abductions have begun with a beam of light. The Betty Andreasson abduction (to be discussed later) began after a pulsating reddish-orange light shined through the kitchen window. The Travis Walton abduction also began when a beam of light suddenly appeared from a craft and knocked him unconscious. The Schirmer abduction case involved a green light that seemed to be a sort of tractor beam.

Could a laser, or several lasers working together, or some kind of field produce complex scenes such as these? Could the strange lights be a marker for other types of forces?

Some psychological effects also accompanied these sightings, for example Barney remarked:

Later, when Barney listened to the playback of the tapes, he likened this event to the feeling he had when he went into hypnosis with the doctor...If this is true, was he being put into hypnosis by these "men," and if so, was his amnesia caused by this?) DOCTOR: Are you asleep at the time? BARNEY: My eyes are tightly closed and I seem—disassociated. DOCTOR: Disassociated? Is that what you said? BARNEY: This happened after I was in the road at Indian Head. I thought I had driven quite a distance from Indian Head when I got lost and found myself in the woods. DOCTOR: You got lost after Indian Head, is that it? BARNEY: I was not on Route 3 and I couldn't understand why.

Betty had also remarked about this, "Betty, straining to remember, thought that Barney had made a sharp left turn from Route 3, but could not in any way identify where this might have been." Neither knew why Barney turned off Route 3 just before the abduction.

And in another comparison, Betty, as had my sister, noticed the erratic movements of the object and this is why she had tried to call Barney's attention to the object, "And as they got closer, there seemed to be more of this jumping back and forth in the sky."

Also, as mentioned the Hill object seemed to take on several appearances. When it went in front of the moon, they saw it as it as odd shaped and flashing all different colored lights and with something like searchlights rotating around it. Betty said you could see those long beams of white-and they were different colors. These were bright colors like a bright orange light, with an almost a reddish beam. And there was also a color like blue. When they first saw it more closely, they described it a cigar-shaped object and drew it with seven windows. Later in the sighting, it displayed a disc shape and when it left, it appeared as a bright, huge, orange ball and they described it as a beautiful, bright ball.

Although this memory is disconnected, I remember us watching our object leave and being very happy that we thought it did not us. The Hills expressed this feeling when their object left, saying they both seemed so elated, really happy and thinking it isn't too bad. They saw a bright moon, laughed and said they were happy.

Still another comparison of these events might be made with the events associated with Betty Andreasson – Luca. This abduction took place about 50-60 miles from the place of our sighting and occurred in 1967.

Her events, like ours, began with a childhood sighting of a small ball of light. As mentioned we were both written about in Randle's *Star Children*.

The earliest encounter that she recalled was when she was seven years old. While she waited for a girl friend to come to play dolls with her, a small ball of light zipped into the play hut, zipped around her head and landed between her eyes. After she awoke, she thought a bee had bitten her and could not remember anything else concerning this experience until many years later.

I asked her if she consciously remembered this event and if she had any idea what the ball of light was. She said that she was conscious of the ball of light and at first thought it was a bee. She did not, however, know what it was or how it functioned.[80]

As had happened to us, she had additional sightings during her childhood. Her only conscious memory of something unusual was getting bitten by a bee, seeing the moon growing larger in size and an animal trap that was missing from where she had set it up. Many years later, her subconscious UFO memories were recovered through hypnosis.[81] She had no idea that such little, insignificant experiences were connected to this phenomena.

Later on January 25, 1967, she had the abduction experience at South Ashburnham, Massachusetts.[82] Betty was in her kitchen, with her seven children, mother and father in the living room. Around 6:35 p.m., the house lights suddenly blinked out for a moment. After that, a pulsating reddish-orange light shined in the kitchen window. She calmed the frightened children while her father rushed to look out the kitchen window. They saw a group of strange-looking small beings approaching with a hopping motion. These five small humanoids passed through the wooden door. Her family was placed into suspended animation. The leader established telepathic communication with Betty. Betty was taken outside and taken on board a small craft. This machine was about twenty feet in diameter and looked like two saucers, one inverted upon the other; with a small superstructure on top (she drew this with windows). The craft accelerated and apparently merged with a larger parent craft and there Betty was subjected to the effects of strange equipment and a physical examination. Afterwards she was taken to an alien place and given a bizarre object lesson that caused her to undergo a painful but ecstatic religious-like experience.

The aliens told her that certain things had been locked in her mind and she was instructed to forget them and her experience until a certain time. She consciously remembered only a small fraction of the encounter; the power failure, the colored light flashing through the window and the beings entering the house.

She did not know anything about UFOs and thought this was some sort of religious experience, except that the beings she saw looked nothing like angels. It was many years before she reported it. At first her account was so fantastic that it was not believed. Eventually researchers came across it again.

Among the many other oddities is the ball of light that she saw when she was seven. When we saw our small object, I worried about what would happen if it hit us. In her case, she said that it landed right between her eyes. This would have been very dangerous, or might have even killed her, if it had been ball lightning, because it has a lot of energy. Thus, this did not fit the idea of ball lightning.

She was conscious of losing consciousness when the ball of light landed between her eyes. She had many unusual experiences, "I felt uncomfortable each time I had to call Ray and report another unusual experience happening to us."[83]

Because of the resemblances to the Hill sighting, I was also in contact with Kathleen Marden.[84] She is recognized as the world's leading expert on the Hill abduction and researcher of contact with non-human intelligence and an author and lecturer. She is the niece of Betty Hill, who with husband Barney, had the world's first widely publicized alien abduction. She has written books with nuclear physicist/scientific Ufologist Stanton Friedman–*Captured! The Betty and Barney Hill UFO Experience, Science was Wrong* and *Fact, Fiction and Flying Saucers* and *The Alien Abduction Files*, with Denise Stoner. Her essays have been published in several additional books. She has also spearheaded an extensive research project, with Denise Stoner, to identify commonalities among experiencers and is currently working on MUFON's Experiencer Survey. She has given expert testimony on the *Discovery, History, H2, National Geographic and Destination America* channels and on documentaries and news shows.

Her comments were very interesting and helped me to understand the phenomena immensely.

She read our reports and said that because I recalled possible missing time and close encounters, I have the most significant markers that experiencers share.

One thing I was curious about was the appearance of the light through the windows, the colors and intensity of the light and what the interior looked like in the Hill sighting, because it had begun the same way ours had, with someone looking through the windows of a similar-shaped craft. My very first impression when I first saw it and when I looked through the windows close-up was of light from a mercury vapor lamp. This is because in college I had worked as a negative stripper (everyone jokes that that means they made me put my clothes back on) for a blueprint company. They had mercury vapor lamps so that I was familiar with this light.

In a December 3, 2017 letter, Marden said, "Barney had used the words mercury vapor lamp or light to describe the intensity of the light he saw through the windows of the craft as he stood in a farmer's field in Lincoln, New Hampshire, looking up at the craft." I had not seen this description previously, but we must have experienced something similar. She added, "The examining rooms were not as brightly lit and the walls, through which the light emanated, had a bluish white cast. More blue than white. However, at one point during their examinations, both mentioned a bright light. This is unusual. Today, most people describe the Grey's examining rooms as dimly lit."

We could not find a reference in the literature where he used the term mercury vapor, but we both thought that she had probably heard them say that.

In *Interrupted Journey*, Betty had mentioned that during her examination, "the light is very bright so my eyes aren't always open."

I had also asked her about light fixtures or how the Hill's object was lit and she said that the light emanated through the walls. This was our impression also.

Marden also added that she had found reports that others in the area had seen objects on the same night as the Hills had.

Another thing I wanted to ask about was the difference between conscious and hypnotic recall. For example, in the Buff Ledge comparison drawings, the drawing that Barney made right after his encounter resembled the sketches my sister and I and the Sharon witnesses had made more than the sketches that he made after hypnosis did. These original sketches by Barney had been published later than the others, so there was no chance of memory contamination. However, the sketches he made after hypnosis differ. She said that more attention should be paid to Barney's conscious recall.

About this sketch, Marden said:

Betty told me that she and Barney each drew a sketch of the UFO on the day after their sighting, 9/20/1961. Barney's sketch was much more detailed than Betty's because he alone walked into the close encounter field and he was using binoculars. He saw the figures that he described as "somehow not human" (Walter Webb's NICAP report). Betty was seated in the passenger seat, the driver's side door was open and the inside light was on. Therefore, she was unable to see the detail that Barney saw.

I have always maintained that more attention should be paid to Barney's conscious, continuous recall of the event. There is no doubt that he was a credible, high functioning person. Betty was as well, but the debunkers have torn her to shreds in their attacks upon her.

I, of course, also wondered about the lighting that they saw. She said:

Betty and Barney said that the lights they saw through the craft's windows were very bright and blue-white. The light inside the craft was bluish and radiated from the walls. They did not find additional information about the red lights on each end of the craft. With regard to the darkness and then light, I was referring to the craft's spinning appearance. It seemed to have lighted windows on only one side, so when it rotated, the Hills could see the lights and then darkness and then lights and darkness.

I read your "Uncommon Commonalities" paper. I am pleased that you were able to find other cases where the craft matched the Hill's craft. Great job!

This was interesting because the light we saw in our object was extremely bright.

Because Budd Hopkins had investigated us in relation to family sightings, I had also asked about this subject. She had paid some attention to this subject and had some very interesting observations:

I haven't personally studied the genealogy of experiencers. Derrel Sims discovered that many experiencers originated in Turkey. He also found a Celtic-Native American connection. Others have discovered an elevated level of Rh-negative blood type, but there are plenty of O positives as well. Most of this research is cost prohibitive. Most of us fund our own research on a small amount of money.

Dr. James Harder was the first researcher, as far as I know, who discovered that genetically related individuals were experiencing serial abductions. I've collected anecdotal evidence that supports his claim. When a parent has been abducted, the children are usually taken as well. I've spoken with other researchers about my findings and they have also noticed this trend.

If the parent was single at the time of his or her first contact, the children might be taken from the time they are very young. These are the only cases, as far as I know, where the initial contact occurs in a home. If the initial contact is made in an external environment, such as from a car, fishing spot, hiking spot, etc., additional contact is usually made inside one's home. The results of my commonalities study at http://www.kathleen-marden.com/commonalities-study-final-report.php indicate that 36% believe they were under age 5 when their first contact occurred. 83% indicated they were under 20. The participants were self-identified experiencers, but 88% stated they had conscious recall and 76% stated that they had someone with them. 67% had conscious recall of observing a craft at less than 1000 feet prior to an abduction. So, if they are being truthful, they meet the criteria for having experienced a physical abduction. I have more research to do and should attempt to obtain statistics on this topic. So far, I have anecdotal reports but have not quantified it. But virtually everyone I've spoken with who have children, have stated that they believe their children have been visited (except those with seriously handicapped kids). Many of these children are very fearful during their teenage years when the experiments become sexual and sometimes painful. This experience of possible missing time, but no knowledge of a UFO or abduction, as happened to us, is experienced by others as she described above. It is not unusual for a missing time event to appear almost seamless. Unless you're acutely aware of the time on your watch and you check it immediately after the sighting, it could simply slip by. As you know, the close encounters and lights in your car are often precursors to an ET contact experience. These experiences might have begun for you at a very young age. There appears to be a pattern for experiencers to be taken for study and tracking along family genetic lines. It might be interesting to develop a questionnaire for close encounter experiencers and missing time experiencers and ET contact experiencers with recall. Many people are aware of missing time, but did not observe a UFO. I spoke with a couple over the weekend who were sitting in their car with their doors open, preparing to go to his apartment. They were dating at the time. They had checked their watches in order to determine if they had time to watch a movie, as she had children at home who were waiting for her. Suddenly, they woke up and realized that half of their clothing was wet and they were missing 3 hours. The parking lot had been empty, but now it was full. They had not observed a UFO. I receive reports similar to this one from time to time. I also wondered if there were any relationship between such experiences as seeing small objects and UFO close encounters or abductions and she replied:

I've received several reports of light orbs inside an experiencer's home immediately before an abduction. A few experiencers have observed the orbs rapidly expand into ETs. I've spoken with three physicists about this and other high strangeness events. It is possible that they use technology to raise their vibrational level until they become invisible and able to pass through solid matter. It is just a matter of getting things in alignment to get them to inter-penetrate, making it possible for matter to pass thorough matter. The trick is to match up both frequency and phase of the human and solid object. We've already done something like this on a very small scale in a laboratory.

Important findings–UFOs may have lights out of the visible range.

Some important effects were noticed during our sighting. Besides the many aspects mentioned, several additional important disco variations can be found in this event. For one example, from our photography it appears that this object was shining a light that was not in the visible range. Maybe this photography is the first good evidence that UFOs can have lighting that is not in the range that the human eye sees. This photograph was taken before the digital age, I have the original and it could not be altered digitally.

Lasers can emit light at variable wavelengths, which includes the invisible range and perhaps this is what produced the double trace. In addition, lasers can be used to make holograms. Perhaps some of the unusual sightings that often accompany UFO events are holographic or volume display images created by laser.

There is very little photography showing light coming from UFOs or even aircraft in the invisible range (it is not known if aircraft even carry lasers). About the only one is a 2017 video purporting to show a UFO firing a laser at the International Space Station. The station was unharmed and the video is thought to just show lens flares.

In addition, the object near the ground may have also made the inside of our car light up using laser light. We may have been exposed to laser light from both objects.

So far, there is little evidence that aircraft carry lasers, "Industry has struggled for about a decade to make a laser small enough to be installed on a vehicle or aircraft."[85] Thus it is unlikely that this photograph is of an airplane and it certainly did not behave like one.

Our report also led to another sighting–the DIA.

Our Massachusetts event may have had additional consequences beyond its weirdness. For example, I was extremely disturbed about the experience and afraid I might have gone crazy. This led me to mention the subject of UFOs at work–but certainly nothing about having a specific sighting.

At that time I was working for the DIA in a GS-11 position that is considered PhD-level work and I had very high security clearances. I certainly did not want to say anything about seeing a UFO and when I just mentioned the general subject, I expected the normal harassment about this. However, the people I worked with in Air Order of Battle, told me that they had recently reported a UFO they found on our satellite photography.

Thus, our sighting had actually led me to discover another one–and this was in the DIA. Just before our sighting, my supervisors had reported a UFO on the satellite photography that we were working on to their superiors, which I will describe below.

Because today some UFO literature and investigators suggest that the government may have some relationship with aliens. I also wondered whether there could been any relationship between my supervisor's reporting a UFO on the film and our UFO sighting soon afterwards. There is a definite relationship in time, but it is unknown if any other relationship existed. Also, later I discovered that the DIA was actively investigating UFOs when this happened.

CIA, DIA and UFO Photography

In July 1968, I mentioned this subject to my colleagues. As I recall they included Mr. Reams, a high-ranking civilian; William Carlisle, an Air Force Major; and Rick Shackelford, a civilian. I think Mr. Reams may have had a high position, such as GS-14. To my surprise, no one ridiculed me. This was because in early 1968 (before I'd begun working in that section), they had observed a UFO on their TK photography. I looked at these photographs and made copies for use at the facility, but because they were classified, I could not take them home or record any identifying information.

This, however, led to my own smoking gun experience while working for the DIA, as Timothy Good reported in *Need to Know: UFOs, the Military and Intelligence*.

I did not even think of reporting my sighting or talking about it because I had some top security clearances. The subject of UFOs was looked down upon; people thought you were mentally disturbed if you thought you saw one and this could lead to losing your security clearances. If you lost your clearance you lost your job.

The event is described below:[86]

In 1968, I worked with satellite photography for the DIA under code word security clearances that were above Top Secret and some of which were the most highly classified in the government. Two of these code words were "Keyhole" and "Talent" (TK). This work was done in a vault in a windowless building, where we had to work a safe combination, pass before a one-way mirror and through a security check just to enter the workplace. The work involved identifying all flying objects over certain airspaces.

This work was very secure and vital because the 1960s were a time of the Cold War with its intense vigilance by the US in the face of a perceived Soviet threat. The US maintained reconnaissance operations via satellite technology and aircraft over flights of the Soviet Union and elsewhere. Jeffrey Richelson's *America's Secret Eyes in Space: The U.S. Keyhole Satellite Program* (1990) describes the Keyhole Program as one of the most significant military technological developments of the last century and perhaps in all history. The photoreconnaissance satellite played an enormous role in stabilizing superpower relationships because it helped dampen fears of weapons that the other superpowers had available and because it showed whether military action was imminent. Much information about photoreconnaissance satellites and similar technology is still classified. Photoreconnaissance satellites are crucial to the military and satellite and aircraft imagery also can provide new and valuable intelligence about UFOs. This work remains some of the highly secured in the government and according to Dr. Bruce Ashcroft also takes place in the extremely secure WPAFB areas, the NASIC, building 856.

Today it is still exceptionally classified and recently has been in the media because of e-mail news. Its current status the "'TOP SECRET//SI//TK//NOFORN' level must be handled with great care under penalty of serious consequences for mishandling. Every person who is cleared and "read on" for access to such information signs reams of paperwork and receives detailed training about how it is to be handled, no exceptions—and what the consequences will be if the rules are not followed. In the real world, people with high-level clearances are severely punished for willfully violating such rules."[87] So I did not carry away or mention any of this specific information.

In 1968, I was working in a section called Air Order of Battle in the Soviet/East Europe Division, Eastern USSR Branch. Our duties included identifying and recording all flying objects viewed via this satellite photography in this area, such as aircraft and missiles. I think the CIA was the recipient of our reports.

The object that my supervisors had reported was in photographs that were taken over water and I could tell by the water's wave pattern that the object was above the water and not in it. As I recall, the object was over the Black Sea. It was to the west of a mountain range that had a group of buildings, there might have been a Soviet military installation on its other side. The object was photographed on at least two missions (a mission was one 90-minute satellite pass around the earth). It was in a slightly different place during each of the two passes, but it was in the same general area in both.

I made enlargements of the photographs and manipulated the object's size until I had two photos that showed the object from two different viewpoints with the object the same size in each. Thus, I could examine the object's shape stereoscopically. It was saucer-shaped, with a dome. This dome was tall in comparison to the brim—almost like that of a top hat. However, the shape may have been distorted by my method of reproducing and enlarging the photos.

The protocol required us to report the results of our photographic analysis to the CIA and the supervisors of my area said they'd reported the object as a UFO. I am unaware of any time that our supervisor's professional opinion about the identity of objects in the photos was questioned because they were the government's own top authorities. However, the CIA did not accept this report. The CIA insisted the object was an illusion caused by an imperfection in the film. The DIA analysts protested that because the object had been photographed on two different missions, there could not be such a photographic imperfection.[88] The CIA, however, was adamant.

To determine whether the object might indeed be an illusion caused by an imperfection in the film, the analysts sent the film to sensitometry and densitometry specialists. These experts analyzed it and reported that there was no imperfection and that a real object had, in fact, been photographed. My supervisors reported these results to the CIA, but the CIA continued to insist the object did not exist and was an illusion caused by flaws in the film. The specialists who analyzed the film thought this was highly unusual behavior on the part of the CIA. As far as I know, the Air Order of Battle section was the DIA's top organization for analyzing over-flight information and I know of no other time that the section's professional opinion was questioned.

In this case, what should have happened is that the CIA should discuss the material with the experts in a courteous professional manner. If the experts were wrong, the reasons why should have been pointed out. This would improve the country's proficiency in photointerpretation.

But what did happen is interesting–instead the CIA gave an explanation that was weirder than the UFO–almost as if it were taunting the professionals. The images were very, very definitely not film flaws. If the CIA experts knew what caused them, they should have given constructive information, rather than ridiculous replies.

Moreover a misidentification in the government's Photographic Interpretation Office could potentially start WWIII. This was highly classified and significant work. Because our work could easily involve UFO phenomena, I think we should have been informed in some way about it. We had a need to know, but we did not. Instead, we experienced something that could be seen as harassment from the government. This suggests that a much higher government agency can interfere with and maybe actively harass even people working in the government in areas that should be concerned about UFO phenomena.

In addition, I later discovered that the DIA has a significant, maybe vital, role in both UFO investigation and its cover-up. For one, many suspect that it might be the agency that collected UFO reports after Project Blue Book was terminated on December 17, 1969. For example, John Greenewald, of the Black Vault in "The Defense Intelligence Agency's UFO Files" said:

The Defense Intelligence Agency, their mission is to provide timely, objective and cogent military intelligence to the decision makers and policymakers of the U.S. Department of Defense and the U.S. Government. Did they take an interest in UFO sightings? They sure did and The Defense Intelligence Agency has hundreds upon hundreds of blacked out investigations into the UFO phenomenon.

Moreover, some of its released documents show that in 1968, when this occurred, the DIA was actively investigating UFOs; thus, some department likely was aware of our report.

In other documents, he said that the Central Intelligence Agency and Defense Intelligence Agency have conducted UFO investigations that have not been publicly released. This might be the majority of their documents on the subject.

And these agencies have been involved for a long time; the CIA sponsored the 1953 Scientific Advisory Panel on Unidentified Flying Objects, also known as the "Robertson Panel."

Our experience with this DIA behavior suggests that a department monitors UFOs along with other flying objects. Because their response to our report was ridiculous and insulting to the specialist's professional expertise, it may also cover-up and debunk UFO reports. These activities also reminded me of the Kenneth Arnold events, where it appeared that a higher government echelon acted independently of the rest of the government.

Many investigators, such as Timothy Good, have backed up this DIA information. This experience suggests to me that somewhere in the government is or was a group with knowledge of UFO activity. Moreover, it's likely that our Air Order of Battle section would have been monitored because it possessed widespread and the most recent coverage of the earth's surface and air space. And we should have been the agents to find the UFOs.

This inside the DIA experience certainly made me think that the government was involved in cover-up activities. In fact, it even made me slightly wonder if aliens were running the government.

This program is likely vital for UFO study, for as Stanton Friedman has observed, the government probably knows the most about the UFO subject and its best evidence might be its photoreconnaissance programs. He mentions that the best equipment for monitoring UFOs is satellite or ground-based radar or high performance cameras and these are operated by government agencies.

He added that much of the data generated by spy satellites is born classified. Government agencies are always on the lookout for equipment coming in from orbit and recovery teams are instantly alerted when information comes in.

Because of the technical expertise exposed through this photography, it is among the most classified material in the country and this is regardless of whether UFOs are involved.

Moreover, as more information becomes known about DIA overseas investigation, UFOs associated with water and UFO activity in the Black Sea area of the world, perhaps this information might help to shed light on our DIA experience or our experience might help in the examination of additional little-known UFO events there.

Thus, my conclusion about this is that the DIA lies. No matter what was on the film that the DIA Air Order of Battle sectioned turned in as a UFO, it was definitely something that had been photographed. It was not a flaw on the film. The DIA used a lie that was patently obviously false when they said it was a flaw on the film. It is unknown why they would use such a blatant lie about this, rather than a more sophisticated version. This ridiculous response, of course, made me think that some government organization was aware of UFO phenomenon and we had experienced part of the cover-up. But this debunking strategy seems to work, such as in the 2017 report about Harry Reid's UFO investigations. I did find a report of a UFO over the Black Sea in this time-frame:

Trabzon (Turkey)

Sighted on Wednesday 15. May 1968

Reported on Thursday 04. January 2007

Shape: Disk | Duration: 10 minutes

Source: NUFORC

Memorable experience brought back to mind by the recent O'Hare UFO report and how national news is trying to dismiss it (Fox news, for example, had a crawler stating that FAA said it was likely a lenticular cloud)....Then, in 1968, I was assigned to an Air Force 'outpost' in Trabzon, Turkey.... I saw a dull metallic looking 'disk' shaped object hovering in the distance. While I had little to judge size and distance by, it appeared to be pretty good sized and several thousand feet up in the air. As I watched it, I became sure that I was seeing an actual lenticular cloud formation. I did not see anything like ports or windows and did not hear any engine sounds, etc….Then, after several minutes of observation, during which the object hovered in one spot, it pulled the same maneuver the United Airline employees observed at O'Hare. Suddenly, it shot off at an upward angle against the prevailing wind direction...directly into/through the approaching front. Punched a hole clear through it, like drilling a tunnel. I was dumb-founded and realized this was no 'lenticular cloud'. ((NUFORC Note: Witness indicates that the date of the sighting is approximate. PD) There is additional evidence that the offices that investigate UFOs include the government photographic interpretation departments. For example, a CIA document gives the information:

Declassified in Part- Sanitized Copy Approved forRelease2013/09/18: CIA-RD…

17 February 1967 MEMORANDUM FOR: Director, National Photographic Interpretation Center

SUBJECT: Photo Analysis of UFO Photography

    1. This memorandum is in response to Project Number 66120-7,

    submitted by Deputy Director, NPIC, requesting

    that TID/NPIC perform a photo analysis of photographs imaging an…[89]

Indeed the CIA itself was formed very soon after the Kenneth Arnold and Roswell events. It was created under the National Security Act of 1947 that President Truman signed on July 26, 1947. Truman appointed the Deputy Director of CIG, Roscoe H. Hillenkoetter as its first director. Hillenkoetter is listed on many Internet sites as among notable people that have publicly stated that UFO evidence it being suppressed. After retirement, he became a member of the board of governors of NICAP, a UFO investigatory group, from 1957 to 1962. He wanted public disclosure of the UFO evidence.

Thus such government photographic interpretation offices as I worked in are important in investigating UFO events and photography. But it appears that the government does not even disclose UFO information to those working in pertinent fields.

Figure 1: This shows photos along the Massachusetts trip, which began in Washington, DC, at around 6:00 am Saturday, then to Madison, NJ, next to Boston, next we took Route 3 into New Hampshire, then we returned to Boston–and on our way back to Madison we viewed the mystery objects, we then arrived at Madison around 6:00 am Sunday. Photo 1 is my sister talking to my DIA coworkers, photo 2 is a lake in NH, photo 3 is a fern forest and photo 4 is my sister as we returned to New York. A mystery is why my co-workers were unable to contact me on Sunday for the ride home, when they knew who we were, had the phone number and had been at Drew University talking to us.

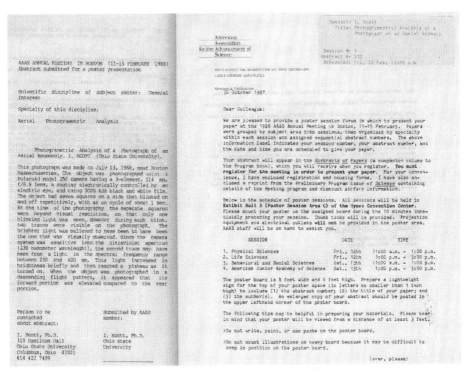

Figure 2: This shows the acceptance of my paper about the photograph I took during this trip of a mystery object that we watched. The American Association for the Advancement of Science accepted this work. The photograph showed that this object carried lighting that was not in the visible range. This is the first photograph showing this that has been accepted by scientific peer review and it may be the only photograph showing this also.

Figure 3: Another of Sue Postle's write-ups describing the same object. She described a strange color of light inside the car at the time we stopped to watch the object. She also described the blinking pattern of the lights on the object's side and its amazing speed.

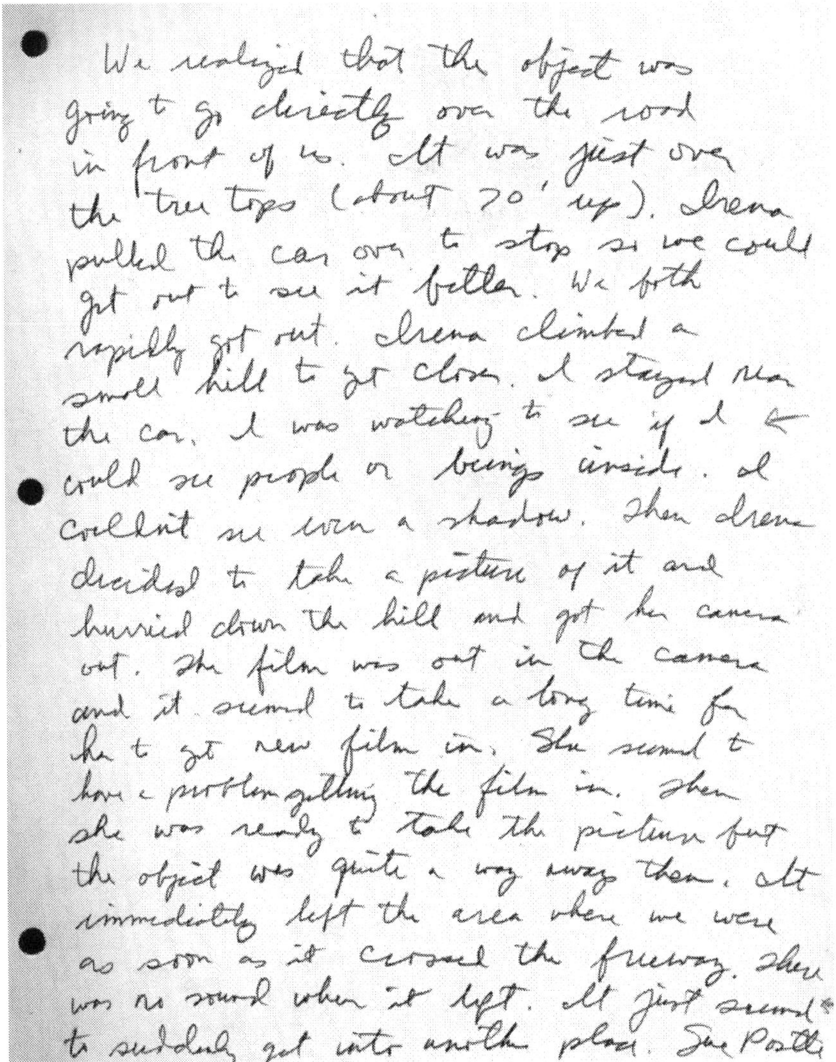

We realized that the object was going to go directly over the road in front of us. It was just over the tree tops (about 70' up). Irena pulled the car over to stop so we could get out to see it better. We both rapidly got out. Irena climbed a small hill to get closer. I stayed near the car. I was watching to see if I could see people or beings inside. I couldn't see even a shadow. Then Irena decided to take a picture of it and hurried down the hill and got her camera out. The film was out in the camera and it seemed to take a long time for her to get new film in. She seemed to have a problem getting the film in. Then she was ready to take the picture but the object was quite a way away then. It immediately left the area where we were as soon as it crossed the freeway. There was no sound when it left. It just seemed* to suddenly get into another place. See Postt

Figure 4: This is one of my sister's write-ups about our trip that includes a description of the mysterious object that we saw. In it, she described the object's incredible speed, "It just seemed to suddenly get into another place." We watched it travel at this speed a number of times. She also describes my going up a nearby hill twice.

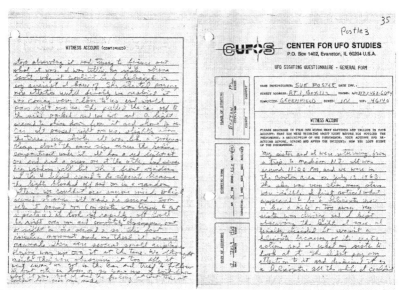

Figure 5: Sue Postle's CUFOS report. She describes how low and close it was, the light that it shone down on us and in our car, the red and green lights on each end and the seven large windows that showed a blinking pattern. She also described the objects was soundlessness, how it seemed to be right over us and then disappear by showing up somewhere else and the airplanes we saw above it.

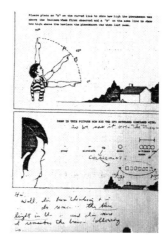

Figure 6: Sue Postle's CUFOS report showing her drawings of the object

246 W. 16th St.
New York, N.Y., 10011
Sept. 4, 1986

Dear Irena,

I am very sorry to be so late in writing to you to thank you for the photographs and other information you sent me. The photographs are especially helpful, and I appreciate the way in which you sent me a xerox "map" to clarfy locations. Do you have any objection if I should use one of the photographs in my forthcoming book? It would be unattributed, of course. I may only use photos of scars which we are rather certain from hypnotic and other recall, but I would like to know in any case. I would use one of the calf photos if I did publish one.

My as yet untitled book will be published in April or May by Random House, and will include photos of scars in a number of cases, drawings of humanoids and photos of ground traces.

I am truly sorry, Irena, that we didn't have more time in a more relaxed situation to try another hypnosis session when I was visiting Jenny and interviewed you there at her home. I feel certain that another try will be more successsful.

I thank you for your continuing support and interst in my work, and I have been very admiring of your research on Ohio cases. Keep up the good work, and let's keep in touch.

Thanks, again, for the photos.

Very sincerely,

In which the person recalls the U.F.O. omitted origin of the mark.

Figure 7: Budd Hopkins found that some abductees had a scar on their calf. I looked at mine, found a similar scar and sent him a photograph. He asked about using it in his forthcoming book (Intruders: The Incredible Visitations at Copley Woods) as shown in his September 4 letter.

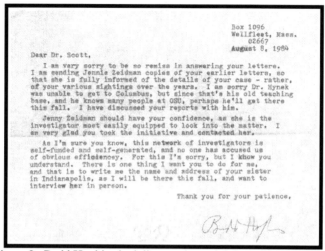

Box 1096
Wellfleet, Mass.
02667
August 8, 1984

Dear Dr. Scott,

I am very sorry to be so remiss in answering your letters.
I am sending Jennie Zeidman copies of your earlier letters, so
that she is fully informed of the details of your case - rather,
of your various sightings over the years. I am sorry Dr. Hynek
was unable to get to Columbus, but since that's his old teaching
base, and he knows many people at OSU, perhaps he'll get there
this fall. I have discussed your reports with him.

Jenny Zeidman should have your confidence, as she is the
investigator most easily equipped to look into the matter. I
am very glad you took the initiative and contacted her.

As I'm sure you know, this network of investigators is
self-funded and self-generated, and no one has accused us
of obvious efficiency. For this I'm sorry, but I know you
understand. There is one thing I want you to do for me,
and that is to write me the name and address of your sister
in Indianapolis, as I will be there this fall, and want to
interview her in person.

Thank you for your patience,

Figure 8: Budd Hopkins had discussed our sighting with Dr. Hynek.

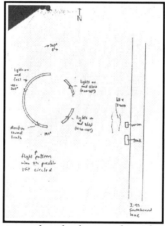

Figure 9 : After I took the photographs, the larger object began to circle. It appeared to be circling Norwood Memorial Airport to our west. We watched it circle and watched airplanes flying above it, which did not land while it circled. It had a very complex pattern. When it flew in a semicircle north to south, it traveled to rapidly to see. Then in the south to north semicircle, it blinked its lights on twice. It circled in this pattern for about 20 minutes. During the time it circled, the truck driver chased us south; we got away and then turned around and headed north. When we returned it was still circling, but afterwards it changed direction and traveled to the north. It could not have possibly been human-made because nothing could travel that fast.

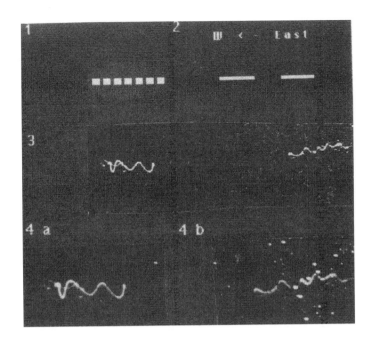

Figure 10 : This diagram is from page 13 of my IUR article 9/10 1990. It shows the photograph of the larger object that I took from the hilltop (3 and 4) and a computer sketch of what the object I saw (1 and 2) should have looked like. The object's appearance is shown in part 1 (it had seven lit squares but it was so far away that these merged into 1 light. Part 2 shows its expected photographic trace (during two blinks and moving east to west). Part 3 shows the actual photograph of it during two blinks (and part 4 a and 4 b show an enlargement of this). It did not show the expected straight path, but showed undulations–these were not mysterious but caused by the hand-held time exposure with nothing with which to stabilize the camera. But what is mysterious is that although only one object was visible by eye and through the viewfinder, each blink was composed of two traces, thus one trace had not been visible. It appeared that the brighter trace was the visible one, but the dimmer one had not been visible and therefore in a frequency that was photographed but not seen.

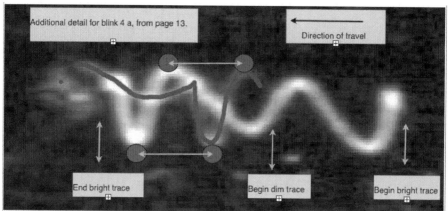

Figure 11: This is a diagram of blink a. It shows that the brighter trace came on before the dimmer trace and then turned off sooner than it did. The brighter trace was somewhat consistent in its brightness. The dimmer trace came on slowly, reached a peak and then became dimmer and then turned off.

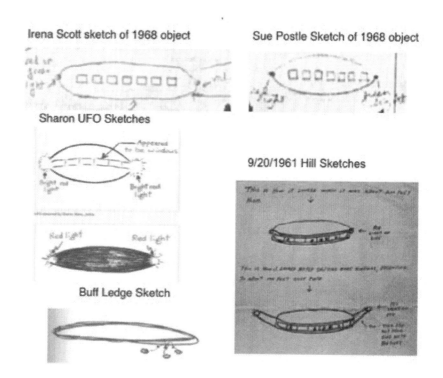

118

Figure 12: The original witness sketches of the Bluff Ledge, Hill, Sharon and the Massachusetts objects show their similar and unique attributes, such as the general cigar shape, the large windows and the lights in the area to the side of the windows. The sketches clockwise from upper left show the similarities of the objects as described in these possibly related sightings. Sketches of the 1968 MA object by my sister, Sue Postle and me (from IUR 9/19/1990), the Hills' original two September 20, 1961 sketches (Kathleen Marden published these original sin 2013 "Betty and Barney Hill: Where the Debunkers went Wrong."), the sketch of a Buff Ledge witness showing the cigar-shaped object releasing three satellite objects (from Encounter at Buff Ledge) and the Sharon witnesses' two sketches
(http://www.ufoevidence.org/cases/case548.htm). In the Massachusetts, Sharon and Buff Ledge reports, similar circular, satellite objects, with bands rotating and changing color across the spectrum, were associated with the larger objects.

******

CHAPTER FIVE: AIRPORT AND OHIO STATE UNIVERSITY SIGHTINGS

My next sighting was in 1984 and took place at work in the daytime, with the object over an airport landing slope and a university. This was several years before the noted Chicago O'Hare sighting. Although I was unable to take a photograph of the object, I have good drawings from five people as shown in the figures. My witnesses and I held academic positions in the OSU College of Medicine.

Sightings of UFOs over airports are extraordinary. For example, the Chicago O'Hare International Airport (November 7, 2006) sighting became one of the Chicago Tribune's most-viewed stories on its Web site. Not only are such sightings astonishing in themselves, but objects in the area where aircraft are landing and taking off are very hazardous.

Besides this one's being over an airport, this was an unusually good sighting for additional reasons: the object was in sight for a long time, it had numerous witnesses, the witnesses were very high caliber, it was investigated as it took place by a well-known investigator, it was unexplainable and for numerous other reasons.

I published the object's description in the peer-reviewed scientific literature the, "Description of an Aerial Anomaly Viewed over Columbus, Ohio" in the OJS (Figure 1).[90]

This information was also published in the *MUFON UFO JR*; [91] "UFO activity over Ohio;" *UFOs and the Millennium*, pp. 109-113; *FATE* 4, 1985;[92]and the *MUFON of Ohio Newsletter*, "An Improbable Airport Sighting Could this be mind control?," [93]

I was contacted and interviewed by many people after I made this report, including Budd Hopkins, Leo Sprinkle, Dr. Hynek and others listed above, as mentioned.

I was fortunate to have very credible additional witnesses. These witnesses all have PhDs and have been or are university professors, Dr. Dean, Dr. Curris, Dr. Boulant, Dr. Curry and myself. All worked in the OSU Medical School at that time. A number of other people were in the room (the Physiology Department office) watching it. No one had any idea what it was. The witnesses that I asked, wrote and signed descriptions and made drawings of the object right after the sighting. I sent these to CUFOS with my own report.

The sighting was investigated by Warren B. Nicholson of Battelle as it progressed and he called the airport and looked for the object himself. Later he told me that he had another report with photographs and high caliber witnesses.

Although this probably has nothing to do with UFOs, there had been a power failure, no electricity, in our house right after the sighting when I had returned home. This did not affect the neighboring houses. I checked the circuit breakers, but this did not help.

This sighting was significant for me, because I viewed it at the exact time during which I was filling out reports on previous sightings by my sister and me. I in no way expected it. At the time I was living a normal life, working for OSU, Battelle Memorial Institution and *Popular Mechanics* magazine and living with my family on a farm with a tree business. I had paid little attention to UFO phenomena and even thought people no longer saw them.

Suddenly in late 1983 for no reason at all, I became very afraid of UFOs. This was so bad that I did not want to go out of the house and when I did, I kept hiding under trees. Our dog disappeared, but I was too fearful to look for her. (I can remember also having these feelings when I was around age 10-17, but do not know why.) I did not know why this happened, but it caused me to contact the Center for UFO Studies to report our previous sightings.

Because I had always intended to report the sightings and because I had developed the intense fear at that time, I decided to report our UFO sightings. Among others, I contacted CUFOS (2/10/84). They sent report forms and amazingly as I began filling them out (2/23/84) at OSU, I had this daytime sighting and fortunately had extremely good additional witnesses.

There were a number of other sightings in the area at this time and they even made the newspapers.

An improbable airport sighting, could this be mind control?

This sighting took place about 4 P.M. on February 23, 1984, at Hamilton Hall on the OSU campus and lasted about 25 minutes.

I first saw the object over the approach slope for what is now the John Glenn Columbus International Airport, Columbus, Ohio's principal airport. It was somewhat like the later sighting over the O'Hare International Airport (November 7, 2006). The *Chicago Tribune* had filed an FOIA request and Jon Hilkevitch investigated in a story that climbed atop the paper's list of most-viewed stories on its Web site. Like this object, ours was rotating or undergoing a regular appearance change.

The sighting seemed extraordinary because of its location, because it occurred in the daytime, was visible for a considerable length of time and, for me, because I viewed it at the exact time that I had begun filling out reports on previous sightings by my sister and me (but I in no way was expecting to see or was looking for anything).

The witness drawings and write-ups, not only show the appearance of the object, but show its change in appearance as the sighting progressed. Also at the time of the sighting, the wind was coming from the east and several of the witnesses mentioned that it traveled to the east— confirming that it traveled against the wind.

Figure 2 of Chapter 5 is my own sighting. I saw the object first and was looking upward at more of an angle (maybe 80 degrees) than when it was seen later. It at first looked like a building with girders and a bright light under it floating through the sky. It was rotating or changing its appearance at a regular sequence of time, not randomly. Later when I viewed it from the office, it appeared as a rotating rectangle on a bright light.

Figures 3 and 4 are drawings of M.C. She was the second person to see it and also at first looked at it from more of an angle. Her first drawing was of a shiny round object, which rotated regularly about 30 to 60 seconds. She said that she also had seen the rectangular configuration. And mentioned that it was traveling east.

Figure 5 was the description and drawing of J.D, who watched it from the department office. He also mentioned that it was rectangular and rotating around its long axis.

Figure 6 is the description of J.B. He described it as a rectangular object with something very bright on the bottom and also mentioned the object's rotation. He also said that it traveled to the east.

Figure 7 was a drawing by J.C.

Figure 8 is a drawing by J.D showing the window we were watching it from and its relative size and shape. It had an extended apparent diameter. Its position above the OSU buildings shows that it was in the airport landing slope area and should have shown up on their radar. A similar drawing (not shown) was made by M.C.

Figure 9 is a comparison photograph, showing a balloon near the OSU campus. It looked nothing like a balloon.

So far, the object has never been identified. This sighting is unique because it is possible that no other sighting has been made that reported such elements as visibility for a long time of an object having an extended apparent diameter and as viewed by witnesses having such a high education level

This sighting is also strange because, as mentioned, in late 1983 I had developed a sudden unexplained fear of UFOs. Because of this, in February 1984, I contacted the CUFOS office. I received a letter from Michelle Baumeister (Figure 10 of Chapter 5)) asking me to list any strange experiences in my life (as shown) I listed about 10 pages, but did not send anything in because I thought no one would believe me. They sent the forms about a week later. Then very strangely when I began to fill out the forms, I had the following sighting (but luckily had other witnesses or I might have felt that I was crazy). Soon after that, there were many sightings among my neighbors and family and even a mysterious burn. I had no sightings for a long time after that year, but just before my book was to come out in 2017, I had another sighting, so I certainly had some strange experiences.

As a detailed written description of the events, when I first saw the object, I had glanced up out an east-facing window. The object looked like an upside down ice cream cone, with the ice cream (one scoop) part glowing a brilliant white (Figure 2). It was moving so slowly that, at first, I thought it was a balloon. The object appeared to be in or above the approach slope of the Port Columbus airport to the east and a low jet plane that was landing appeared to pass under it as I watched.

During most of the sighting, the object looked like either a solid rectangle or a rectangle on top of a light. It would repetitively–in a regular cycle (~ 60 seconds), not in the random pattern of a windblown object–appear to rotate (or change its appearance).

But it appeared somewhat different when I first spotted it. This might have been because I was closer to it and looking up. Later we saw it from a more sidewise angle. At first, it had an incomprehensible appearance like a construction made of Erector Set-like beams/girders just floating in the sky. This "girder" appearance had a fog surrounding it. The fog was not like a cloud; it was small and traveled with the object. The object changed appearance in a regular fashion. At first, there would be a shape I could not understand; looked somewhat like a rectangle–constructed of metallic beams like a building framework. Then, it appeared somewhat like a vertical beam with three horizontal girders sticking out from it–looking like a capital E. After this, a real clear and obvious rectangle would appear that lasted for a while. Then, it would either look like a thin line, or disappear, or go toward its large shape (I can't remember which). It had a white light and made a complete cycle of shape change at totally regular intervals of perhaps once a minute. It did not just twist randomly in the wind.

The beams seemed to be red, or black, or brown, but they were thin and difficult to see.

I went to the third floor and asked MC to look at it with me. I asked her if it looked like a balloon and she did not know (Figures 3 and 4). We went to the physiology department office (room 312), where more people began to watch it.

We opened the window to get a clearer view. We asked Dr. C, a professor, to watch. He watched briefly and said maybe it was a box kite (Figure 7). We then asked Dr. B, another professor, who watched it for a while and asked if it were a balloon (Figure 6). There was no balloon shape above or below it. Also, a balloon should not be in an area where airplanes were landing. After several more minutes he said, "Maybe it's a UFO." JD watched and discussed it with us (Figure 5).

When I first watched the object, it seemed to be headed straight east. Near the end of the time, it was to the northeast and looked as it had traveled quite a distance (its apparent size was smaller). It then appeared to be a little north of the airport (which was almost directly east).

During this time, for the most part it looked like a rectangle that would undergo a very regular appearance change about once a minute. I assumed this was caused by rotation. During this rotation, it would look like a clear rectangle with its long axis up and down, then disappear and then reappear as a rectangle. It continued this appearance for some time.

By then, I could clearly see it traveling and was sure it wasn't a box kite. There were buildings, trees and electric lines in the way. It would have been impossible to fly a kite on a string around these obstacles. In addition, the air was still.

MC and I asked several of the people that were watching if there was a telescope in the building. We were unable to find one. While we watched I called Warren Nicholson, a scientist at the nearby Battelle Memorial Institute (holds several U.S. Patents, etc.) that was also an experienced UFO investigator (e.g. investigated the classic Coyne Helicopter incident, was head of a UFO group and others), to tell him what we were witnessing. I do not know how the object disappeared. After I talked to him, I looked again and could not see it.

Many people should have seen this object, especially some of the thousands of students at OSU. It was one of the first warm days of spring and many people were outside. (I would investigate it differently now with experience as a UFO investigator. Because the professors wanted anonymity, I did not call the news media or get other publicity in seeking additional witnesses.)

Mr. Nicholson later told me that he had checked with Port Columbus immediately after I called him. They told him the wind velocity was 0, so our object shouldn't have been a box kite.

They could not see it. That was strange, because it had been in the Port Columbus approach slope. Mr. Nicholson also had climbed to the Battelle roof to look (on the opposite side of Hamilton Hall from the airport), but had been unable to see it.

Mr. Nicholson called me that night to say a family had also seen something odd later that afternoon. They saw four lines in the sky. The father had taken pictures through a 1200 power telephoto lens with ASA 400 color film. The wife described the lines as tear drop shaped and the husband described it as shaped like an airplane's wing section. In general, the lines seemed comma- or oblong-shaped. They were in the west and were dark. They were not objects reflecting light. They then flew away in four different directions. Mr. Nicholson thought that many sightings in one day were a "flurry" of activity.

The sighting was quite odd. It's unknown how the object remained suspended in the air. No witness saw or drew a balloon shape and should have if it were a balloon. During one part of its rotation/phases, it would completely disappear, also indicating that it wasn't a balloon. It had no visible wings or propellers. It had a strange appearance–its shape seemed fluid, or changeable. It was unrecognizable as a known object–either in descriptions or drawings.

Also, it rotated in a regular pattern the entire time. The other witnesses commented on this in their reports. Its rotation was smooth and regular. It would need some kind of power plant and maybe a computer to keep this rotation going, regular and stabilize it. If it were a balloon, it should have exhibited random twisting in the wind. I've found nothing in the literature similar to the object and no information that balloons can rotate in this manner.

The object traveled against the wind, which is another indication that it was powered. The official Port Columbus weather report was that at 4:00 pm, the visibility was 10 miles and the wind was 5.8 mph from the East with scattered clouds, "4:00 PM…[Wind Dir] East5.8 mph…Scattered Clouds."[94] "The term "wind direction" is defined as the direction from which the wind is blowing."[95] The object should have traveled west, rather than its observed direction toward the east. Thus it was traveling toward the wind. Several witness reports also mentioned that it traveled to the east. The weather station is close to the OSU campus.

It seemed extremely strange that the airport was unaware of it. It could have been a very dangerous obstacle to aircraft. It was in the landing slope of a major airport, well within their radar and visual range during the entire sighting and there for a considerable time. Mr. Nicholson said he called the airport immediately and they hadn't seen anything visually or with radar. However, they should have. For example, even small objects (geese) over an airport can cause a disaster, such as when Chesley Sullenberger saved his passengers and airplane when it hit geese. When I first saw it, it was lined up with the glide slope. The airplane that I watched at the same time seemed lower. It took much longer for the object to pass over than the plane, thus, it probably was higher.

The airplane pilots should have seen it. It was comparatively large with an extended apparent diameter–not a point source. It was large enough to be visible for nearly half an hour. All witnesses drew an object of extended area containing features.

Unlike a balloon, it had a very bright light; balloons usually do not carry lights or reflectors and hot air balloon gas jets do not look like that. I assumed at first this was a reflection. However, as it traveled it was at different angles to the sun, but the bright light was still there, thus, this might have been a real light, or some sort of directional beacon. Although it was daylight, the light was strong enough to be visible most or all the time the object was observed and seemed brighter than aircraft navigation light. It was stable, in phase with the object's rotation and did not fluctuate in brightness when it was visible (not like a dangling piece of metal or mirror twisting in the air). The witnesses watched it for shorter periods than I did, but reported the bright light at different stages. It was not a Chinese lantern and no ad plane was seen towing it.

It was in the path of airplanes swooping low over OSU and landing at Port Columbus. This was so close that when I used sensitive instruments to detect neuronal impulses, the equipment would sometimes pick up airplane-tower communication. At such a close distance to both the airport and university, it could have been a security breach.

It is still unidentified; there was no evidence that it was a balloon–no balloon was visible, it rotated regularly, it could completely disappear, it appeared to be powered and there was no evidence that anything had been released at that time. It traveled against the wind. There was no evidence that it was a drone, because they did not fly in those days and it looked nothing like one.

I vaguely wondered if the electricity going off in our house right afterwards could have been some form of poltergeist affect and mentioned this to my husband.

This sighting is also interesting because it is part of an historical site. The object's trajectory would have been over Battelle Memorial Institute right before we saw it. Battelle has played a crucial role in UFOlogy. Battelle's scientists had conducted a massive study, Project Blue Book Special Report No. 14 (SR-14), which may be the best scientific study of UFO phenomena ever done and one of a few that show the reality of the phenomena. A Battelle physicist named Howard Cross is said to have reported viewing a UFO over Battelle. Cross is thought to have headed Battelle's Project Stork under which *SR-14* was done.

In addition, Cross authored what is known as the Pentacle Memorandum. This memorandum may be the most significant existing documentation of the US government's approach to UFO phenomena.[96] Battelle and OSU had been Dr. Hynek's original home ground.

Thus, another sighting over Battelle may be associated with the best UFO study ever done.

Confirmation and Discussion

It seemed strange to see a possible UFO as I filled out the report, but a 25-minute daytime sighting over a populated area and airport with no one noticing, seemed unreal. I was certainly glad that I had witnesses.

But this strangeness has been reported by other people and may be even seen as a sense of humor. For example, Dr. Harley Rutledge, who made an extensive scientific study of the phenomena, wrote to me that "Surely they have a sense of humor."[97] And he said further that he knew that they played "games" with the researchers and this behavior was observed under precise circumstances with additional witnesses. The scientists sometimes even wondered if the UFO events were being staged for their benefit.

And I was certainly lucky to have extremely credible witnesses– the five of the academics in the medical school and Warren, Nicholson's witnesses.

Ohio State University again

Soon after this sighting, I had another one. This sighting occurred on February 29, 1984 at 3:27 P.M. (and was previously reported in *FATE* 4 1985, shown in Figure 11) on a slightly cloudy day, after a bad snowstorm on the previous night. I saw the object from the northern most fourth floor east facing window in Hamilton Hall. Unfortunately, the object flew away before I had any chance to get other witnesses.

The object was a small, black and slightly brownish, round, dull, rough-textured, object that was seen over Neil Hall–across the street. It looked to be about 1-2 feet in diameter and maybe 20 feet higher than Neil Hall. The object was probably less than 100 feet away from me. It was amorphous, like a pillow, bread dough, or a beanbag and seemed to change shape as it moved around. It seemed to have more or less a random motion around but stayed pretty much over the same spot. Its shape change reminded me of bread dough being kneaded. It moved up/down and around in same general area for around two minutes, then seemed to "tighten-up," became blacker and flew away rapidly to the southeast. I watched it recede until it disappeared by about 3:30 am.

It took off rapidly to the southeast in a straight line, not fluttering in the wind. I watched it recede. The sighting took about three minutes (I timed it using my watch). When it took off, it flew rapidly and assumed a spherical shape. It seemed to contract its outside surface, or become firmer and did not change shape. It also looked a little darker. I could not believe that I was seeing it and tried to see if the window glass was distorting anything, but did not notice this. Afterwards, I watched birds flying in the same area. The object was larger than and did not fly like birds (no wings or movements associated with wing flaps). I also watched a helicopter and this had no resemblance to what I saw.

In my CUFOS report, I mentioned that I had stopped thinking about the UFOs, because having the earlier OSU sighting when I was thinking about them had scared me so I stopped thinking about them. Having another sighting so soon after the last one seemed very strange.

The wind direction would not be relevant, because at first it moved in all directions around a somewhat stationary point. It gave me a horrible feeling as if I had just seen the devil.

Discussion

As with the Massachusetts sighting, there might have been some commonalities between this UFO sighting and this UFO experience. Possibly, the sighting on the 24th might have been prolonged into even the 29th as the Massachusetts one seemed to have been prolonged for several days.

The only odd thing in the papers around that time was the controversial Columbus Poltergeist activity, which made national headlines for several weeks (for example in the *Columbus Dispatch* 3/3/1984).

Another oddity is that, as I mentioned, I became very fearful about three months before this happened. When I was alone on the farm, I kept trying to hide. I seemed to be fearful that something would happen when I was alone. However, the sighting too place in a very public location. I wondered if something were telling me that the UFO phenomena could appear anywhere and there is no way to hide.

Yet again at Ohio State University

This sighting occurred in the daytime north of Hamilton Hall on August 24, 1984. I have my drawing on the CUFOS report form (Figure 12 of Chapter 5) and comparison photographs of balloon clusters (Figure 13 of Chapter 5).

I saw what looked like five bright objects in the sky to the southwest. There were five objects each looking like Venus or Jupiter when they are visible around sunset. I at first thought the objects as a group were slowly moving to the northeast.

I immediately thought that they might be a cluster of balloons. However, unlike the type of balloons that have a half reflective surface and change as they twist in the wind, these had an even appearance. Individually they sometimes moved slowly, sometimes darted, (moved quickly and then stood still), sometimes hovered and sometimes several remained still, while others moved. Part of the time they were near a cloud. This cloud was thin and wispy so I could not tell whether they were behind or in front of it.

One thing that made me think this was odd is that sometimes two would come together. I could not tell whether they merged, or whether one was behind another. Sometimes when one would blink off another would blink on at the same time. This would happen repeatedly for a period of time for just two of the objects, but it happened with different groups of two several times during the sighting.

I stood there watching the objects for about five minutes. It was finals week for the OSU summer quarter and there weren't many people nearby for me to get as confirming witnesses. Because I was standing by Sterling Loving Hall, which housed part of the OSU psychiatric facility, I did not want to be too obvious in trying to get another witness. However one person walked past me and I asked her to look. She acted as if she thought I was doing something spooky, did not look up and hurried on by.

I then went upstairs for three flights of stairs in Hamilton Hall and down the hall to my office. I did not find another witness. I looked out the window just as the objects traveled out of sight.

I, at first thought the objects as a group were moving to the northeast. However later they moved to the southwest. The wind direction might have not made any difference because individual objects seemed to dart in different directions.

Discussions

I have the report and sketches I made at the time. I had at first thought the objects might have been a cluster of balloons. To examine this further, I have photographed clusters of balloons under different circumstances–loose balloons floating in the wind, loose balloons with one shiny side floating in the wind, clusters of balloons floating in the wind and tethered balloons (Figure 13 of Chapter 5).

The objects that I saw looked nothing like a cluster of balloons. The balloons in clusters are close together and you can see both sides of the ones that are shiny on one side. Balloons do not appear and disappear, or do this synchronistically with other balloons. These did not look or behave like the objects I saw.

Board F
@ 9:00 a.m.

SPATIAL ANALYSIS OF HIGH TECHNOLOGY
MANUFACTURING EMPLOYMENT IN METROPOLITAN OHIO.
CLARKE, Audrey and MILLY, Brian P., Kent State
University, Kent, Ohio 44242.

This study assesses the recent changes in high technology
employment in Ohio's Metropolitan areas, forecasts near
term changes in high technology employment and evaluates
the spatial distribution of high technology employment in
light of selected factors thought to influence the location
of such activities. These goals are accomplished by
measuring the levels and changes in high technology
employment within Ohio's MSAs since 1973, using a shift-
share model to identify the components of these changes.
The paper further projects likely future changes in high
technology employment and relates the location of those
industries, in terms of employment, to selected MSA
characteristics which are thought to be reliable
indicators of locational influence. The paper ends with a
discussion of the prospects for high technology in mature
industrial regions and the policy implications for regional
industrial development.

Board G
@ 9:00 a.m.

THE EVOLUTION OF THE DARBY CREEK LANDSCAPE:
A GRAPHIC DEPICTION OF LANDSCAPE CHANGE
OVER TIME. Professors John W. Simpson and
John C. Billing, Department of Landscape Architecture, The
Ohio State University, 190 W. 17th Ave., Columbus, Ohio,
43210

This seven panel illustrative wall display, measuring
approximately 4'x 11', graphically depicts the evolution
of the Darby Creek landscape through geologic time.
Developed as a stand alone public educational display, as
well as a supplement to other on-going research projects
regarding the same area, it attempts to trigger deeper
understanding of the landscape's dynamic nature by
graphically representing many of the earth's primary
physical, biological and cultural processes on consistent
time scales. The environmental effect of each process is
illustrated on a separate time line, all drawn at the same
scale, and all aligned in parallel on the display, thus
enabling easier visual correlation of their cause and
effect relationships. The time lines illustrate biological
evolution, cultural evolution, global climate, sea level,
glaciation, magnetic pole orientation, natural
catastrophies and upheavals, and the deposition and mass
wasting of sedimentary deposits. The time lines are
supplemented with numerous diagrams and drawings, and by
supporting notes. In addition, a set of idealized
vignettes illustrate how the Big Darby landscape may have
appeared at various, critical stages in its evolution.

Board H
@ 9:00 a.m.

DESCRIPTION OF AN AERIAL
ANOMALY VIEWED OVER
COLUMBUS, OHIO. J. Scott,
Department of Physiology, Ohio State
University, Columbus, Ohio 43210.

On February 23, 1984 at 1600 an unusual
aerial object was sighted at 40.00° N and
083.00° W. Five witnesses made written
descriptions of the object. The object
initially appeared to be cone-shaped with
its apex oriented upward. During the
initial few minutes of the sighting, the
cone appeared to be surrounded with a
fog. Its base was a bright area.
Approximately every 60 seconds during the
20 minutes that the object was viewed, it
passed through a regularly timed cyclic
appearance change. In one phase of this
cycle, the object appeared as a distinct
rectangle, and in another phase of the
cycle it became nearly invisible. It
appeared to drift several miles to the
northeast during the period of
observation. The ground wind velocity was
reported to have been 0. After a search
at Port Columbus, it was reported that
the object was not seen and was not
detected by radar. Other aerial anomalies
were reported later in the day by
different observers. The object could not
be explained as a natural source,
balloon, or known aircraft.

Reform Movement. Responses to the need for teacher education
improvement are as diverse as the experts and advocates
themselves. A teacher's sense of efficacy has been positively related to improving student learning. Because most
research dealing with the area of teacher efficacy has been
conducted with experienced teachers, this research was conducted with preservice teachers in the clinical setting of
microteaching regarding their sense of personal teacher efficacy.

The problem investigated was as follows: the relationship
between personal teaching efficacy and microteaching success
in initiating a discussion was examined. The investigation
included looking at the relationship between demographics
such as sex, age, grade point average (GPA), class rank,
(freshman, sophomore, junior, senior, or post baccalaureate),
and teaching specialty and the personal teaching efficacy
of preservice teachers in microteaching success.

Research in the area of teacher efficacy at the preservice
teacher level may better serve educators in teacher education to identify problems to develop intervention strategies
with this population.

9:15

THE GREAT LAKE ERIE: AN INTERDISCIPLINARY
REFERENCE TEXT FOR EDUCATORS. Victor J. Mayer
and Rosanne W. Fortner. Department of Educational Studies, The Ohio State University, 1945 N. High
St., Columbus, Ohio 43210.

Fifteen experts in the sciences, geography, history,
economics and resource management have combined their
efforts to produce a reference text for educators and media
communicators. Funded by The George Gund Foundation of
Cleveland, The Great Lake Erie contains over 150 pages of
information about the importance of the Lake in the
development of Ohio, the economy and culture of the
continent, and the lifestyle of those who live in the
region. Several chapter authors will be on hand at the
Academy's Annual Meeting to discuss their work and the
anticipated uses of the book.

9:30

Operation Bluebird: An ODNR Funded Nongame
Wildlife Project. Robert E. Rohrbaugh,
Jackson Memorial Middle School, 7355 Medbrook
Street, N.W., Massillon, OH 44646.

During the Spring of 1987 approximately 300 Jackson
Middle School seventh grade science students and several
Jackson High School industrial arts students were involved
in making the nesting season for the Eastern Bluebird in
northern Stark County potentially more successful by con-
structing suitable nesting boxes.

Not so many years ago bluebirds were a common sight in
Ohio. But, due in part to a decrease in their natural
nesting cavities such as dead trees and wooden fence posts,
their numbers have drastically declined. The nesting boxes, designed specifically for the Eastern Bluebird, were
constructed in an attempt to provide artificial nesting
cavities.

Thanks to citizen contributions through the "Do Something Wild!" checkoff option on the state income tax return form, Jackson Local Schools received $1,409 from the
Ohio Department of Natural Resources. "Operation Bluebird"
was one of 25 nongame and endangered wildlife projects
approved for funding during 1987.

9:45

A SIMPLE TECHNIQUE FOR THE TRANSFER OF
PLASMID DNA BETWEEN SPECIES OF BACILLUS.
Spencer E. Beames. Benjamin Logan High
School, Box 98 (Logan Co. Rd #5), Zanesfield, Ohio 43360.

Biotechnology techniques are often difficult to
demonstrate at the high school level due to the lack of
specialized equipment. A potentially important, yet
very simple, method of transferring plasmid DNA between
members of the genus Bacillus can be conducted without
any specialized equipment.
Bacillus thuringiensis is a bacterium which produces

Figure 1: The information about a 1984 UFO sighting from the OSU campus is acceptable scientifically by peer-review and has been published in the scientific literature, "Description of an Aerial Anomaly Viewed over Columbus, Ohio" in the Ohio Journal of Science (88(2)-23, 1988 p. 23). The object continues to be acceptable as a UFO after scientific examination because no explanation has been put forth to explain it. This sighting took place on February 23, 1984, of an object that was over the OSU campus and in the approach slope for what is now the John Glenn Columbus International Airport. It was a daytime sighting of a rotating object and resembled the well-known Chicago O'Hare International Airport (November 7, 2006) sighting.

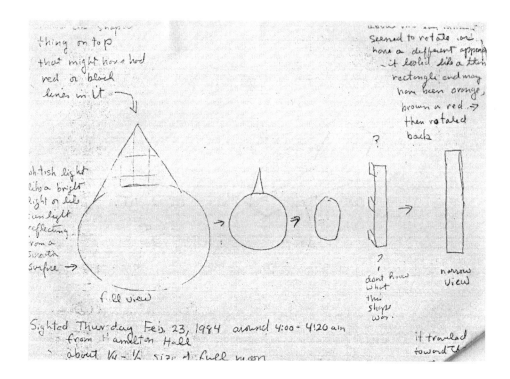

Figure 2: The following figures show the witness' drawings and write-ups for this February 23, 1984, sighting of an object over the OSU campus and in the approach slope for what is now the John Glenn Columbus International Airport. These drawings not only show the appearance of the object, but show its change in the appearance as the sighting progressed. The first figure is my own sighting. I saw the object first and was looking upward at more of an angle (maybe 80 degrees) than when it was seen later. It at first resembled a flying building with girders and a bright light under it. It was rotating or changing its appearance at a regular sequence of time, not randomly. Later when I viewed it from the office, it appeared as a rotating rectangle on a bright light traveling toward the east.

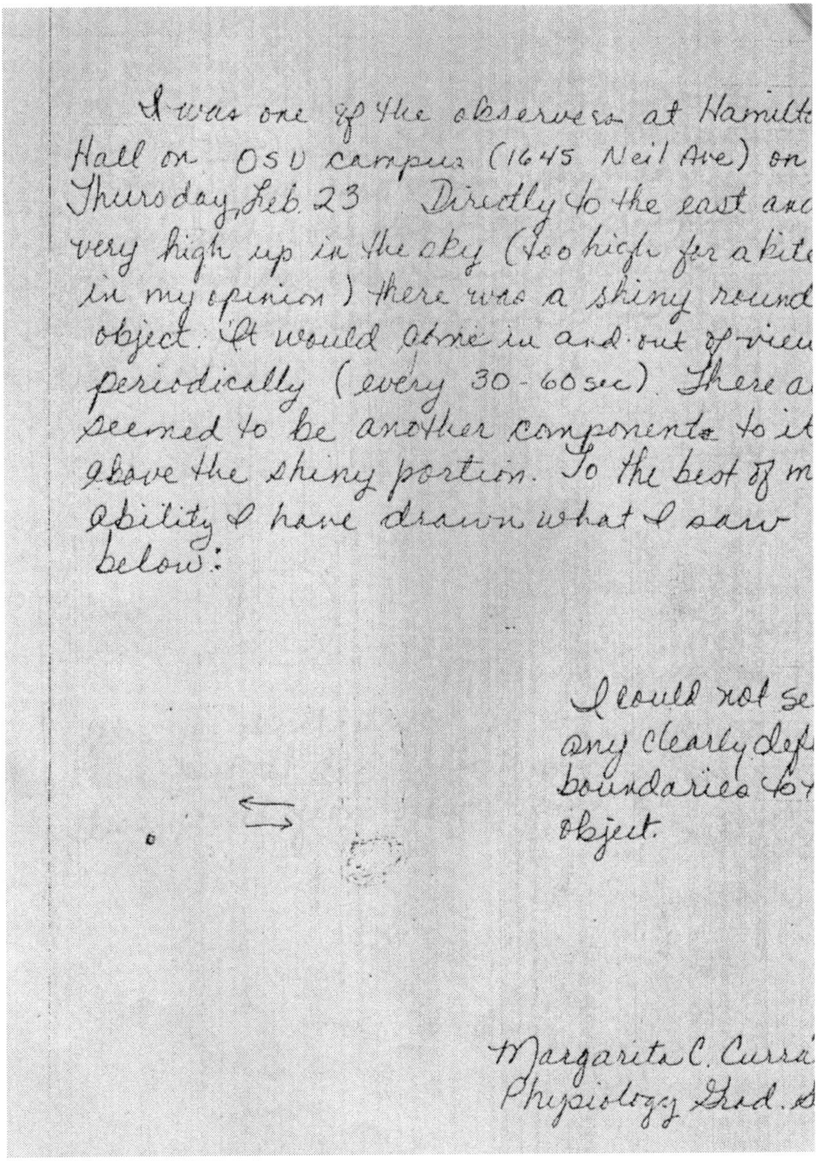

I was one of the observers at Hamilt[on]
Hall on OSU campus (1645 Neil Ave) on
Thursday, Feb. 23. Directly to the east and
very high up in the sky (too high for a kite
in my opinion) there was a shiny round
object. It would come in and out of view
periodically (every 30-60 sec). There a[lso]
seemed to be another components to it
above the shiny portion. To the best of m[y]
ability I have drawn what I saw
below:

I could not se[e]
any clearly def[ined]
boundaries to [the]
object.

Margarita C. Curr[á]
Physiology Grad. S[tudent]

Figure 3: This is MC's the first drawing. She was the second person to see it and also at first looked at it from more of an angle. Her first drawing was of a shiny round object, which rotated regularly about 30 to 60 seconds. She said that she also had seen the rectangular configuration and mentioned that it was traveling east.

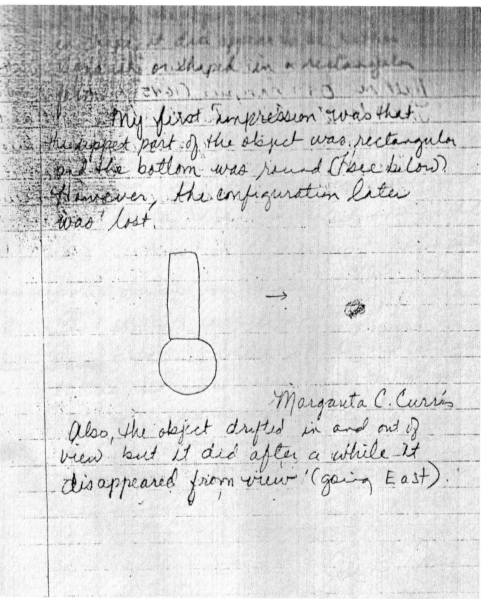

... or shaped in a rectangular ...

My first impression was that the upper part of the object was rectangular and the bottom was round (see below). However, the configuration later was lost.

Margarita C. Currie

Also, the object drifted in and out of view but it did after a while it disappeared from view (going East).

Figure 4: This is a second drawing by MC.

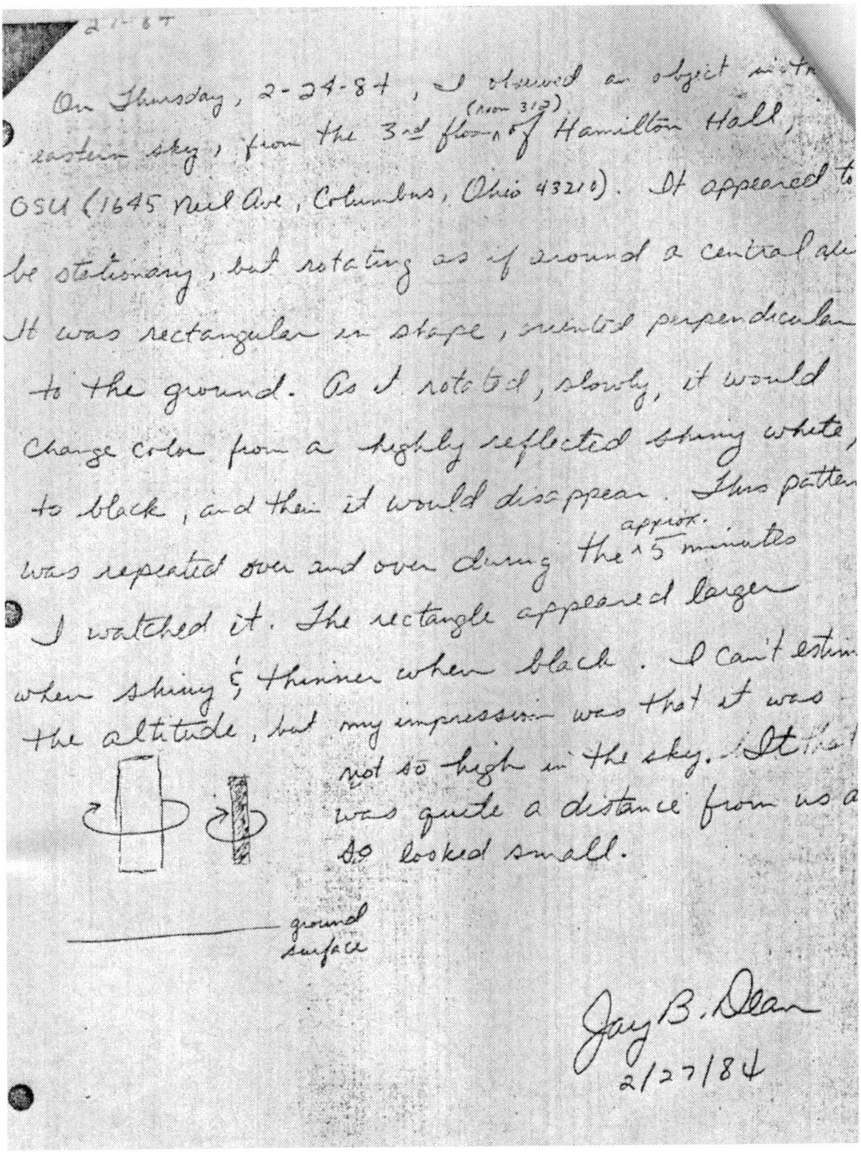

2-1-84

On Thursday, 2-24-84, I observed an object in the eastern sky, from the 3rd floor (room 319) of Hamilton Hall, OSU (1645 Neil Ave, Columbus, Ohio 43210). It appeared to be stationary, but rotating as if around a central axis. It was rectangular in shape, oriented perpendicular to the ground. As it rotated, slowly, it would change color from a highly reflected shiny white, to black, and then it would disappear. This pattern was repeated over and over during the approx. 5 minutes I watched it. The rectangle appeared larger when shiny & thinner when black. I can't estimate the altitude, but my impression was that it was not so high in the sky. It that was quite a distance from us so looked small.

ground surface

Jay B. Dean
2/27/84

Figure 5: This was the description and drawing of JD, who watched it from the department office. He also mentioned that it was rectangular and rotating around its long axis.

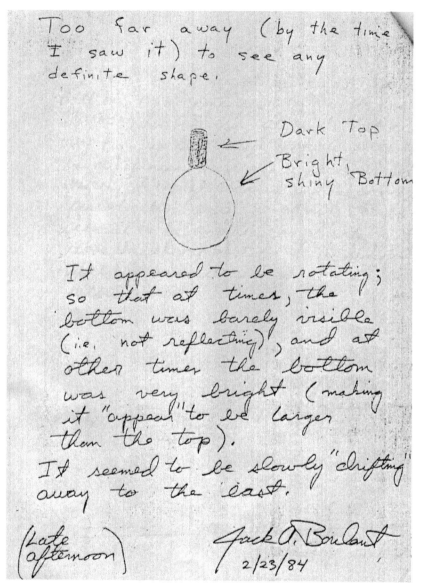

Too far away (by the time I saw it) to see any definite shape.

Dark Top

Bright, shiny Bottom

It appeared to be rotating; so that at times, the bottom was barely visible (i.e, not reflecting), and at other times the bottom was very bright (making it "appear" to be larger than the top).

It seemed to be slowly "drifting" away to the east.

(Late afternoon)

Jack A. Boulant

2/23/84

Figure 6: This is the description of JB. He described it as a rectangular object with something very bright on the bottom and also mentioned the object's rotation. He also said that it traveled to the east.

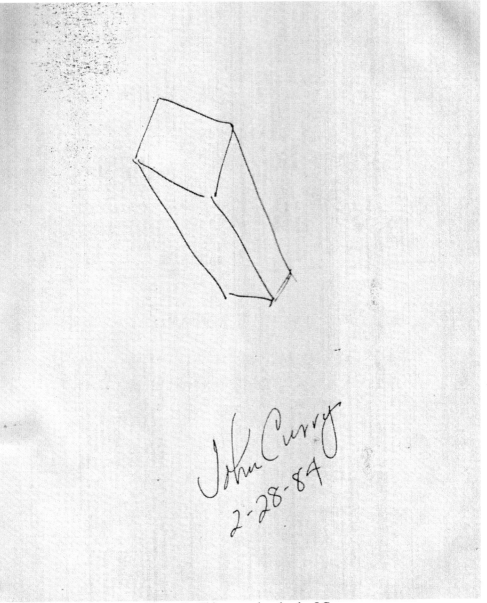

Figure 7: This was a drawing by J.C.

Figure 8: This is a drawing by J.D, which shows the window, in Hamilton Hall room 312, from which we watched the object and the object's relative size and shape in comparison to the buildings. It had an extended apparent diameter. Its position above the OSU buildings shows that it was in the airport landing slope area and should have shown up on their radar. MC made similar drawing also showing the view from the window, and object's relative size, shape, extended apparent diameter and its position above the OSU buildings (not shown).

Figure 9: This shows a comparison image of a balloon near the OSU campus. The object we saw looked nothing like a balloon and, unlike a balloon, ours was also flying against the wind and rotating regularly.

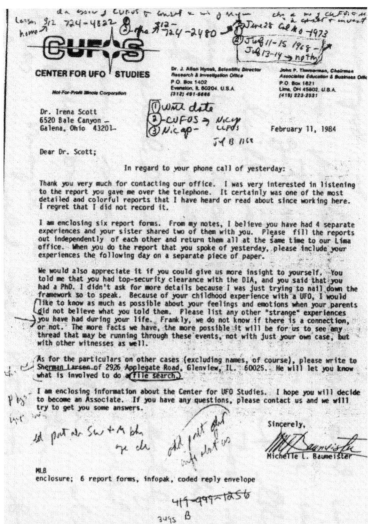

Figure 10: In late 1983, I developed a sudden fear of UFOs for no reason at all and in February 1984, contacted the CUFOS office. I received the following letter and they sent the forms about a week later. Then a really strange occurrence happened because when I began to fill out the form, I had a sighting. This gave me the creepy feeling that maybe something was watching me, maybe something had a sense of humor, or maybe something was trying to make me look crazy (and I remembered the man in the Massachusetts sighting pointing to his head).

Figure 11: I wrote this sighting up in FATE magazine looking for additional reports at that time, but received no comments. The only other odd thing in that time frame was the controversial Columbus Poltergeist activity, which made national headlines for several weeks. An article in the Columbus Dispatch told of another person who saw a UFO at that time and wondered if it had anything to do with the poltergeist. I was unable to contact her.

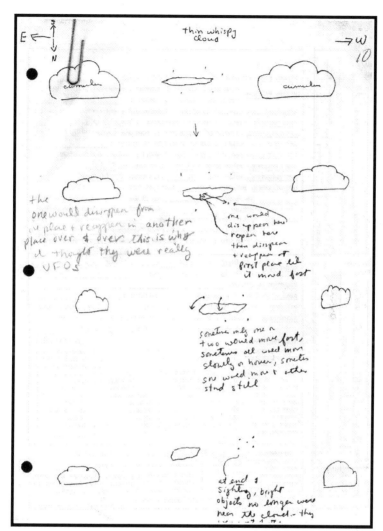

Figure 12: This shows my CUFOS report and drawing of a daytime sighting I made north of Hamilton Hall on August 24, 1984. I saw 5 objects looking like Jupiter or Venus, when they are visible around sunset, moving as a group. At first I thought they were balloons, but they did not behave like balloons. Later I photographed clusters of balloons for comparison (Figure 30) and these looked nothing like the objects that I saw. These objects were separated by some distance, did not show any evidence that they were connected and made maneuvers that a cluster of balloons could not do, such as appearing and disappearing, or moving too rapidly to see.

Figure 13: To further examine the idea that these objects might have been balloons, I observed and photographed clusters of balloons under many different conditions–loose balloons floating in the wind, loose balloons with one shinny side floating in the wind, clusters of balloons floating in the wind, tethered balloons, unusual shapes and sizes of balloons and also took a balloon ride. These objects looked nothing like a cluster of balloons. The balloons in clusters are close together and you can see both sides of the ones that are shinny on one side. Balloons do not appear and disappear, or do this synchronistically with other balloons. The objects that I saw did not look or behave like balloons.

******

CHAPTER SIX: MANY SIGHTINGS, MYSTERY BURN AND DANCING LIGHTS

A mystery burn mark and many additional sightings

During the summer of 1984, I discovered that a number of my neighbors also had sightings around the time that I had mine at OSU. There were so many that several people jokingly commented that everyone had been seeing UFOs.

In addition, a newspaper article also was published about the sightings, "Flying object seen in Galena."[98] This sighting was made on May 18 at 9:30 pm, by a retired army colonel and a nurse. He described it as, "something 'flying at tree-top level in a westerly direction...12 feet long, black and ignited rockets from the rear lit up the whole sky, burnt out and disappeared in a westerly direction."

The colonel made a report to sheriff's office and I have a copy. This was close to the time and place a mark appeared in a farmer's field. The object was traveling in the direction where the burn was found in a nearby alfalfa field around that time. Although an intensive scientific analysis was made, the cause is unexplained.

William Jones, J.D. and I made a survey of sightings of people in my neighborhood (published in the *OJS*, 1987, as mentioned).

My sister and I discussed it with Budd Hopkins and he was interested because it resembled the one featured in the beginning of his book, *Intruders*.[99] [100]

I later published an investigation about it in several *MUFON JR.* (9, 1991 and 5 and 8 /86) issues.

As in most other such reports, there were no witnesses. However, there were UFO observations within a mile and within a month of the approximate time of the trace's appearance. The trace was located in an area that was not visible from any habitation.

I turned in to CUFOS the reports from the many people who thought they had seen UFOs at that time. I have a letter to John Timmerman that described these activities. Budd Hopkins in his book *Intruders*, described the unusual mark he wrote about and said that although it was found after the abduction, that it was associated with it. Below is my *MUFON Jr.* Write-up:

Tracking Traces–Burn in field

Irena Scott State Section Director Scott is a MUFON consultant in Physiology.

Crop circles and other traces have been of intense recent interest in UFOlogy. Many of these crop circles are in England and are composed of bent over grain. Other traces are similar to the one in Budd Hopkins' *Intruders*: "The main area was a circle, eight feet in diameter, in which all the grass had turned brown and was now crumbling away. Extending out from this circle was a 49-foot-long swath that ran perfectly straight and was nearly three feet in width. Here, too, the grass was dead and disintegrating. This long track ended in a nearly perfect arc and seemed absolutely artificial. Two smaller 'jogs' appeared to emerge from the main circle and one of these contained a deep crack which looked, superficially, as if it had been caused by intense heat." These traces are rarely seen being made; however there are often reports of UFOs in the area.

I investigated a trace similar to, but larger than, the one Budd Hopkins described. I first found out about it in August of 1984, while conducting the survey described in Ohio Jr. Sci. 87 (1) 224-26, 1987 and described it briefly in the *MUFON UFO Journal* (May 1986). Budd Hopkins subsequently expressed an interest in it to my sister. Because of the current high interest in such "circles," more detailed information might be helpful in comparisons and studies of this kind of particular physical trace. As in many other such reports, there were no intermediate eyewitnesses; however, there were some related UFO observations (including an extreme close encounter in which the UFO "was followed by a jet-like rocket propellant, which was a bright white rocket exhaust," and which left, or came down, in the approximate direction of the burn) within a month of the approximate time of the trace's appearance and within a mile of its location. The trace was located in an area that was not visible from any habitation.

Discovery

A farmer discovered the trace in June 1984, in a field of knee high green alfalfa. He believed that it had not been made much before then. This field had been in alfalfa for several years and had shown no previous damage in this or any other area. The field was not plowed or replanted for four more years and the trace remained devoid of alfalfa. The burn was invisible to anyone except people standing in the field–there were farm fields and trees all around the area, so no one on roads or by houses could see it (Figure 1 shows the trace in September. It was quite evident after several cuttings of hay).

Its initial appearance was that of green alfalfa which was blackened and charred into its roots. The plants were standing, but charred. Nothing in the area had been bent down. The area of the burn was very localized; plants next to the burned area were undamaged. I obtained this description from the farmer and his two workers, who also saw the burn before the hay was cut (Figure 2 shows their descriptions and drawings). All of them said that nothing had been applied (e.g. no fertilizer or pesticides) to any area of the alfalfa. There had been wet weather during this time and water was standing in the fields.

There was a large high-tension power line, about ¼ mile south of the burn, which was near a freeway. Several times these power lines had broken and come down, creating a highly dangerous situation because of the freeway. The farmer was worried that people might have trespassed on his property and shot the power lines down. Because of this, he kept the only lane to the field blocked by a steel gate and cable locked to a post. He kept the only key himself. No one could have taken machinery on this property without his knowledge. The farmer was mistimed about the cause of the burn. He said that he had never seen anything like it in 70 years of farming. He had reported it to the fire department. When asked about UFOs, he and his wife were strong skeptics, they did not think that they existed and did not link the burn to UFOs. I know the farmer well. Neither he nor his wife wanted attention; in fact, they did not tell me about the burn, another neighbor did.

When I first saw the area in August 1984, several cuttings of hay had been made. However, no alfalfa grew in the area of the trace. It was a swath about 130 feet long and around six feet wide. Like the trace described in *Intruders*, it consisted of a central circular area (the farmer referred to this as a "blast area"). But it was larger with more burned area than the one in the *Intruders*. There was a secondary smaller circular area beside it. The largest was around 6-8 feet in diameter. Extending from it to the south was a swath, which ran straight for around 20-25 feet. It had a clear-cut strip of vegetation down the center. Extending in the other direction from the circular area was a distinct swath that curved over the hillside and slowly became less distinct. As in the *Intruders* trace, the central area contained deep cracks (Figure 3).

I discussed the burn with the farmer, his wife and his two farm workers (Bill Rammelsberg, Richard McCammon and Brad Barker), the fire chief (Virgil Newell), a senior industrial chemist

(Art Sill) and government employees in the Department of Agriculture, such as James Diuguid. The farmer and his wife could not think of a way for the burn to have been made. They did not believe lightning would make this pattern. If a hot air balloon had landed, turned over and blasted its burners sidewise, it would have mashed the hay. Also, it is doubtful if the gas would blast for 130 feet (over the side of a hill) or leave two discrete traces. If an airplane had dumped gasoline, it would need to have flown higher than the power line and would most likely not be able to make such a discrete mark either, because the gas would disperse in the air. There is no evidence that helicopters burn the ground. Both the farmer and the fire chief said that green alfalfa does not easily burn. The fire chief said that in order to burn green alfalfa it has to have had the water vaporized first since it is chiefly composed of water (the fire chief had also had a sighting). It would be almost impossible to set a fire in the area and burn this vegetation without the use of special equipment.

The area was on the other side of a very long, steep hill from the freeway. It would have been a very poor site for someone to have carried something from the freeway and dumped it: (1.) There was a lot of tall vegetation, such as barbed, blackberry plants; (2.) It was up a tall hill, with a tall fence with barbed wire on top of it on the hill top; (3.) Then the person would need to have carried the substance out into the field; (4.) It would have taken quite a bit of substance to kill that much vegetation; (5.) The person would be visible climbing the freeway hill and would need several trips; (6.) and there were no tracks, either coming from the freeway, or in the field; (7.) It would be a poor place to hoax a trace, because there were few people in the area and the only place it was visible from was the field itself; (8.) There were many other places where something could have been dumped downhill from the freeway that would have made a much better site.

When I discussed the burn with the farmer, he said that hauling a liquid or other chemical component would have required a considerable amount, necessitating several trips up and down the hill, all within full view of the freeway.

I was reminded of certain other effects associated with the trace case mentioned in *Intruders*: "The hedge in the immediate area of the bird feeder also began to wither and (they) had to cut the plants back almost to the roots to force new growth. In the spring, the Davis family had planted a few tomato plants in the general vicinity of what became the burned circle. The fruit these plants eventually produced were abnormally large and so mealy as to be inedible." They believed microwaves or some other form of radiation had possibly affected the area.

In order to investigate further, I took a sample of the soil and of nearby soil from an undamaged area. Seeds grew in both samples. Thus, there was nothing in the soil that interfered with plant growth.

Later on in the field, however, as a few dandelions began to grow around the edges of the area (possibly from seeds that had already been in the soil) and an unusual number looked somewhat deformed. A more than normal number of dandelion stems seemed to grow together so that there would be large-diameter dandelion stems with numerous flower heads. Many of these crept along the ground instead of growing up. So, while there did not seem to be anything in the soil that damaged new seeds, some of these already in the ground seemed somewhat abnormal. I noticed this only with dandelions. Not much else grew there. The alfalfa did not grow back, but it might have needed to be replanted.

Several years later, I noticed that portions of the soil, the clay-like parts and some of the rocks in the area were red. This red color was not visible in other areas.

Analysis

For further analysis, I sent a sample (taken in August) of the soil to a PhD senior organic chemist, Dr. Art Sill. He analyzed it using mass spectrometry. For separation, he used a fused silica capillary column. He injected vapor from the heated soil sample into it, heated the column from 50 to 300 C. at 15 c/min. to drive off the separate compounds and then collected them. For analysis of the separated peaks, he used electron impact and chemical ionization spectrometry. Since we wondered about gasoline, he also analyzed for gasoline residue. He found no trace of gasoline in the area (Figures 4 and 5).

I took the chromatograms to several agricultural experts. They said there was no trace of any products or degradation products of pesticides or herbicides (Figure 6). Most of what they found were common organic chemicals from farm plants and weeds. They thought two of the chromatograms might have been from DMSO (dimethyl sulfoxide). This might be a somewhat strange find. DMSO is used as an industrial solvent and produced by the oxidation of dimethyl sulfide (Me2S). At present, there are only very few reports of MezSO being found in nature. It is under increased use in the manufacturing processes to produce microelectronic devices. In medicine because it can penetrate the skin and other membranes without damaging them, it is used carry other compounds into a biological system. It protects against freezing and is an important constituent of cryoprotectant vitrification mixtures that are used to preserve organs, tissues and cell suspensions. And it is important in the freezing and long-term storage of embryonic stem cells

Therefore, there is no indication that the burn was made by any commonly used or known chemicals.

I used a Geiger counter (August 1984) to look for radioactivity in some samples, but if there was any it was close to background and not enough to detect that way. I was not able to use a gamma or scintillation counter at that time, but still have the samples. Although the seeds that I planted grew in the burn area and in the control soil, several weeds grew in the control soil only, again suggesting that seeds in the burn area might have been damaged. Later after a rain, algae grew in the control sample soil, but not in the burn area sample. Thus, there may have been a difference in the microfauna in the soil–the algae for example might have been destroyed by heat.

There may have been a physical difference in the soil because when I watered them, seeds in the control sample only sometimes floated to the top and needed replanting.

One thing I was curious about was lightning. I have seen lightning hit an open field, but have not noticed that it leaves a trace, except when it starts a fire. Once lightning hit my neighbor's transformer. Several neighbors, my husband and I saw the fireball. Others saw it short down the ground wire. This ground wire had poison ivy climbing it. This poison ivy remained alive and healthy. Thus, it is unlikely that lightning or an electrical field would have produced the effects mentioned above.

Budd Hopkins suggested microwaves as a possible cause for such burns. Others have suggested an electromagnetic force or some still undiscovered energy, such as a plasma vortex, might be related to the formation of crop circles (*MUFON UFO Journal*, 8/1991).

I placed alfalfa, some of which was green but growing in dry ground and some of which looked somewhat dry and desiccated, in a microwave oven. It did not produce a charred appearance in either after several minutes of microwaving on high. The somewhat desiccated alfalfa looked pretty much the same after seven minutes (stopping a few times to check it) of microwaving. Neither looked charred several days later, but they both looked desiccated. The stems remained stiff and did not bend or fall over. I also tried to burn green alfalfa and it definitely did not burn.

Thus, it appears that it would take quite a bit of energy to produce this appearance in that type of vegetation. It also appears that this trace was made from above, because of the lack of any other pressed down vegetation anywhere in the area. There was no evidence that the trace was made with chemicals. Therefore, although crop circles may be the best known and most common kind of trace, this type of trace is difficult to explain also, or reproduce and needs further study.

The chemist had very good credentials. He had a PhD and was first employed by Battelle. After that he was a senior chemist at what became Merrell Dow Pharmaceuticals, Inc. He also taught chemistry at the University of Cincinnati.

Several years after the burn was made, the ground was plowed. When I looked in this area again, some of the soil and some of the rocks (plowing mixes the soil) were reddish. I read once that extreme heat can turn some rocks red. Possibly the burn was what it looked like: something had heated the vegetation enough to kill it, but also was hot enough to affect the rocks and soil. The farmer had reported that the roots of the plants had been charred. Thus, the effect had gone down into the ground.

This trace was thoroughly studied. The mass spectrometry would have shown if it had been made by such means as gasoline, pesticide, too much fertilizer, or other chemicals. There were no traces of these substances. This confirms what the farmer and his employees said, that nothing had been applied to the ground. The evidence suggests that the area was subjected to heat, or some type of radiation that was accompanied by heat. The fact that the new plants that grew from seed were deformed again provides suggestive evidence that the area was damaged by heat or by some kind of radiation. Some kinds of radiation are external and would not cause radioactivity e.g., gamma rays are radioactive. They come from an external source and do not normally leave radiation. Radiation normally is left when the radioactive substance is left. Also, microwaves or other kinds of radiation that produces heat may have heated the area. Different forms of radiation, or even heat itself, might damage the development of embryo plants in the seeds.

The burned streak was accompanied in Budd Hopkins' *Intruders* by a power failure in near-by homes. In this case, the area was not near any houses. It would not be possible to determine if similar electrical changes occurred.

So far I have found no explanation for it. My family has lived on this farm since about 1803 and no one has ever reported anything like that.

Below for comparison is the description of the burn and witness report of the events associated with it as discussed in *Intruders*.[101] Although there were no witnesses when our mark was being made, it resembled this mark,

On June 30th, 1983, as Deb stood at the kitchen sink and looked out the window, she noticed an odd light coming out of the swimming pool pump house. She knew the door should be closed because she had just closed it. The light was not like light from the incandescent bulb inside. It appeared more like florescent, white light that was very bright. As she was leaving, she checked the light again and it was off but the door to the side garage was open. As soon as she arrived at a neighbor's house, she called her mother to check on her and she said she was okay. She hung up the phone and it instantly rang from her mother, who sounded strange, frightened and wanted her to come home. (Her mother did not remember why she called until a week later when she suddenly said that she had seen a basketball-sized ball of light near the bird feeder.)

Deb, with a shotgun, looked around and found her dog, firmly lodged under a truck. Something had really scared her–she was yelping, whining and tearing at Deb's hands. Later the dog became very ill and died–it seemed to have radiation exposure symptoms.

Then suddenly she felt as if she were on fire. She was hit in the chest by something that was very bright and electrifying. She said she had never been hit by lightning, but if she could imagine what it would feel like, she would say it was like this. This burning, electrical feeling slowly moved down her legs, out her arms to her fingertips and around her head. She could feel every molecule of her body vibrating and could not move. She could not see because the flash was so bright. She thought she might be dead and was shaking and burning like she was vibrating to her very core. The brightness wore off fast, but she was vibrating and could not move. Then she felt someone pulling on her right shoulder, as if to pull her down a bit. Then, she could hear someone telling her it was unfortunate that she had to feel pain.

She could see a soft, white ball of light directly in front of her–about the size of a basketball and hovering about as high as she was tall. The light slowly moved up and down, as if it were looking at her from head to foot. Then, it moved into an egg shaped thing and disappeared. The egg-shaped thing was maybe 8 to 10 feet tall. And then she saw six people in the yard in front of her at various spots in the yard. Then, they all seemed to line up and slide to the left, back to this egg-shaped thing in front of her. They were smaller than she was but large in the head.

With each step back to the house, the memory of what had just happened, faded until by the time Deb reached her mother at the back door, she did not remember anything after she had entered the garage. She said to her mother that everything's cool. With that, her mother became animated again, as if she was standing there, in a daze, until she heard Deb's voice.

Then she returned to the neighbors' house and found them upset because she had been gone about two hours but she remembered only about 15 minutes.

When she woke up the next morning, she could not open her eyes. Her mother took her to the emergency room. The doctor was stunned at the extent of her injuries.

No one noticed anything until the 4th of July weekend, when her nephew noticed the mark in the yard. This was an 8-foot circle with a 20-foot swath coming off it. It ended in a perfect arch and was exactly 2 feet wide. The grass in the mark was brownish gray and wilted and the dirt was gray and hard. There were deep cracks around the edge of the circle.

Then to Deb's astonishment, the first thing her mother said when she saw that mark was, Oh, that's where our UFO landed. She thought her mother was nuts and wondered what was wrong with her.

The mark in the yard remained for about five years. Every year the snow melted off it, animals would not walk on it and there were no bugs in the soil.

She also noticed the dandelions. Those that grew around the mark were three times the size of normal ones. The power line above the mark had shorted out, blown a transformer, melted the wiring and blew out the tubes on a HAM radio in the basement of the house, which was right next to the place in the yard.

Thus, this mark resembled ours in a number of ways. Theirs had the same general appearance including a burn or swath area with tracks coming from it. She said the vegetation in the swath area was wilted and our witnesses described it as standing but burned to a crisp into the roots. There were deep cracks in both marks. No plants grew back in the area of either mark for many years. And as in ours, the dandelions were noticeably different.

I had done a very thorough investigation of this mark and found nothing to account for it. Although there were no witnesses, it had a lot of similarity to the mark discussed in *Intruders* and there had been a number of UFO sightings in the area at that time. Most such marks, such as crop circles, do not have witnesses to their formation.

Others have reported similar marks, for example the *National Geographic* reported:
Possible physical evidence of encounters with alien spacecraft. The 1968 University of Colorado report, compiled by a team headed by James Condon, documented numerous instances of areas where soil, grass and other vegetation had been claimed by witnesses to have been flattened,

burned, broken off, or blown away by a UFO. A report by Stanford University astrophysicist Peter Sturrock, who led a scientific study of physical evidence of UFOs in the late 1990s, describes samples of plants taken from a purported UFO landing site in France in 1981. French researchers found that the leaves had undergone unusual chemical changes of the sort that could have been caused by powerful microwave radiation—which was even more difficult to explain, considering that they found no trace of radioactivity at the site.[102]

The well-known Lonnie Zamora sighting involved burnt vegetation and an egg-shaped object:

On Friday, April 24, 1964, at about 5:50 p.m., on the outskirts of Socorro, New Mexico. Several primary witnesses emerged to report their version of the event, which included the craft's approach, conspicuous flame and alleged physical evidence left behind immediately afterward. Lonnie Zamora, a Socorro police officer who was on duty at the time, claimed to have come closest to the object and provided the most prolonged and comprehensive account. Some physical trace evidence left behind—burned vegetation and soil, ground landing impressions and metal scrapings on a broken rock in one of the impressions—was subsequently observed and analyzed by investigators for the military, law enforcement and civilian UFO groups.

The event and its body of evidence are sometimes deemed one of the best-documented and most perplexing UFO reports. It was immediately investigated by the U.S. Army, U.S. Air Force and FBI and received considerable coverage in the mass media. It was one of the cases that helped persuade astronomer J. Allen Hynek, one of the primary investigators for the Air Force, that some UFO reports represented an intriguing mystery. After extensive investigation, the Air Force's Project Blue Book was unable to come up with a conventional explanation and listed the case as an "unknown".[103]

The *New Scientist* reported, "But many others involving multiple sightings – in at least one case involving thousands of people across France – and evidence such as burn marks and radar trackings showing flight patterns or accelerations that defy the laws of physics are taken very seriously."[104]

Thus, although such burn marks are less well-known than crop circles, they may be mysterious also and have no evidence of what caused them.

Bright red and white flashing objects and barbells and triangles

The following is a recent sighting. I did not formally report or publish this happening until a year later, but discussed it with several people and posted the information on the internet the day it happened to seek additional witnesses.

I did not want to report it because it was close to the time my book was to be published and I thought it might appear that I was hoaxing to get attention for my book if I said anything at that time.

The sighting began while I was taking nighttime photographs of several planets and that is why I had cameras set up already. The photographs were taken with an iPhone camera and a camcorder. The photographs of the planets showed up well.

I show both the photographs from the camera and the video recorder on YouTube in https://youtu.be/P1Cge5TpIyc and more details of the videotape recording in https://youtu.be/7FJ6RrPC5rM, but the recording was in HiDef which took quite a large number of megabits, but I was unable to get even near this much detail on YouTube.

I have recently reported it to the Black Vault site of John Greenewald, Jr. They investigated and classified the sighting as Case File Status: Unexplained and posted it on their site.[105] They also showed the photography, although the video on YouTube showed much less than did the actual HiDef video–which contained many more megabits of information.

It appears that I am still experiencing the pattern described by Randles, of people who have childhood sightings continuing this trend as adults. But despite many years, I still have no idea what any of this of means or why it takes place.

Several other people have looked at the objects that I photographed and also said they were unidentified.

The sighting, November 4, 2016, took place at approximately 7:22-7:26 pm EST to the south of my house. It began while I was standing in my back yard photographing astronomical objects. Thus, it was not some mistaken astronomical object as is often used to explain UFOs, because when it happened I was photographing Venus, Mars, Saturn and the Moon and I labeled them on some of the photographs. I am an amateur astronomer, have worked professionally in photography and because it was a very clear night for good photography and several planets were visible at once, I had two cameras with me. The cameras were an iPhone 6s and a HiDef

Camcorder that also records sound. I have made much wildlife, astronomical and aircraft photography from this location and am very familiar with it. Everything I saw was against the sky, nothing was against background trees or anything.

The location is a family farm where I was born, lived for many years, go out nearly every night after dark to check things, have taken many photos and videos at this location and have never seen anything like this. (This house was next door to the one where I had experienced the childhood sightings.)

It started when I was looking southwest at Venus and then saw two bright red glowing objects approaching from the west. They flew smoothly, were completely vertical in orientation to each other, were soundless and there was no evidence of an airplane or aircraft lights (Figure 7). There were no strobe lights, green lights, sounds, or anything vaguely like an airplane. The objects' lights did not blink or change in intensity or brightness. The movements were in complete synchrony and the objects looked exactly alike. From this first second of the sighting, I was mystified.

The objects approached Venus and because they stayed together so smoothly and completely, I thought they had to be connected. I watched for what would happen when they passed Venus. They were in a position of one precisely above the other in a straight vertical line. When they went by Venus, it appeared that the top one was about a full Moon's apparent diameter above Venus and the lower one about the same distance below Venus–the angular distance between the two was about a degree or more with Venus in the middle. They moved so synchronously that I expected them to be connected. Although I could not see any connection, I thought they might be connected to each other by something thin in a barbell-like fashion.

But when they passed by Venus, I saw no dimming, so I did not know whether they could have been two objects moving in exact synchrony or whether they were like barbells and connected by a thin strand (that wouldn't show up much when they flew past Venus). They did not even slightly sway in the wind and just moved smoothly and steadily together. They looked nothing like Chinese lanterns or any type of balloon.

They flew in a controlled fashion–they stayed in a vertical position. I do not know how they flew. I did not hear engine noises but they must have had some kind of power because they were red and glowing. I was amazed because they looked like something that could not happen-like one would see in a cartoon or a computer simulation. Also because they took up such a large degree of arc, probably a degree or more, I thought they might have been close or of a huge object and expected a sound, but there was none. I do not know their altitude, but they showed against the sky, not the background.

I had been taking photos of the planets with my iPhone in hand when I saw them. But I was so completely dumbfounded in amazement at first that I did not do anything except stand there frozen. When my brain finally re-activated, I realized I needed to take photos so I took pictures–snapped three photos in very rapid succession at 7:22 EST each 5 seconds after the previous one. This was after the red objects had already passed. I did not see anything unusual when I took these photos. I did not use a flash.

Then I noticed a huge area of the sky light up with all kinds of blinking, gyrating, dancing, flashing objects. The objects blinked in random patterns–nothing like an airplane. This display took up a large area of the sky–maybe 20-30 degrees in width and height. It spread from the tree to my southeast to west of Venus, which was to my west.

Because the objects in this display were flashing and seemed to be moving around, I ran for the video camera to try to capture this motion. It took some time to run to the camcorder, set it up, get it turned on in the dark and wait for it to come on. It was mounted on a tripod. By the time I had the camcorder going, most of the objects had flown behind a tree and a building to the east so I could not see them. I thought the tail end of the objects was still there. I pointed the camcorder and tried to videotape the dancing objects. When I had seen them with my eyes they appeared to flash, move around–sometimes synchronously, blink, etc. All this was soundless. There seemed to have been a number of red and other objects that constantly changed configuration. These were definitely not like any standard aircraft lights. I took a 26-second video (although that doesn't seem like much, you can do a lot with it using a computer).

The size of this display of the group of objects was many, many times too large to be the lighting on an aircraft. A very low aircraft (such as ones coming in for a landing at John Glenn Columbus International Airport, about 20 miles away) might be about the apparent angular size of the Moon or smaller. The size of the Moon when compared to size of the display of the group of objects in the video images was very much smaller. Another estimation of the apparent size scale can be found at the end of the video. It shows the length of a car on the road in a wide view. The car is approximately 0.13 mile away, but the length of the car is many times shorter than the display of the group of objects. If the group of objects had been the lighting on an airplane, the airplane would have been either tremendously large or so close it would be almost crashing into the camera.

There was nothing there that would cause a group of objects to appear. This is a large family farm area surrounded by agricultural fields with no one around. The neighbors are my relatives and I know what they are doing. I am very used to seeing airplanes, blimps, blimps with lighted sides and all kinds of aircraft here and photographing them in the dark.

These objects seemed nothing like airplane lights or other commonly photographed objects. The sighting was nothing like viewing a drone–I have a drone, fly it, photograph with it and repair it, so I am familiar with drones. The objects were nothing like lasers or flashlights, because these need something to reflect against to be seen (such as cats chasing a laser on a wall). Of course these could have been holograms or volumetric displays produced by laser. What I saw were bodies against the sky. It was nothing like fireworks. I have recorded fireworks from this general position using this camera and they look nothing like this. This was nothing like Chinese lanterns–several Chinese lanterns have landed in the field I filmed in and I have them. They weren't birds, because some glowed red, they blinked on and off, there was no wing motion and birds do not light up at night. I saw no green lights at all any time during the sighting and it is standard for aircraft to have green lights. I read that all aircraft built after March 1996 must have an anti-collision light system (strobe lights) turned on for all flight activities in poor visibility. There was no continuous track of strobe lights as seen with aircraft–just white flashes at random all over the sky. In addition, aircraft show a patterned sequence of flashing their lights and there was no form of pattern with these objects' blinking.

The white flashing objects were nothing like stars. When one looks at the sky, one can see stars and they often twinkle. But they do not completely disappear and new stars do not appear in different places as they did in the video. The stars and planets have stable locations. Thus, the phenomenon wasn't photographs of stars or twinkling. Both cameras can photograph stars at night. Also I have seen meteor showers and northern lights and this sighting resembled neither. I have also seen flares such as airplanes sometimes send out–I may even have one that I collected here years ago. These last longer than a split second and they travel downward, not in all directions.

The camcorder records sound very well, but there was no sound except for when I rustled the grass, fiddled with the camera and from the road traffic.

I'm not sure about the colors–whether they were just red and white or whether there were more colors.

The objects I watched by eye seemed to dart, dance and gyrate and because of that and the flashing, I had gone to the video camera to photograph the motion. In the video, the white objects seemed to just give very quick flashes and it appeared that all I captured of these was just the flashes. Occasionally, there appeared to be double white lights.

After I recorded the views, I brought the IPhone and camcorder into the house and e-mailed the camera photos to my computer and downloaded the camcorder video tape recording into the computer. I still have the original e-mails and camcorder tape. There was a game going on at the school several miles to the west and so I contacted someone there to see if anything had been released. The answer was no and I did not think so to begin with but checked anyway. Later I called the airport to see if anything unusual had been flying here or if anyone had seen anything. They said no and suggested calling the Bigelow organization that collects UFO information. I think I called them twice and left a message. They returned the call several days later, but I did not get back to them. I immediately on November 4 posted the video on both YouTube and Facebook and also did the next day in order to find out if anyone else had seen or knew anything, but I did not find out anything. The original November 4 YouTube videos and other posts are still on.

I also checked the weather   ;
(https://www.wunderground.com/history/airport/KCMH/2016/11/04/DailyHistory.html?req_city
=Port%20Columbus%20International&req_state=OH&reqdb.zip=43230&reqdb.magic=6&reqdb
.wmo=99999), which said: "Wind

Wind Speed 4 mph (North)

Max Wind Speed 14 mph

Max Gust Speed 17 mph

Visibility 8 miles and from the North at 7: 51"

The wind was blowing from north to south. The objects traveled from west to east. If the wind were coming from the north, the group of objects would have been blown to the south and stayed in view if they had continued to be lit. Instead, the group flew behind the tree and building to the east and quickly disappeared. Thus, because they were not flying in the direction the wind would have blown them, they may have been operating under some form of power.

Because this was my backyard, I have taken many other videos in the same area, with the same lighting conditions, in wide and narrow view, with a tripod, including videos of different aircraft and have not seen anything like this. For example, airplanes photograph as discrete continuous objects following a path; they do not look like randomly scattered blinking lights. These other videos do not show the white and red objects as seen in this one and could be used as control videos to compare normal videos to this one.

Immediately after I made the photography, I wondered if I had photographed anything, because this was difficult photography. It was dark, which made it difficult to use the iPhone and even to turn on the camcorder, let alone focus it. But when I uploaded everything to the computer, I was amazed that everything had worked–the cameras had come on instantly and in focus.

I had taken three photos by iPhone immediately after the red objects had passed on 2016.11.04 at 19:22:27, 19:22:32 and 19:22:37. These three turned out well and although I thought I had photographed nothing because I did the photography after the 2 red objects had passed and I did not see anything when I took the photographs, the camera appeared to photograph some sort of splotches passing in front of the camera.

The videotape also turned out much better than I expected. I might have seen a few flashes when I made the video, but the actual video showed much more. When I clicked through it, one click at a time on full screen in the dark it showed many flashes and also a pair of red objects. I had set the camcorder to daytime photography to try to get the colors of the planets and this allowed me to photograph the objects in color and it did photograph red and white flashes.

When I uploaded the three photographs into the computer, I noticed bright spots in them that photographed the same way objects would (Figure 8). They were generally to the east of Venus. Although the photographs were taken only 5 seconds apart the spots were not in the same place; thus, it appeared that they were moving (as the two red objects had done).

In order to check whether the spots were in the same place, I made computer transparencies and overlaid them. This showed that the spots were not in the same place in the photographs. Therefore, they had been moving and this would make their outlines in the photographs less clear.

In order to find out if the spots were part of some natural background, I looked at the photos that were taken right before I saw the two red objects. There were several of these photographs and no such spots were visible on any of them. The spots did not appear to be part of the natural background. They also wouldn't be some form of camera artifact.

With this camera, I can easily photograph such objects as Mars and Saturn and have even photographed dimmer objects such as Neptune and asteroids, so I'm familiar with the camera's performance. The stars and planets, of course, stand still whereas these objects were moving and thus more difficult to photograph, with less distinct outlines. I saw no airplanes at the time I took the photographs and I would have noticed them because I was looking at Venus. Moreover, it would be unusual to see three airplanes together at once and I would definitely have noticed. The only things I had seen near Venus were the two red objects and that was a few seconds before I took the photographs. Also, I doubt if my camera would have taken photographs of birds or insects, because it was dark. The objects showed up as bright spots that looked like lit objects such as Mars. The trees photographed as dark bodies that were barely distinguishable from the background. In addition, the trees were much larger than birds and do not move around.

Although the only objects I saw were the two red ones, it appeared that I had photographed several other things. Because I had seen the red objects with my eyes, I thought the spots might have also been objects traveling with the red ones. I think they weren't the red objects because these had been exactly vertical and the spots I photographed were in more of a horizontal configuration.

Thus, it appeared that more unlit objects might have passed after I saw the two red ones. I did not see these when I took the photographs, so they might have been unlit but traveling with the red object/objects.

These spots were a bright whitish color and this is how the illuminated objects, such as Mars, had photographed. I think if I had photographed birds they would have appeared dark. Therefore, I thought that the objects might have been emitting some form of radiation that could photograph, but not be visible to the human eye.

Although it was suggested that I may have photographed insects or dust, I did not have my flash turned on and there was no background light. Thus the splotches were not something in the air reflecting light; they were lit objects.

I quit photographing with the iPhone, because the entire south part of the sky suddenly lit up with all kinds of flashing lights and I had run to the video camera. This also made me wonder if the bright spots were objects, because the flashing lights would have come from objects, but the only objects I had seen before this were the two red ones. Also, all I saw of the flashing lights were the flashes; I assumed the flashes were from objects that weren't visible in the dark. Thus, perhaps the spots I saw in the iPhone photographs were among the objects that flashed later but were not emitting radiation in the visible range or flashing when they passed Venus.

This photography suggests that some objects might have been traveling with the red ones, but I may not have seen them because they were not lit in a light frequency visible to the human eye. Immediately after this, however, the entire sky lit up with flashing, blinking objects. Thus, the objects in what was likely a group of objects may have changed their frequency (during the flashing) to one visible to humans.

Perhaps this could be a reason why it is sometimes reported that UFOs will suddenly blink out or disappear.

I was able to upload the video recording, which had photographed the tail end the group of dancing objects before they disappeared behind the tree. I was also able to click through this video one click at a time in full screen in the dark and also to modify the lighting on this video to study it further.

The video definitely showed some of the object's flashing as distinct, obvious, bright objects with discrete boundaries. It also sometimes showed dimmer flashes, or bright flashes turning into dimmer ones.

The video showed the blinking and colors of the lit objects. These were red and white blinking objects, but no other colors were evident (but there may have other colors that just did not photograph). These objects appeared real because they showed up against the sky, not against any background. The first two red objects that I had seen with my eyes shined a very bright red– sort of a blood-red color. Two red objects that seemed to be together also showed up on the video, but these were not as red. However, a camcorder photographing in the dark might show a different color than the eye would see, even if it photographed the same thing.

The white objects would blink on and off at random times in random places over a wide area of the sky (Figure 9). The photography was taken over the fields of a large farm. The neighbors were relatives and no one was doing anything odd that would cause objects to appear at that time.

I had initially seen two red objects traveling to the east. Although I did not see this with my eyes when I took the video, it also captured two red objects that flew together and stayed on for a while–the video captured them three times. I do not know if these red objects were the same ones I saw with my eyes at the beginning when they passed Venus. There were several rapid changes in configuration of the red objects and I do not know whether this was caused by a red object darting from one place to another, or if there had been a larger object that turned on different red lights. I had seen no obvious connections between the two red objects in my original observation by eyesight but do not know if these were what I was seeing in the video. Sometimes a third and maybe more red lights would be with the two that stayed together. Many of the flashes were very distinct and clear, whereas some were blurred. I do not know if the blurring could have been caused by motion. I had very little time to film the trailing edge of the group, before they flew behind the tree (but it was still possible to slow down the recording on the computer and find a lot of detail).

I saw the three together on the tape only three times, although there was enough time to see them blink on for a fourth or fifth time. Near the end of the third sighting, the objects appeared somewhat blurred with what looked like trails to the right. It is possible that they rapidly flew away after the third time they were together.

The video showed red objects and it sometimes showed two that would stay lit for a while and traveled together. I do not know whether the two red objects that seemed to fly together in the video were also the first two I saw with my eyes (the possibly barbell-like ones that passed Venus). These were not vertical as the ones I saw by eye were, but were tilted and more horizontally oriented. These two red objects together showed three separate times on the video. Sometimes these two objects would be different distances from each other and in different orientations. The two red objects that sometimes appeared together did not look like blinking airplane lights, because an airplane would travel away in a straight direction and generally have more than just red lights. If these were on an airplane, it was doing unusual gyrations.

I saw no strobe lights with the group of red lights that stayed together, such as airplanes have and there was plenty of time on the video to see strobe lights.

Sometimes these red objects resembled dumbbells, when two stayed together and occasionally triangles, when three were on at the same time. At times, I would see three bright, clear red objects on at once, like a triangle. I could not tell whether there was anything connecting the objects. Sometimes I would see several red objects together and wondered if they could all be lights on one object. I also wondered if some of the objects had quickly moved from one location to another. There seemed to be brighter, sharper, red objects and some dimmer ones that were more like blotches, or maybe rapidly moving objects. I do not know if there were other colors.

The red lights that traveled together in the video did not turn on or off at exactly same time (as seen in the slowed down video), although this timing was quite close to synchronous. In airplanes, such lighting would be synchronous. The first two views of the red objects that stayed together stayed on about the same amount of time, but the last one was shorter. And the time between views was less for the last one also. The distance between the red objects varied. There had been no patterned sequence of blinking lights such as is on aircraft.

Other oddities were that the two red objects would completely disappear between flashes. Nearly all aircraft in the dark keep at least one steady light on all the time. Their blinking pattern wasn't regular. Also, they were higher in altitude each time they appeared. They might have been traveling upward after they had passed me at what appeared to be a fairly low altitude. If aircraft are going over the horizon, they go down. These appeared to rise as if they had just taken off, traveled upwards, or were getting closer, but they did not look any larger as they would if they were becoming closer. And if these were the lighting on a craft, I should have continued to see them because there was a lot of time on the video for them to show up again. But I did not see them again–they showed only three times. However there was time to see them in two more blinks and it appeared that they might have taken off very rapidly to the east after the last blink, because in the last photograph they traveled that way and left a trail.

In comparison to the red objects, when the white objects blinked, they would sometimes be on for just a tiny fraction of a second (they appeared and disappeared in one click), they generally seemed brighter and sharper than the red objects and individual objects did not appear to move together as some of the red objects did.

These were nothing like strobe lights. Although a strobe light may flash on and off quickly as these objects did, a property of strobe lights is that they are regular. There was nothing regular in the flashing of these lights. In comparison, when one watches airplane strobe lights, the strobes continue in a smooth path along with the airplane. These white objects appeared and disappeared all over a large area of the sky. Their strobing wasn't regular, nor did any strobes follow a continuous path.

There were some very distinct, bright red and white objects, but others also looked red and white, but dimmer and more blurred. I do not remember from seeing them with my eyes if there were other colors. In the video, they seemed stationary when they were lit up, but some were a little blurred as if they had started to move rapidly.

No object's flashes were recorded in exactly the same place twice, so I photographed nothing that was fixed or stationary. I think I taped only one blink twice in almost the same location.

There was no smooth movement like an airplane flying away from the camera. In several instances, an object would look double as if it were two objects together or had very rapidly moved while blinking on. The planets never appeared as double, so this double appearance was not an artifact. Some of the objects' lighting seemed to have trails as if this were showing motion. Sometimes UFOs are reported as merging or coming apart. These double images suggest that the objects could be close together, or possibly even be merging.

There were several indications that these objects had some form of power. One reason is that the group took a definite direction and was not simply blown with the wind. The ability to move in a different direction from the wind indicates that some form of power is in use. Also, they glowed and this glowing would take power. In addition, they were able to blink off and on. Blinking lights such as strobe lights use different forms of power and some form of control is needed to make the light flash on and off. The ability to light up and to flash indicates that some form of both power and control existed in these objects.

Discussion and Confirmation

I saw two red objects fly past Venus at the beginning of the sighting and was able to capture several other objects going past Venus with my iPhone at the beginning of the sighting.

Then over a whole large area of the sky a group of objects began to flash lights. I was able to videotape this display with the video camera on HiDef video. This display also included two red objects that showed up together three times. I do not know if these were the original two objects that I saw.

The following applies to the videotape and includes some technical information about the photography. It does not have to be read to understand what happened. The reader can skip this—it is given as information for people watching the videotape in HiDef.

During the time the video was made, the camcorder was toggled between a wide (wide-angle) and a narrow (telephoto) field of view. The first portion shows a wide-angle view that includes the tree silhouettes below and to the left side of the picture. Venus and the Moon are a distance apart. Venus appears to move to the right, when the camcorder setting is changed from a wide to a narrow field of view (it doesn't really move). A number of the flashes showed up in different places in the wide-angle view and this showed how large a portion of the sky the flashes took up (Figure 10 shows the wide displacement of the flashes of this display by showing six photos that were made from the video during a two second time period. The time is shown on the timeline and the much smaller amount of displacement of a car during the same time can be seen on the bottom left).

Because this wide view covers such a large angular distance, if this display of the group of objects had been of aircraft lighting, it would take up a much smaller angular distance. For example, the angle covered by the diameter of the full Moon is about 31 arcmin or half a degree. A close airplane would subtend about the angular size of the Moon. The display of this group of objects was many, many times the angular size of the Moon. (Figure 11 shows the displacement of these flashes during a two second interval and Figure 12 shows the displacement of an airplane during the same time. It is evident that the flashes' displacement took up a large section of sky; whereas the airplane's displacement were almost in the same place).

These objects' flashes could also be compared to the general background (Figure 13 shows the apparent size of the display compared to Mars and Figure 14 shows that objects such as airplanes take a continuous path forward–they do not flash all over the sky). I took the video of the tail end of a group of flashing objects that were headed east. Thus, there are more of these flashes on the left side. The background is dark with large irregular blotches of black, red, green and purple that changed shape constantly and were darker, dimmer and less defined than the flashes. The objects that flashed differ from the background because they are generally obvious, bright and circular-shaped with well-defined edges and smaller than the background blotches, rather than just large amorphous, changing blotches.

Because the background is not white, I think most of the white flashes are from objects. Unlike the background, with the white flashes some are very clear and sharp, although some are smaller and dimmer. The red objects that photographed the best were also circular-shaped with fairly well-defined edges. However, both red and white objects could transform from well-defined into less well-defined flashes. An instance here is where two of the red objects that traveled together began as sharply defined, but became less well defined later. At 00.08 – - 00.17 two sharply-defined red objects and then three were seen at first. Then the third one blinked off, but the other two continued together. But as they continued, they became less well defined. At 00:10 – -00.15 the two red objects that traveled together showed for the last time. On their last blinks both objects showed as bodies that seemed to go to the left with trails to the right. Then they disappeared and did not show up together again, even though there was time on the video for this to happen. It appeared that they had suddenly sped off.

The white objects would often light up for only a small part of a second. They often would appear for only one click. Because they were on for such a small amount of time, it is best to go through the video one click at a time, else these very short flashes wouldn't be seen.

The bright, clear objects with distinct outlines are most frequently on the left side and middle of the video images, because the group was heading east and few bright, clear ones were on the right side by the time the video was taken. However, the right side could be used as a control to show what the sky would normally look like if no blinking objects were present. Although the sky is the same on the left and right side, the blinking white and red objects are generally visible on the left side. If these objects were some kind of camera artifacts, the objects would be visible on both sides. (When I had first seen the display it was to the west of Venus and heading east and then the flashing objects covered a wide area of the sky but they were drifting to the east and by the time I had the camcorder on, I was just photographing the tail end of the group. When I took the video, I thought it might have been too late to get anything, but I did photograph some of it.) Thus, because the flashing was mainly on the left side of the video, the right side might be used as a sort of control for how the normal sky would appear. I have many videos that could be compared to this one and used as controls also.

I disregarded the area at the bottom of the video, near the line of the tree silhouettes, when looking for objects' flashes, because there was some background lighting, which might have caused some form of photographic artifacts.

The video began with a wide-angle exposure. A white light appeared at 00:00 – -00.25. It was below the Moon and to the left of Venus. Because the camcorder was recording at the wide-angle setting and shows both the Moon, Venus and silhouettes of the trees, it demonstrates that even at this stage (as the group of objects flew east) objects could appear far enough west to show that the display took up a considerable angular distance.

Two (or maybe three) white objects appeared at 00:02 – -00:23, then more flashes appeared. Increased activity begins at about 00:07. One of several apparently double white blinks occurred at 00:08 – -00:17, another was at (00:08 – -00.07) and another at 00:015– -00:10. These may be two white lights that were near each other when they flashed. One white object flashed twice in about the same location (00:16 – -00.09 and six clicks later also at 00:16 – -00.09). At 00:11 – -00.14 four fairly dim white objects flashed; two of these were quite close together.

At 00:13 – -00.12, a white object appears in a wide view above a tree silhouette and three clicks later another white object appears to its right and some distance away compared to the tree silhouette. Nothing was visible during further clicks. One trailing, dim white object appeared to show on the right side as late as 00:19 – -00.06.

The first two red objects appeared at 00:07 – -00.18, they then continue to appear together through eight clicks until the object furthest to the left blinked out at (still at 00:07 – -00.18), then another one appeared below the former position of the left one (still at 00:07 – -00.18). After that two red objects appeared together again at (00:07 – -00.17) and then after another click a third red object appeared ((00:07 – -00.17). The two red objects appeared together again at 00.09 – -00.16. Sometimes a red object would appear by itself such as at 00:09 – - 00.16. At 00:08 – -00.17 two red objects that have stayed together are visible. In one click the one on the left becomes fainter and sort of appears as if it is moving down; in the next click a red object appears under the right red object, that is still on, as if the left object moved to the right and under the right object which stayed lit. Because several red objects sometimes came on together, possibly they were lights on a larger craft. Sometimes they would form a triangle. (Figure 15 shows the configuration of one set of red objects during a two second video recording.)

Both white and red objects sometimes appeared to have trails, for example, white one at 00:03 – -00.22.

These red objects were sharp, but others sometimes appeared that were less sharp and I do not know if these were just photographic artifacts, or objects with dimmer lights, or red objects in motion. Some of the white flashes were much clearer and more distinct than others. When I am recording stars or airplanes with this camera after dark, I see no flashing objects like this, so they weren't camera artifacts. (The main time there are camera artifacts on this camera's videos is when the battery is low. These artifacts are normally rectangular-shaped and sometimes they contain colors or designs. They aren't flashing objects like these. I just watched the video portions that were above the tree line at the bottom. There may have been artifacts along the tree silhouettes and higher because of background lighting.)

I posted this video on YouTube on that day and have posted more several more times. Because one could see a lot less on YouTube than on the HiDef video, I just posted several slowed down, enhancements of the video to show what some of the blinking objects looked like: https://youtu.be/tedrg9GINRE, but they did not work well and I received no comments.

I think my iPhone was pointing in the general area of the southwest when I took the photos and the photos were in full high definition.

The camcorder was mounted on a tripod and pointing south. It was a Sony HDR-HC5 HDV 1080 4MP MiniDV Hi with 10x Optical Zoom and digital zoom. The recording was made in 1080p full high-definition video on DV cassette tape. The camera has night vision, but I had it set for day vision, so I could see the colors of the planets. The video was transferred to an iMac computer using iMovie. The video is large, 425 MB and I do not know how to send it. The YouTube video upload shows much less than the actual video.

I have the original photographs that I sent from my iPhone to my computer and the tracking information. I think I had GPS turned off, but the coordinates were latitude: 40.174204 and longitude - 82.964062. I also have the original videotape. My camera taped over the video, but I had downloaded it before this happened and I have heard also that an original video can be retrieved even if something is taped over it.

A second reason I have not yet reported the sighting was that I had the photos on my iPhone, but then purchased a new iPhone. The technician assured me that everything would transfer from the old phone to the new one. But later I discovered that everything had transferred except these three photos and several before. I felt terrible because I thought I could not verify the photos. But I just (2017.10.11) found out about EXIF and tried this with the photographs. This worked and I was able to extract the digital information from the photographs, as shown below:

I used the Internet program https://camerasummary.coms to extract the EXIF information and that for the first iPhone photograph is: "The image on the left is your original image and the image on the right is the thumbnail stored within the image file. Resolution Unit: Inches File Size: 621022 bytes File DateTime: 10-Oct-2017 12:45:22 Flash Used: No Flash Make: Apple Model: iPhone 6 Plus xResolution: 72.00 (72/1) 0 yResolution: 72.00 (72/1) 0 Software: 8.2 File Modified Date: 2016:11:04 19:22:27 Exposure Time: 0.250 s (1/4) (1/4) F Number: f/2.2 Exposure: program (auto) Iso Equiv: 500 Exif Version: 0221 DateTime: 2016:11:04 19:22:27 DateTime Digitized: 2016:11:04 19:22:27 Component Config: Does Not Exists Aperture: 2.2000001213747 brightness: 3718580.87 (4294960908/1155) Exposure Bias: 0.00 (1/256) Metering Mode: Spot Focal Length: 4.15 (83/20) Maker Note: NOT IMPLEMENTED sub Section TimeOriginal: 945 sub SectionTime Digitized: 945 Flashpix Version: 0100 Color Space: sRGB Width: 3264 Height: 2448 sensing: One-chip color area sensor Scene Type: Exposure Mode: Auto Exposure White Balance: 0 Zoom Ratio: 3.01 (816/271) Flength 35mm: 87 Screen Capture Type: Standard Is-Colour: 1 Process: 192 Resolution: 3264x2448 Color: Color Jpeg Process: Baseline."

The photographs that I had originally mailed to my computer provided a complete EXIF. However, another portion of the photographs did transfer from my old iPhone to the new one and these are still on my iPhone.

I also just found out about RAW data. This was lost during the transfer because the three photos did not transfer. Since everything on the old phone was transferred at once (not separately) by an electronic process, it is strange that just the UFO photos did not transfer. It might be interesting to try to investigate this; I still have the receipt for the new phone.

An odd coincidence with this is that I had investigated a sighting called Dancing Lights with Paul Burrell, Delbert Anderson and Bill Jones (Burrell, Paul, Delbert Anderson, William E. Jones and Irena Scott. "Dancing Red Lights, Logan, Ohio, October/November, 1995." : 4-5 MUFON of Ohio Newsletter (November, 2009)), as was also mentioned in my book and written up separately on the Internet by Paul Burrell. The Logan sighting was somewhat similar to this sighting, because it involved dancing, blinking, red lights or objects. I realized this July that November 4 was the exact date of the witnesses' second sighting of the Logan dancing lights. Bill and I may have actually interviewed the participants earlier in the day of November 4. These witnesses videotaped the second appearance of their dancing lights on November 4th, but did not use a tripod, so that this video is confusing although the report is excellent and involved many witnesses. [106]

I do not recall reporting this event, but discovered that a sighting report existed for it anyway in the National UFO Reporting Center, http://www.nuforc.org/webreports/ndxloh.html. This may have been taken from my YouTube posts or I may have reported it when I was searching for other sightings. There are a number of sightings on November 4, 2016 on the Internet.

Discussion and Confirmation

Several people looked at this information and one made the comments: "I wonder if that was specifically for you to see? Amazing sighting Dr. Irena. Would you like that to go into the MUFON archive/CMS? It's an impressive sighting. I'd give it an Unknown personally."[107]

Dr. Harley Rutledge had also commented on flashing and blinking objects and had even given some a name: "Not all the lights we saw appeared to be plasma balls. Some were single or even multiple xenon gas-like flashes. I categorized the multiple flashes into three types: RFEX (Random Flashbulb Effect Xenon), JSLX (Jumping Strobe Light Xenon) and ERSX (Erratic

Strobe Light Xenon)."[108] He said that some physicists have explained these as an entoptic effect in the retina of the eye. However, since I took pictures with a camera, I know this was not that.

My very first impression of this from the second I saw the red objects is that this was unreal and could not happen, but it was certainly real because it could be photographed. It gave me the impression of a computer simulation or cartoon. This made me wonder if it and much else in our environment that is unexplained might result from a simulated reality. This is the theory that our reality could be simulated—such as by quantum computer simulation—to a degree indistinguishable from "true" reality. Such a reality could contain even conscious minds, which might or might not be aware that they are a simulation. This idea differs from the current, concept of virtual reality, which generally can be distinguished from the experience of actuality. Simulated reality would be hard or impossible to separate from our "true" reality. Much debate has taken place over this topic, ranging from philosophical discourse to practical applications in computing. No one has ever proven that our reality is real and this might not ever be possible, unless something can take us to the outside of our reality. But perhaps UFO phenomena can exist because we live in a simulated world. Perhaps it could provide even a bridge to true reality.

Although this sighting has not been much publicized, some general conclusions might be drawn that fit this data. When I took the iPhone photographs, I had just seen two red, glowing objects passing Venus. Then I took photographs of Venus and these captured additional objects flying by Venus, however, I did not see these objects. Because I had already seen the red objects and these other objects were moving, they may have been traveling with the red objects. Thus I appear to have photographed objects that were emitting radiation, but not in the visible range.

The idea that objects/UFOs could be in our environment, but not visible to humans, could suggest several explanations. One is that they are advanced images made through such mechanisms as laser created volumetric display technology or holograms.

Another possibility is that they might not be in the form of matter that we view as normally composing our world. This could help to explain a plethora of UFO data. For example many people report that when they are watching a UFO, it can suddenly disappear, or an object or entity can suddenly appear. This data suggests that objects such as this can vary their emitted wavelength such that they can be visible or not visible to us. Or if the objects are holograms, they can obviously be made to appear and disappear by something controlling the light they emit or the light from which they are formed. Holograms can be photographed.

The idea that they could be images created by holographic or volumetric display, or composed of something that differs from our normal concept of matter could also explain the difficulty that numerous people have reported in photographing the objects. For example, Dr. Harley Rutledge, who conducted an extensive scientific study of UFO phenomena (to be discussed later) in his book, *Project Identification: The First Scientific Field Study of UFO Phenomena*, [109] discussed the difficulty in photographing UFO phenomena.

These researchers discovered numerous reasons why studying UFO phenomena is difficult. In Project Identification, although scientists spotted numerous unidentified flying objects, they frequently could not photograph such subjects as Class A UFOs (the best documented events) because the UFOs would disappear, would appear when cameras could not be brought to bear on them, or would not show up on film after being photographed.

The information from this photography might help to explain such results. It might also help to explain the object's power, propulsion and ability to defy gravity.

For example, if one aims a camera at a tree and takes a picture, the tree will show up in the photograph. This does not necessarily happen with UFO phenomena however, even under intensive scientific examination, as described above. This difficulty could be caused by the ability of the objects to adjust the wavelength of their emitted light, so that they can come into and out of the human visual range. They may have mechanisms that interfere with photography. Or some objects may be holographic/volumetric display images and thus can be changed by changing the light used to form them.

After I photographed the objects traveling past Venus, suddenly a wide area of the sky lit up with flashing lights. I saw no objects, only flashes, although I had seen what appeared to be objects in the iPhone photographs. Thus these flashes likely came from objects. This conclusion can be drawn because the flashes photographed, which they would not do if they were just images in my eyes or brain.

For the white flashes, the video camera just photographed flashes; it did not appear to have captured objects (its sensitivity to different wavelengths of light may differ from that of the iPhone). This again leads to the conclusion that the flashes came from objects. It appeared that these objects were traveling in a group.

Although the white flashes were just brief flashes, there were red objects in the video that could stay in view for a while. It is unknown if these were the same red objects that I saw by eye. These objects seemed to have an extended apparent diameter.

It appeared that these objects may have had control over what a human could see and photograph.

In addition, Rutledge even mentioned telepathy in association with the phenomena that he studied. He thought that the objects seemed to pick up the thoughts of the researchers. This could also be explained using the idea that the UFO phenomena could control what humans could see of it. Thus, the phenomena might be right there with the scientists, but they would not know it. It could not only pick up human communication, but also intentions and thoughts.

This might help in some way to explain that a difference might exist between orbs and lightning balls. Some lightning balls seem intelligent. Some even are reported to turn into other things, such as an orb turning into an alien, or a monster. Perhaps they are two different things. Perhaps many lighting balls are just regular prosaic lightning balls. Perhaps others are a manifestation of UFO/poltergeist phenomena. Those that appear to be UFO-related might images such as holograms, or volumetric displays, or even some unusual form of matter. This could explain the bedroom visitor aspect of balls of light, orbs that turn into something else and the similar phenomenon associated with sightings of UFOs, bigfoot and other manifestation. Also, we might not understand distance very well. Perhaps an object can not only vary the frequency of its emission, but also the appearance of its size and distance.

And although it seems strange there is much in our universe that is invisible to people maybe even most of it, for example one well-known form is gas–it is a physical material that has mass and occupies space.

Another example is Dark Matter, which comprises most of our universe and as hypothesized by theoretical physicist Dr. Lisa Randall might even contain life:

Scientists have mostly ruled out all known ordinary materials as candidates for dark matter. The current consensus is that dark matter lies outside the Standard Model of particle physics, currently the best description of how all known subatomic particles behave. Specifically, physicists have suggested that dark matter is composed of new kinds of particles.

Randall and her colleagues propose a more complex version that they call "partially-interacting dark matter," where dark matter has both a non-interacting component and a self-interacting one. A similar example in real particles can be seen with protons, electrons and neutrons—positively charged protons and negatively charged electrons attract one another, while neutrally charged neutrons are not attracted to either protons or electrons.

"There's no reason to think that dark matter is composed of all the same type of particle," Randall says. "We certainly see a diversity of particles in the one sector of matter we do know about, ordinary matter. Why shouldn't we think the same of dark matter?"

One intriguing possibility raised by interacting dark matter models is the existence of dark atoms that might have given rise to dark life, neither of which would be easily detected, Randall says. Although she admits that the concept of dark life might be far-fetched, "life is complicated and we have yet to understand life and what's necessary for it."[110]

There is also energy:

There is no manifestation of energy that is visible. Even light itself is not visible...We see things only if they are sources of light with the light coming into our eyes or if they reflect light. Consequently light itself can't be seen we can't see energy, but we can often see the effects of energy.

We note that something is moving relative to us and conclude that it has kinetic energy. We see a moving object, but we can't see kinetic energy itself.

We see that something has been raised far above the Earth and conclude that the work done in raising the object has produced additional gravitational (potential) energy. We see a raised object, but we can't see the gravitational energy...

It's just like time. You can't see. So wherever there is a chance of electron changing its orbit or colliding or forming new bonds with other elements, you will see light. When it is decelerated from high velocity, it will emit light which you can't see.

Mostly because energy is a model we invented to make our physics easier. It doesn't physically exist, it's just something we created to show how things behave.[111]

Thus there are many possibilities that might provide an explanation for the objects that I photographed. One immediate possibility is that the objects were created by holographic/volumetric image display. Scientists today would be able to create this in a small way. Another is that we may live in a simulated environment with UFO events being created by the creators of our simulation. Also because some UFO phenomena might be created under self-organizing abilities, it may be endowed with much else such as intelligence.

Other possibilities include the existence of both invisible matter and energy. In addition, it has been scientifically hypothesized that Dark Matter might even encompass life forms. Thus such inferences are within the purview of today's science. These are draft inferences. I have a feeling that this sighting might be "instructional," as Sprinkle had expressed and that much might be learned from it. Many interpretations of this data can also be made.

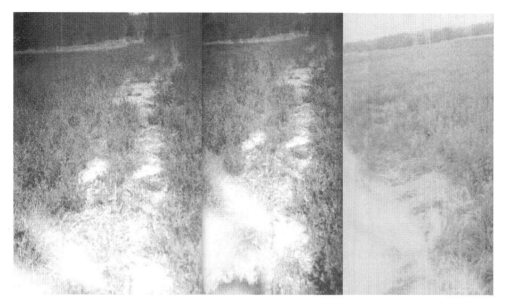

Figure 1: A farmer discovered this trace in June 1984, in a field of knee high green alfalfa and thought it had been made recently. It was a swath generally about 130 feet long and around 6-8 feet wide. It was located in an area that was not visible from any habitation or road and consisted of standing plants of green alfalfa that were blackened and charred into the roots. Nothing in the area had been bent down. The area of the burn was much localized; plants next to the burned area were undamaged. The photographs were taken in September after several cuttings of hay. The first two views are to the north (from the "blast" area) and show its isolated location. The third is to the south and show a nearby high tension power line. (I do not know why some parts of the photography look foggy.) The farmer reported it to the fire department and several members were mystified as to its cause.

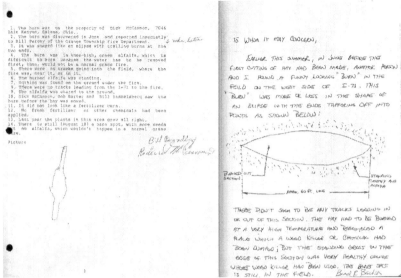

Figure 2: Three witness who saw the burn before the hay was cut made drawings and descriptions of its appearance. Nothing had been applied to the area. My sister and I had discussed it with Budd Hopkins, who was investigating a similar burn. Like his description in Intruders, it consisted of a central circular area around 8 feet in diameter (the farmer referred to this as a "blast area"). This was larger than the one Hopkins examined and had a secondary smaller circular area beside it. The farmer and others had never seen anything like it.

Figure 3: As had the burn in Hopkins' book, Intruders, this area contained deep cracks.

652C Bale Kenyon
Galena, Ohio 43021
June 28, 1984

Mr. Jim Dinguid
Department of Agriculture
8995 E. Main Street Bldg 4.
Rennoldsbury, Ohio 43068

Dear Mr. Dinguid!

    I have enclosed my Uncle's mass spectronometer
analysis of the soil sample from the burn in the alfalfa
field. He also analyzed gasoline residue and this is
enclosed. For separation in all of his determinations, he
used a fused silica capillary column. He injected vapor
from the (heated) soil sample into it, heated the column
from 50 to 300 C. at 15 C/min. to drive off the separate
compounds, and then collected then, For analysis of the
separated peaks, he used electron impact and chemical
ionization spectronometry. Pages 1-12 show the peaks
analyzed by electron impact, pages 13-15 show the peaks
analyzed by chemical ionization, and pages 16-17 show the
gasoline spectra. He didn't know what volume of the sample
to use and probably used too much (possibly causing some of
the peaks to be overloaded). In the chemical ionization
run, he thought his injection needle might have bumped
something, causing his whole sample to come out of the
column right away instead of in peaks. The spectrum curve
looked pretty flat, so he just sent the graphs.

    We wondered if the burn might have been caused by
gasoline. He did not detect gasoline residue in the soil
sample. He thought, if gasoline were used to burn the
alfalfa (the burn was discovered in June and I put the
samples in a jar in ~~October~~), possibly some gasoline
residue could have remained. He said that the molecules
listed by the computer were approximations because the
computer just goes through commonly known compounds and
lists the relationship. (not that same Uncle who did the mass spectonomics)

When my Uncle found the burn the alfalfa
was knee high and ready to cut. It was charred
to the ground in a very discrete area, shaped
like this [sketch] He thought it had been

Figure 4: To test for any chemicals that might have caused the burn, samples from the burn area
were sent to a senior industrial chemist. He performed a mass spectrometer analysis and tested
for a number of compounds, such as gasoline, poison and fertilizer. The letter to the Department
of Agriculture describing the techniques he used, a request for help interpreting the results and
some notes on the analysis are shown. (The date on the letter is incorrect–the analysis was dated
October 26, 1984.)

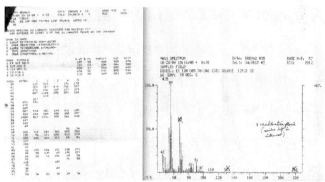

Figure 5: Two examples of the many pages of the mass spectrometer analysis done by the
chemist are shown. This was done on October 26, 1984.

OHIO DEPARTMENT OF AGRICULTURE

DALE L. LOCKER
Director

8995 E. Main Street
Reynoldsburg, Ohio 43068
TELEPHONE: (614) 866-6361

RICHARD F. CELESTE
Governor

December 20, 1984

Dr. Irena Scott
6520 Bale Kengon
Galena, Ohio 43021

Dear Dr. Scott:

I have talked and showed several of my fellow workers the chromatograms you sent to me. We can not find any products or degratation products of herbicides or pesticides in the list of compounds. On page 5 compounds 2 and 5 could also be a solvent known as DMSO. On page 9 compounds 4 and 5 are found in oil of many plant seeds. Sorry that I cannot help more in identifying the problem.

The method we use most in checking problems like this, is to do a solvent extraction of the soil, then concentrate the solvent, and shoot the concentrate in a G.C.

Sincerely,

OHIO DEPARTMENT OF AGRICULTURE

James Diuguid
Formulation Laboratory

JD:las

Figure 6: The mass spectrometer results were sent to the specialists in the Ohio Department of Agriculture. This analysis was very precise–it was difficult, costly and took the chemist a long time to do it. The scientists at the Ohio Department of Agriculture found no trace of herbicides or pesticides in the results. Thus, the cause of the burn remained unexplained.

Figure 7: This sighting began as I was photographing planets and astronomical objects using an iPhone and a camcorder. I was thinking about what a nice clear sky it was for photographing the planets. The photograph (lightened) below is one I had just taken–the planets are labeled. Then I saw two bright red, glowing, objects traveling across the sky toward Venus–these are drawn onto the photograph. They were soundless and reminded me of a computer simulation. This looked like something that could not happen and I was so dumbfounded that I did not immediately take a photograph, although I had the iPhone in my hand. All of the objects were seen against the sky.

Figure 8: Then I realized that I should take a photograph, but the red objects were out of sight. I did not see anything but I began taking photos in case any more objects appeared. I took 3 photographs in rapid succession, below. Although I had seen nothing when I took the photographs, when I uploaded them to the computer all three showed glowing objects. When these photographs were resized and overlaid, the objects were in different positions in the 3 photographs, thus, they were moving. They appeared to be flying past Venus as the first two red objects had done. These objects had been invisible to me and, thus, were emitting radiation in a frequency that I had been unable to see. Below are the three figures showing the objects and their change in position during the few seconds, when I took the photos. None of the photographs before, such as shown above, or after showed such objects.

Figure 9: Then in a wide area of the sky to the south, I suddenly saw many flashing lights. I assumed these flashes came from objects like I had seen passing Venus and thought that the ones I saw must have been part of a group. I ran for my camcorder, which was already on a tripod and tried to photograph the flashing objects and their movements. By that time I could see just the tail end of the display as they traveled behind trees. The photograph shows 2 of these flashes and Venus.

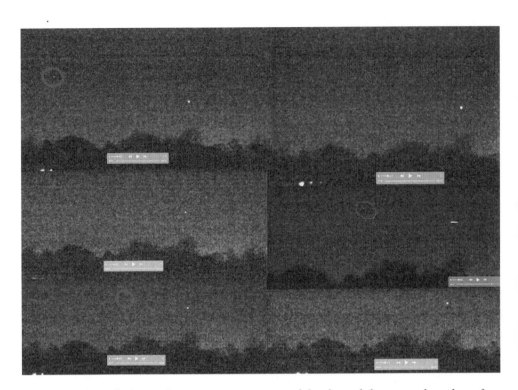

Figure 10: These flashes took up an enormous area of the sky and there must have been from many objects. They flashed in red and white. The figure below shows white flashes on 6 photographs. All 6 photos were made from the video during a 2 second time period. This short time period can be seen in both the timeline and in the small amount of displacement of the car driving by (lower left). Despite such a short time frame, the flashes were quite a distance apart both horizontally and vertically. In one photograph three flashed at once. There is much more displacement between the flashes than can be seen in the car–which might show a much greater displacement because it may have been closer. Also the car showed a straight, continuous path on the video; the flashes were intermittent and in different places.

Figure 11: Below is a comparison of the position of the flashing objects when they are overlaid as transparencies. The objects were not insects (it was November) or birds because the flashing was in visible light. Because this was a lot of displacement for 2 seconds, the flashes were most likely from different objects. In one photograph, 3 flashes had occurred at once. No airplanes were seen or heard.

Figure 12: A second way to compare these flashes to a known object is shown below. This shows 3 photographs of an airplane at about the same angular diameter as the flashing objects. These three photographs were also taken during 2 seconds. In these three photographs, one can barely detect any change in the position of the airplane. It is not all over the sky as the flashes were.

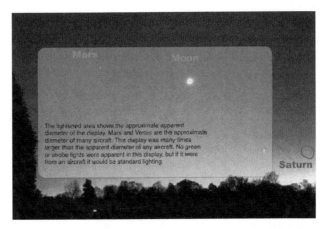

Figure 13: The figure below shows the approximate apparent size of the flashing light display when I first saw it. This display was very much larger than the apparent diameter of an airplane would be (about the apparent size of Mars). There were many flashing and dancing lights in this area and they were traveling quite rapidly to the left (east). There were no aircraft sounds, no green or strobe lights and no evidence of aircraft.

Figure 14: A daytime photograph also provides a comparison to the apparent area of the flashing lights. This shows an airplane contrail. Airplanes photograph as objects traveling forward in a straight, continuous path such as shown by the contrail. They do not appear as flashing lights over a large area of sky.

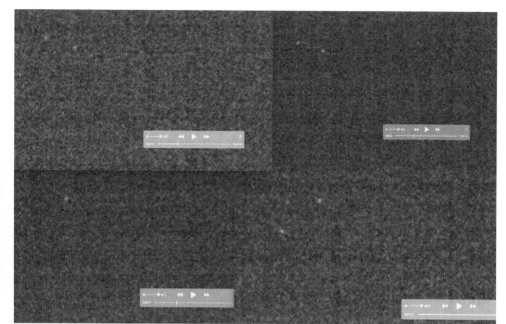

Figure 15: There were also red objects in the display. Some flashed quite quickly as did the white flashes, but some stayed on for several seconds. Sometimes two of these red objects appeared to travel together. They could change in appearance quite rapidly, as shown below during 2 seconds of video recording (on the timeline). Going clockwise from the upper left, 2 objects were visible which both stayed on for several seconds, after this it appeared that 3 or 4 objects flashed and then only one appeared. There were no green or strobe lights or sounds in any part of the display, although if it were from airplanes there should be.

******

CHAPTER SEVEN: MYSTERY SOUND AND DELUGE OF UFO EVENTS

A sudden flood of sightings among neighbors and family members at that time. Why?

A letter I wrote to John Timmerman of CUFOS sums up my knowledge at that time (November 13, 1984).

William Jones, J.D. and I had made a survey of people to see how many thought they had had UFO sightings in this neighborhood that was later published as a paper, "Survey of Unidentified Aerial Phenomenon Reports in Delaware County, Ohio," in the scientific journal, *OJS*. I had sent the witness CUFOS report forms to CUFOS. Ufologist Jennie Zeidman had come out to re-interview several of the people.

Also my sister had told me about having Budd Hopkins visit her and her family. The person with him, as I mentioned was Debbie Jordan-Kauble, who he wrote about in *Intruders*. He was interested in our sightings as a family, the burn in the field here and the sightings of my sister's children. Two of them had experienced sightings the same year. Her daughter had seen five red objects come down from the sky and Hopkins said the other people had had a similar sighting. I think this event had been written about in the newspaper.

Her son had seen a small blinking object under his window one night and had watched it for several hours. They knew of nothing that would have caused him to see anything. They lived in the country away from other houses.

They also talked about a burn that resembled the one here. I do not know if this was the one in the book, *Intruders*, or another one.

Sue said that Budd Hopkins thought that I had been abducted, but thought she might have been put into suspended animation, while this was being done to me.

I also asked about why there should be so many sightings. There had not been sightings for a long time, but suddenly there seemed to be a flood of sightings. A number of neighbors had not only seen things but had what appeared to be close encounters, the trace appeared and people in my sister's vicinity in Indiana also began to see things. There were so many sightings here that there were articles in the newspaper and a police report about the sightings. The events in *Intruders* happened in Indiana during this time-period also. I was trying to understand this:

I have another question…in February [I reported] to your office. Neither Sue nor I had a sighting before that for 16 years. I reported part of the Boston sighting in 1968 to NICAP and neither of us had reported the other sightings to anyone. Then suddenly right after reporting them, I had three sightings in six months. Sue's children began to see things and my neighbors (who didn't even know that I had reported) began to see UFOs and there was reported poltergeist activity in Columbus. Is it common for people and their neighbors to have sightings after people make UFO reports? I didn't understand why I had three sightings right afterwards. There seemed to be a lot of sightings right around here by neighbors; enough anyway, that people were talking about it. Would it just be a coincidence that they seemed to be around me right after I made a report? Also between December 1983 and March 1984, I was scared and kept having nightmares about UFOs even though I hadn't read or heard any current reports about them and was under the impression that they were no longer around…I just wondered if it is a common experience for people to get scared first and then see UFOs.

He did not answer, probably had no idea and I am still wondering. In thinking back, maybe this was some kind of a flap or wave or something. It did not continue.

In these events there also had been quite a bit of hard evidence. One was the mystery burn. I had had the airport sighting and there were many witnesses to the sightings on and near our family farm. Moreover there were also quite a number of sightings in Indiana, such as the ones that Budd Hopkins had investigated, but also ones in our family also (they lived near the area that Budd Hopkins was investigating).

Timmerman had said he would discuss the reports with Dr. Hynek.

These reports included:

My sister's sightings

My sister was a missionary in Brazil for four years. She and another missionary viewed an object: "

This incident happened in Brazil in 1971. It was late at night, maybe 11:00 P.M. on a hot summer night. He was driving our jeep and we were going north on an isolated country road. Ahead of us we saw what we thought to be another car, so Marvin pulled over to the side so we could meet the car (there were no driveways or turn offs where a car could go). We both realized something was strange and I asked Marvin if he had seen a car coming and he said he had. So I asked him where it was and he said, 'Let's get out of here.' So he really stepped on the gas and we returned to our homes. Usually at that time of night there would be no traffic of any kind.

Another of her sightings was of an object above a nearby relative's house. It suddenly disappeared. This is the object that we discussed at the beginning of our 1968 sighting. I did not pay much attention to her sighting at first, but I interviewed these neighbors when I made the survey in the *OJS*. I found that this family had experienced a number of UFO events, even including a landing and a written description by the father. They said that more had happened but they did not talk about it.

The son had seen an object in 1967 and the family had also independently reported close encounters. There was no way to check whether he and my sister might have viewed the same object, because no one remembered the date (except it was at dusk in the fall of 1967).

These were good witnesses. Both the father and son had training in aircraft identification. The son said that he had training to identify hundreds of aircraft profiles from different views. He was working on the B1 bomber. Both father and son worked at North American Rockwell, an aircraft manufacturing company.

The son reported seeing an object land in a field around 300 feet from the house (he worked in aircraft manufacturing, had Federal government security clearances and aircraft identification training). He said it appeared to have a hard body (silvery, metallic), was disc-shaped with portholes emitting white light and it made a whirring sound. The lights in the house went off while the object was on the ground, but the telephone worked. He was terrified and phoned his parents. After about five minutes, the object rapidly flew away. The next day they found crushed grass there, but did not know whether the grass had been mashed beforehand by cattle. He had told his family and grandparents, but had not officially reported the object. This was especially scary because he was 16 and this was the first time his parents had allowed him to stay in the house by himself after dark.

His parents had previously had a close encounter (6/1955) with a lighted object that hovered near their house that made a whirring sound.

The grandmother also reported a sighting. I checked some other neighbors, who also thought they had seen objects.

How the electricity could be knocked out, but the telephone still worked is under study. Although land lines and the 120 V house lines have different power sources, if the electricity had been knocked out by the UFO, one would wonder why the telephone still worked. I asked an electrician, who said that if the house electricity was knocked out, so should the phone line be by the same mechanism:

The main supplier was Columbus and Southern Ohio, (now AEP) 7600 volts cut down to 120-240 by a transformer on the pole near the entrance to the residence... supplied by aerial cable. No underground lines. So all of this would clearly be easy to shut down or disturb the house power by EMP or other similar method. Now the landline back then in my thoughts might be hard to collaborate. All of this was supplied by aerial cable on the same pole as the house power 7600 volts 60 htz. This is the copper cable, but it has a DC current not, AC as the house. Around 48 volts dc on the telephone if on the hook, off hook 3-9 volts, 20 htz. when ringing 90-130 DC volts. As I remember back in the early days the DC was supplied by a large set of battery's on a rack at the phone exchange. So in my opinion it should have taken the phone down by EMP etc.

However some things can block AC but not DC current such as an inductor. For example, different passive elements can show different electrical properties. An inductor has a property to oppose the sudden change in current flow through it. With DC current the change in current in the circuit under normal operation is zero. Thus it can easily flow through an inductor. With AC current unlike DC there is a change in both magnitude and polarity of supplied current to the inductor. Thus, an AC signal is blocked by it. But it is unknown how an inductor could be applied in this case. However there could be other mechanisms that might do this.

It is unknown if such affects might be done with lasers. The father then made a write-up of another sighting and all three of the family members signed it:

We were sitting in our living room late in the evening watching TV. There was a bright flash of light [that lasted a] few seconds. As it was a clear evening there was no chance of it being lightning. Two neighbors later in the Delaware Gazette [?] my wife and I both read where some of our neighbors saw a UFO. It was bright enough to read a newspaper by. We also noticed a slight interruption in our TV reception. There was also a distinct drop in power we noticed the lights dimmed. This was around the end of July or the first part of August.

This was in 1984 and they noticed electrical effects also. I asked several neighbors and others had seen something also.

My sister's family

Also during 1984 several additional UFO events happened to family members in Indiana

In April on a trip through Greenfield, Indiana, I stopped at my sister's home. Her son told me about a light he had seen, as mentioned. He seemed disturbed about it, talking for about an hour and calling it "not a lightning bug." My sister said he had seen it in February 1984 (it would not be a lightning bug in February). It was a small, blinking, yellow light that he said had been on the ground under his bedroom window during one entire night (she wasn't sure about the date, because she thought he told them about it about a week after he saw it). He had gotten up several times that night to watch it out of his window. They live in the country and had no idea what it was. They did not know of anything that would blink all night. He gave the same description when I asked him several months later.

This happened in the same month as my OSU sightings. Budd Hopkins had been interested in this and talked to him.

Another reason Budd Hopkins might have been interested in my sister's family is that they were near the location of the *Intruders* events. My sister lived near Indianapolis–her husband worked in Indianapolis. I have not been able to find the exact location of Copley Woods, except that it is a suburb of Indianapolis and what appears to be the location is around ten miles distant.[112] [113]

There had also been UFO sightings close to my sister and me that we did not know about until later. One example occurred on a farm about a mile from my sister's place near Indianapolis. It included a power failure and a large 44-foot diameter imprint as written about in *The Daily Reporter*, 11/14/1978, Tuesday Greenfield, Indiana November 14, 1978- 15. [114]

My mother's sightings

My mother, in the 1930s in McConnelsville, Ohio, had a lightning ball come in a window, as mentioned earlier.

When I was young, my family would take turns going out to the chicken house to close the door so no wild animals would eat them. This was on the other side of a windbreak from the house and we did it after dark. We were sometimes somewhat afraid to do this in the dark.

One night my mother returned from this chore looking white and terrified. She did not say anything for quite a while. After some time, my father asked her if she had shut up the chickens. She said no. She said that she had seen red glowing spheres floating behind the windbreak. Dad asked her if they were in pairs (like animal eyes), but she said no. Dad and I went out with a flashlight, but we saw nothing unusual.

Also a relative told me that my mother's brother-in-law saw a UFO land in a field. He was terrified and never talked about it again. This same brother-in-law, Gay Cox and my father were once driving in a car and I think they said lightning hit the front of the car. They turned around and came back real fast.

Mystery sound and UFO wave over a wide area all at one time–hard evidence of the UFO reality

Another instance that my mother was involved in happened when she, in Ohio, called me in Missouri to ask if I heard a strange sound (which I found out later happened on October 11, 1973). This seemed so strange that I asked her if she should check in to an asylum for dementia (jokingly).

Although this seemed strange, it may provide hard evidence of the reality of UFO phenomena.

Later I became curious, accidentally discovered exactly when it occurred and collected numerous newspaper accounts about this 1973 UFO wave and the thunderous roar that accompanied it. I discovered that this was not only a unique event, but also likely good hard evidence of UFO phenomena.

Several individuals, including geologist and State of Ohio seismologist Mike Hansen, PhD, helped me analyze and investigate the events. I accessed Freedom of Information Act (FOIA) material, collected and examined seismograph recordings from different locations and sought information from additional sources (Figure 2).

Eventually I published information about the sightings and the mysterious sound. My "Investigation of a sound heard over a wide area," was published in a peer-reviewed scientific journal, *OJS* (Figure 1).[115]

I also have three *MUFON UFO Journal* articles: my first article, a debunking by a debunker of this article Joseph Tester and a following article where I debunked the debunker).[116] [117] [118]

This abrupt series of events began on October 11, 1973, at around 9:00 p.m. and included the strange booming sound, UFO sightings and entity encounters. It may have been the most widely experienced event ever to have been associated with UFO phenomena.

With the exception of the Krakatoa volcanic eruption of 1883, the 1973 boom could be the most widespread audible sound on record. The deafening boom roared through a multi-state area in the Midwest on October 11, 1973, at around 9:00 p.m. The sound was accompanied by a sudden increase in UFO sightings, reports of alien abductions and other unexplainable events– some at the exact time of the blast.

Police switchboards lit up with calls. Reports of a thunderous boom, close encounters, alien abductions, mutilations and similar events swarmed in and this activity continued over several weeks. Central Ohio law enforcement agencies received 150 UFO reports on October 17, six days after the initial activity and this is the largest number of UFO sightings ever recorded in a 24-hour period. In Wheeling, West Virginia, nearly 100 UFOs were reported on October 17, causing alarm in the city of 60,000 inhabitants. This wave and the nature of the sightings were so extensive that some referred to it as an invasion.

The precipitous increase of multi-state sightings has come to be known as the UFO Wave of 1973, although it was so massive it has also been called the Invasion of 1973 and unlike most UFO events that leave behind little proof; the 1973 events included an unprecedented abundance of evidence. This included Dr. Harley Rutledge's study, which may be the best UFO research ever done. Additional smoking gun evidence includes seismograms of the boom.

The boom was felt in 10 states including Ohio, Pennsylvania, Virginia, Maryland and West Virginia. It was first reported about 8:30 p.m. It first became evident over Indiana and western Ohio and traveled east to the coast. The sound covered a circular-shaped area, extending northward from Kentucky possibly to Canada and eastward from Illinois to Maryland.

A seismograph at the Pennsylvania State University's Seismic Observatory provided smoking gun evidence of this event when it recorded a five-second burst of very high frequency at 8:53 pm, simultaneously with the window-breaking boom. The sound and vibrations could not be attributed to earthquake tremors, nor did the widespread pattern of the boom match that of a sonic boom.

Through seismograms, scientists can find clues to what caused a tremor. Earthquakes and mining blasts can be distinguished through their seismographs–earthquakes begin with relatively weak primary waves when compared to mining blasts. The recording made of the 1973 tremor was reported to have been lost (or possibly in possession of the government) and thus cannot be examined in detail.

Various agencies insisted there were no known aircraft that could have caused such a widespread sonic boom; hence, many concluded a minor earthquake had hit the East. But seismographic information showed no evidence of this.

Shelton Alexander, Penn State geophysics and seismology expert said the only other possibility is that it could have been a meteorite coming into the area. It appeared that the boom represented a physical object entering the earth's atmosphere at a high speed. This was probably an object similar to a meteorite or a craft. However, the expected meteorite wasn't seen. But concurrent with the sound, people began to see low-altitude flying objects that fit neither the pattern of falling debris, nor of a high-altitude cloud, nor other elements that would be associated with a meteor.

The Goddard Space Flight Center in Beltsville, Maryland and the National Aeronautics and Space Administration in Washington said they knew of nothing that could have caused the shock. Air Force officials in Pennsylvania and officers at the Naval Observatory in Washington said they had sighted nothing that could have caused a sonic boom or an explosion.

Information about sonic booms can show how unusual this sound was. I found that the width of the boom "carpet" beneath an aircraft is about one mile for each 1000 feet of altitude. For example, an aircraft flying supersonically at 50,000 feet can produce a sonic boom cone of about 50 miles wide. Thus, this 1973 boom was many times wider than that.

Joseph Tester replied to this in a *MUFON Jr.* article which debunked my writing and explained this boom as possibly that of an SR-71 supersonic plane in the area around that time. Tester's article showed a graph someone made that showed an expanding sonic boom cone that began near Galesburg, Illinois and traveled directly eastward such that its eastern center was around Philadelphia, Pennsylvania; its lower (south) eastern edge appeared to be in North Carolina; and its upper (north) eastern edge was south of the Finger Lake region of New York. He attributed this to the sonic boom cone of the SR-71.

However, the SR-71's sonic boom would have looked much different than this. The SR-71 traveled south of Chicago, north of Indianapolis and then to Griffiss AFB, near Rome, New York. This would have taken it near Cleveland and Buffalo and north of the Finger Lakes, rather than south of them as shown in Tester's graph. It traveled at about 80,000 feet. Thus, its boom carpet would be 40 miles on either side and it would end up farther north of and very much smaller than the boom area that Tester showed for it in his diagram. Tester's diagram is strange, however, because it appeared to show the location of the mystery boom, not the trajectory of the sonic boom carpet of the SR-71.

There were numerous additional things wrong in Tester's article and I then debunked his writing in the following article. For one, the mystery boom might have been around 600 miles wide and would differ vastly from an SR-71's carpet. Tester's diagram also showed a triangle-shaped area that became wider as it traveled eastward, rather than an 80-mile carpet of two parallel lines that would follow the SR-71's trajectory.

Tester gave as a reference, the government's description of the flight to which he referred. But this publication gave vastly different information than Tester claimed it did.

Tester's report was very, very strange for a number of additional reasons:

What Tester presented as the start and arrival points for his SR-71 completely differ from those in his referenced report. The actual report states that the SR-71 took off from Beale AFB in CA. (This is near Marysville, CA.) Tester shows that the SR-71 took off from Galesburg, IL. This is a huge difference. There is a small airport near Galesburg, not military and not where a SR-71 could even think of taking off. The actual report states that the SR-71 landed at Griffiss AFB in New York (This is near Rome, NY.) Tester's diagram in his map does not even have any points near Griffiss AFB, the whole triangle is way south of Griffiss and it shows a boom carpet that is nothing like an actual plane carpet–it is a completely different shape and the wrong size. Many additional things differed from what he claimed the report said and what it did.

He made a few sarcastic remarks about me on an Internet site, but I could certainly find a lot wrong in his article.

One thing that is remarkable about the figure Tester presented as the boom of the SR-71 is that it does not show this boom. What it actually shows is the area of the boom, I am investigating.

Thus, this boom could also supply hard evidence for the UFO reality. It was truly unusual not only for its size, but because it has never been explained.

I also wondered why my parents had the strange mental reaction to it and wondered if others did also.

Not only was there an unusual sound, but beginning around 9:00 p.m. on October 11, police switchboards were swamped with UFO reports and the sightings continued over the next weeks. There's no evidence this wave of sightings was caused by media coverage of the unusual activity. The sightings weren't reported until a day or two after October 11 and accounts appeared even later in weekly and monthly media such as magazines. These reports did not seem to fit the pattern of a military test, where possibly a test cloud might be dispersed high in the sky and over a wide area. The UFO's reported seemed to be localized. Not only UFOs were reported, but also abductions. Right at the time of the sound, the Pascagoula Abduction, considered one of the world's most credible abduction cases, took place in Mississippi on October 11, 1973, at about 9:00 p.m. The two witnesses, Charles Hickson and Calvin Parker, began their report to the sheriff's office by saying they had seen a strange object land while they were fishing.

My neighbor's sightings

Below are some of the interesting reports that we obtained in the OJS survey. I also published the information in the *MUFON UFO JR*. These sightings were all in the location of or near to our family farm.

Orange Disk

This sighting was made on Bale Kenyon Road by the Orange Road intersection, north of Columbus, by a woman and her husband. It was on the day of the full moon (August 26, 1980, at around 10:00 pm) and they saw the full moon at the same time as the object. They were driving down Orange Road and spotted a large round, bright, orange object in the sky. It never moved. They estimated the object to be four times the apparent diameter of the full moon. They did not see any other lights. They drove along watching it and then stopped at their house on Bale Kenyon and went in. They looked at the object out of the house window a few times; it was still hovering there and did not move. They eventually went to bed after watching it hover in the same place for about an hour. They, at first, began to tell neighbors about their sighting, but no one was interested. Both people are well educated and own an engineering company.

Green Blimp

This sighting took place on the Africa Road, just north of where I-71 crosses it, north of Columbus. The witnesses were a woman and her husband, who watched between 1 and 3 am.

She was looking out the bedroom window and saw a large close object that resembled a blimp. However, this object glowed a solid green and hovered over the freeway intersection, not far from their house. They thought it was about the same color as a traffic light and glowed all over. They watched it for about 15 minutes and then went back to bed. They approximated its apparent size to have been about 6 times the diameter of the moon.

She mentioned that she had saved a newspaper clipping and searched for it. Unfortunately, the clipping wasn't dated. It reported "Officer spots 'blimp' in Westerville." It said that a UFO described as a blimp with flashing red lights was reported by the Westerville police about 12:30 Friday. The police sergeant who saw it said that he could not identify it with anything he knew. It was flying south and appeared to be following I-71. The police said they had received about six calls about it. They said the object was soundless.

I contacted the policeman who was interviewed. He said that it wasn't a UFO. I asked him how he knew this and he refused to talk about it anymore. The Goodyear blimp often follows I-71 down from Akron. However, people are familiar with it and know that it takes this route.

The witnesses all said that it was storming that night. This would not be a good time to fly the blimp: (1) There are power lines in the area and it's not a good idea to fly low at dark, (2) They are not supposed to fly during a storm and (3) Blimps do not normally glow all over.

Report from a retired army colonel and a nurse

This sighting was also reported in the newspaper mentioned earlier. It was neighbor's sighting of a black object that he believed was around 125 feet from him. On July 30, 1984, the retired army colonel reported the sighting to the police because, on July 27, a Russian rocket had fallen from space and he thought the object he had seen might have been falling space debris. Both witnesses (the other witness was a nurse) described a streak-shape having a west or northwest trajectory. It appeared several times larger in apparent diameter than the moon, They both thought the object might have come down just over a hillside from them. I checked with the neighbors, who owned this property, but no one had noticed a disturbance. A check with the power company showed no disturbance, there was no record of falling space debris and no one knew of anyone shooting rockets or firecrackers at that time. The people lived near the reservoir close to two airports and were familiar with landing lights, ultra-light aircraft, balloons, meteors and astronomical objects and did not believe they had seen a conventional object. In the newspaper article the nurse said that it was not a UFO. But when I interviewed her, it appeared that she saw the same thing that he saw, she just interpreted it as something that she did not understand. The weather had been clear.

Very large, round object

In order to gather additional information, I asked other neighbors and discovered several other possible sightings. Another had taken place approximately 0.4 miles to the southeast of the location of the previous sighting on a Tuesday in April 1984. The witness, a retired accountant said, "I saw a red flashing light in the sky about the time some trees cut out my view, so I kept driving and then I saw it again. It was a very large, round object. It appeared overhead in the sky about treetop high with amber lights all around it and the rest of it was quite red all over. It kept coming closer, so I stopped the car and turned off the radio and just looked at it because I was frightened and thought that it was going to land in the road in front of me."

She said that it was traveling very slowly and, all at once, it disappeared. Judging by the trees behind the object, she believed it had descended to 20 feet elevation and disappeared when it was around 80 feet away from her. The object was a sphere with amber rays projecting from lights around its periphery and it appeared to be approximately 10 times the moon's apparent diameter. She kept watching for it as she drove home and, upon arrival, dashed into the house. She continues to feel creepy when she drives by the area at night. However, she did not tell anyone about the observation, because her husband had told her not to talk about it. (Several years later when I casually asked her again about this sighting, she said she had seen beings inside the object.)

Independent Witnesses–one an aeronautical engineering students

The first sighting took place on Powell Road, where it intersects I-71, north of Columbus. A woman who saw it when she was in high school, around 1976 reported it to me. She was lying in bed and looked out a window to see a glowing object. She first thought of the moon, but it looked almond- or eye-shaped and was traveling to the south. She called for her parents and then hid under the bed. The next day she asked around to see if anyone else had seen it.

It turned out that a neighbor had. I took his report. He was walking into the house thinking how dark it was when he noticed what he, at first, thought to be a plane. However, its lighting looked different and there were no sounds when it passed over. It hovered over nearby woods and then descended behind them, giving off a glowing light. It then ascended again and hovered for a few minutes. He became scared and his heart began to pound.

The bottom part of it seemed to rotate while the top was stationary. It then moved over the freeway and beyond the trees. Its movements had been crisp. It turned at right angles rather than the normal curves an airplane makes. He said, "The movements...were crisp, but quiet...." He said that it moved in straight lines and right angles as he watched it for five minutes. It was two to three times the apparent diameter of the full moon. He did not examine the area where it came down for ground traces. He said it took the scared feeling several days to wear off.

He was an aeronautical engineering student in his last year of study, so he was quite familiar with the sight and sound of aircraft. He said that once a helicopter had landed in the yard by his house and he could hear that from some distance away, so he was familiar with close-up sightings of craft.

This sighting was several miles down the same freeway as the green blimp sighting; however, because of not having good dates, it is unknown if these sightings might have been of the same object.

Spinning orange object with pipes and lights:

Excerpted from the *MUFON JR.* (August 1986) by I. Scott. This observation occurred around the middle of July in 1985, approximately 1/3 mile northwest of the alfalfa burn (reported earlier). I found out about it from my sister, who said that she had heard J.M., a nine-year-old boy, talking about it. I called him and his parents and later interviewed him on tape.

J.M., camping with his family in a wood on their family farm, got up to go to an outbuilding after the others had gone to sleep. As he approached the small building, he glanced at what he thought was a helicopter in the distance. As the object approached from the southeast, he realized it was spherical.

It descended and stopped just over some trees (he estimated approximately 50-100 feet from him). He believed the sphere to have been around 20-30 feet in diameter.

Its outer portion was a rough white surface with scattered black areas. From spots along the outside flashed rays of white, green, red and blue light, in such a manner that the ray from each spot would be white, followed by green, red and then blue with "about a minute in between each one."

Some rays were directed downward, but he said they "did not touch the ground." The ray that came closest to him was around 10-20 feet away. He joked that the rays reminded him of the transporter beam in the Star Trek TV series and he feared he might be transported into the UFO if a ray illuminated him. He was scared and did not move, scream, or run. After he had watched the object for a while, two orange pipes moved out from one side between two of the spots where the rays were flashing. He did not know what the pipes were, but commented that perhaps they had something to do with the object "getting its direction." He added that he did not know how it did it, but at that time the sphere was spinning and the orange things weren't spinning. I asked him if they looked metallic and he said, "It did not look like metal or iron."

Then the UFO sort of swirled in a circle and flew to the southeast. When asked about noise he said, "I could not hear any because of all the crickets chirping."

Although J.M. wasn't sure, he estimated the sighting to have lasted for 5-10 minutes. As soon as the object left, he ran to his sleeping bag and hid. He was scared to awaken his parents and did not tell them about the sighting, because he "did not want them to think I'm crazy." He told several people afterwards, who confirmed that he had mentioned the sighting that summer and continues to describe the object in the same way.

He is intelligent, doing well in school and everyone that I asked said he is reliable. His story seemed consistent. Several times as I interviewed him I would repeat something to mislead him and he always corrected me. There is no record of advertising airplanes in this area. He is used to seeing helicopters and to being out-of-doors on this farm and has a good reputation.

One might think about some of these sightings that people saw blimps. Blimps frequently travel along the freeway from hangers around the Cleveland area to Columbus for occasions such as football games. However everyone knew about these blimps and these people had all lived in the neighborhood for a number of years.

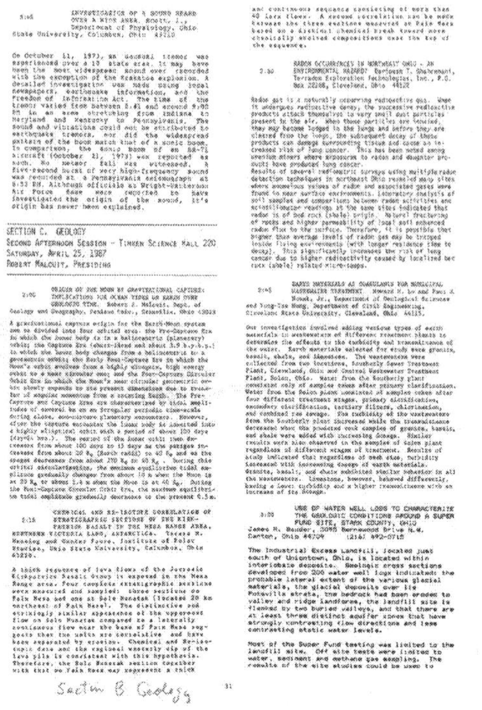

Figure 1: A strange booming sound was audible over a widespread area of the country on October 11, 1973, at around 9:00 pm. My investigation of this mysterious sound was accepted by peer review; "Investigation of a sound heard over a wide area," and was published in the scientific journal, OJS. State of Ohio seismologist, Mike Hansen Ph.D., helped me investigate and analyze the events. With the exception of the Krakatoa volcanic eruption of 1883, the 1973 boom could be the most widespread audible sound on record. Associated with this phenomenon was a spectacular increase in UFO sightings and even entity encounters, such as the Pascagoula Abduction, which occurred simultaneously with the sound.

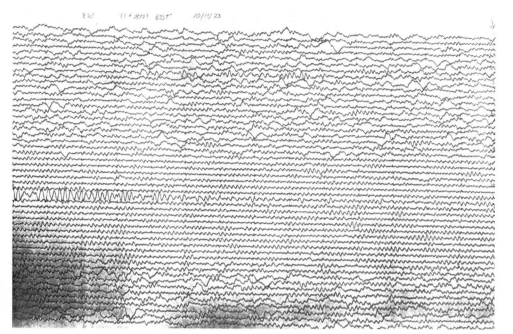

Figure 2: Shown is one of the seismograph recordings we examined in studying the mysterious October 11, 1973, sound. This recording shows the motion of the ground at 11 am EST on October 11, 1973. This event remains unexplained.

******

CHAPTER EIGHT: POSSIBLE PSYCHIC PHENOMENA AND DREAMS

What is going on?

Some people report extensive experiences with UFOs and even entities. Sometimes this is discovered under hypnosis, but at other times the events are remembered consciously. It can involve aliens, contacts, communication, mental telepathy, repeat sightings, abduction, trips into space and to other planets, sperm and egg involvement, feelings of being selected for something, psychic phenomena, being on board a space ship and similar events. These are memories and feelings of which they are conscious.

People are very interested in these events because they may represent humanity's communication with other life forms or possibly with the future.

My sister and I have all the markers of some of these facets and the UFOlogists that investigated us, thought that we may have been abducted, or been contacted. But we do not have these types of conscious memories and do not seem to have the many feelings about the subject that are often reported.

Many people also ask how such UFO phenomena affects you. I have no idea about this either. This is because it may have begun very early in my life, when my personality and even consciousness were forming. It is not something that happened after my mental characteristics had already formed, so that I could detect a change before and after an episode.

Thus, it is unknown why we would have so many markers, but not what is considered by some to be the main event. Perhaps other things besides abduction or contact can occur, but they are too advanced for us to understand–maybe even abductions are a form of screen memory for something else. Or perhaps also nothing else happened.

In the case of Betty Andreasson, the aliens told her that certain things had been locked in her mind and she was instructed to forget them and her experience until a certain time. Perhaps this has happened to us also and maybe we have something in our minds but need some particular stimulus to open it up.

But one important question is; if other beings were communicating with us, why would it be in ways that are often hidden from our consciousness, rather than directly? Why would people need to unlock it?

Although due to my scientific training, I am very cautious about exploring this sort of thing, I think I have some trace of a mental connection with UFO phenomena. It is very subliminal and not something of which I am directly conscious.

There were various events that caused me at least to wonder if I had some form of subconscious interaction with the phenomena.

From my earliest childhood, perhaps starting at around age three, I began having horrible nightmares about flying objects in the sky and this was years before I had ever heard of UFOs. I remember from when I was about three years old, a dream about two red spheres that chased me up a neighbor's driveway. In these dreams, I was probably the most terrified I have ever been in my life and I have experienced some terrifying things, such as being in a riot with live gunfire, coming within two minutes of dying during an allergic reaction and similar events.

When I finally did find out about UFO phenomena, it was a huge relief because then I at least had some idea of what terrified me. I stopped having a very diffuse terror that I had no idea of what caused it–now I had a name for it and could sort of compartmentalize it. I do not know what caused the dreams–it was definitely not from the media at that age.

In looking back, I think some kind of mind control might have been involved in our experiences. For example, in my earliest experiences, I awakened from sleep during a close encounter, but do not know of any reason why I woke up.

In even the first sighting of the object in our bedroom, we did not seem to react as we should have.

We have no idea how the object entered our room or why we woke up at the same time. I think we should have been terrified when we first became aware of it, but we were not. Instead we were curious (although maybe this would be the natural reaction). For some reason neither of us said anything, we just watched it with interest. Later, we both became terrified at the same time and ran shrieking from the room. It was almost as if something could turn on and off our emotions.

In my second experience, with the orange object in the 1950s, I again awakened, immediately looked to the north and saw the object approaching. I do not recall any reason why I woke up. This was also strange. I do not remember exactly when I became terrified, but something happened when it was directly above me. At that time, the dogs in the neighborhood suddenly began to howl and our dog sounded as if she were jumping all over the kitchen, although she would not have been able to see anything.

I think we may have had missing time during several of these sightings, such as when we both awakened in our room with the object there. At the time, we were unaware of the possibility of having missing time during these events. Our memories seemed to be continuous with no gaps.

At the time of our Massachusetts sighting, we were unaware of UFOs and simply thinking about taking a vacation. There were many mysterious elements during this sighting, such as the lights we saw in the car, although we each saw a different light at a different time. The objects, of course, were mysterious, but so were other parts of the event. The crazy man who asked me what I was looking at, twice and then chased us seemed very mysterious. Our driving to the vicinity of the Hill sighting was a bit odd, because although we had heard of it, we did not even know what state it was in. Our both forgetting our watches seemed a little strange: I am a clock-watcher, always have a watch and would be careful to take one during a trip. The fact that the two men who traveled with me were unable to contact me again, also seemed strange because they knew who we were and where Sue was staying.

In the Massachusetts events, I did not realize I was confused about several things and had gaps in my memory until I read my sister's write-up and realized that my brain had missed several things, but maybe my sister simply paid more attention to the UFO.

Obviously the poltergeist experience was frightful but so were my emotions. These were very definitely wrong. I was really terrified, but I kept going back to sleep. This is an extremely inappropriate response to possible danger and very unnatural. I wondered if my mind or emotions were being controlled.

At that time I did not know anything about poltergeist phenomena or that it might be associated with UFOs. I thought that either I had gone crazy or the UFO had done something to my mind. I had high security clearances and was tremendously worried about losing my job, if I had some sort of mental problem. I have read more about it now and realize that it can be associated with the UFO experience.

In the OSU sighting, I had begun with a sudden feeling of terror that came upon me for no reason, several months before the sighting. I was afraid to go outside, hid under trees and did not want to get very far from the house. This caused me to finally contact UFO agencies to make reports.

It seemed quite unbelievable that I would have a sighting at work on the day I began to fill out the CUFOS forms.

Then in the same time frame, many neighbors and relatives also began to have sightings and the large burn appeared on the family farm. And at the same time, similar events happened in Indiana, near my sister's family.

These are all just suggestions that something seemed odd, but maybe they are all just coincidence.

Another oddity, although this also might be subjective, is that our childhood sightings seemed in some ways to be analogous to or even some form of rehearsal or a prescience of our later sightings.

For one, my sister and I both witnessed the bedroom and the Massachusetts sightings. The Massachusetts event in some ways reminded me of our earlier bedroom sighting. Both events took place around 9-11 pm. Sue noticed both objects before I did. I seem to have the image of the object in the bedroom sighting as being elongated, like a throat lozenge, rather than a ball. It reminded me of the shape of the Massachusetts object. (Sometimes I have had dreams about an airplane that would get larger when further away and smaller as it approached–the opposite of parallax). I associated the bedroom sighting with the fourth of July (no one on the family farm set off fireworks or anything) and in our Massachusetts experience; we had planned our trip for the fourth, but waited a week because of circumstances. Our first sighting might have been about twenty years earlier.

In both sightings, the objects showed geometric or patterned behavior. For example, our sighting in our bedroom began with the object taking a random path and then changing its flight trajectory into a circling pattern as it circled the chandelier. This might be somewhat like our Massachusetts sighting in which the object seemingly followed a somewhat random path along a freeway, but later circled the airport and flashed its light in a regular pattern when it did so. The blinking of the windows was also patterned when we saw it closely.

We seemed to have some of the same responses when both objects circled. When the bedroom object circled, we both became terrified and ran screaming from the room. While the Massachusetts object circled our car chase took place, which was very frightening. Both circling seemed a bit patterned. The one circling the chandelier must have received the energy to rise to the ceiling, speed up and make quite a few exact circles, from somewhere. The Massachusetts object circled also in exact circles and in a very patterned way with a precisely ordered blinking and speed sequence. I thought we might have been in danger during the bedroom circling and we very definitely were during the Massachusetts circling. In both instances, the objects circled a prominent environmental feature–the chandelier and the airport. I sort of wondered if the circling had some sort of meaning or could be a symbol, but would have no idea of what. In addition, we seemed to see different things at some points in these sightings. My sister just watched the object circle the chandelier, but I thought it sort of exploded. We also seemed to not see the same thing, during parts of our Massachusetts sighting,

Even my very first dream that I recall from when I was very young was of two red spherical objects chasing me and my last sighting was of two red spheres. Both were on our farm. And I did photograph two red spheres.

Many people that have later events seem to have childhood sightings and I wondered if there is any connection between the childhood and adult events. In ours, the Massachusetts event did remind me in some ways of our childhood sighting. I have not found any reports of a childhood sighting that resembles a later one and have no idea of what this could mean. Jenny Randles had said that the childhood experiences might be "helping to prepare the youngster for the more traumatic things to come in later life. Indeed that may well be another part of their purpose." Perhaps this has something to do with that.

Intelligent UFO behavior, psychic phenomena and dreams

Some scientists have studied intelligent and reactive UFO behavior under experimental conditions. For example physicist, Dr. Harley Rutledge, who was well trained in science. He received his PhD in solid-state physics at the University of Missouri. He later took the position of Professor and Chairman of the Physics Department at Southeast Missouri State University. He was Department Chairman from 1964 to 1982 and then retired from teaching in 1992.

He studied UFO behavior, in much the same way as behaviorists examine animal behavior. He wrote in a letter to me, "In adducing evidence to my book regarding intelligent, reactive behavior by UFOs, I related some of my more recent experiences and appended sightings by military pilots."[119]

Because there was a UFO wave taking place (in 1973 the same year that I mentioned in regard to the UFO wave in the Big Bang articles), he set up a study area with scientists and instrumentation, to be described in the next chapter.

Throughout his book, describing his study, *Project Identification: The First Scientific Field Study of UFO Phenomena*, he gave many instances of possible communication between him, his group of scientists and UFO phenomena.[120]

He also remarked about the many forms of interaction between his scientists and UFO phenomena and ways the UFOs communicated with the researchers. After setting up his viewing stations in the area, he said that:

To summarize the field study, we observed UFO reactions such as lights that (a) turned OFF and/or ON, (b) moved or shot away, (c) avoided our viewing stations by turning through angles up to 180 degrees, (d) disappeared behind trees. The types and number (in parenthesis) of stimuli for the 32 apparent reactions to our observers are: vehicles or aircraft (5), pointing fingers or aiming flashlights, binoculars, telescopes, or cameras (16)), our voices (2), our radio signal (3), telepathy (2) and an awareness by the UFO intelligence of being seen (4).[121]

He mentioned telepathy here and had added: "Surely they have a sense of humor. I know that they played "games" with us in the field...even when near my home. And many people have observed and written about this.

We've all heard stories and rumors of aircraft disappearing, or temporarily being disabled, or being toyed with in the presence of a UFO."[122]

He mentioned a case when a light moved across the sky and he and another observer checked it for undulation. As soon as they terminated their test, the light undulated.

He added that having observed 28 UFO reactions, he believed that these reactions were not all mere coincidences.

Rutledge's observation that the objects seemed to put on a display, or were staged, has been reported before. For example in *Encounter at Buff Ledge* this same type of behavior was reported.

Their sighting began with the witness watching an object described as cigar-shaped, white and incandescent as if glowing by its own light. The object halted and three bright lights emerged from below near its right end. This trio of small UFOs, maneuvered about the western sky over about a 30-degree area and executed zigzag patterns, fluttering motions, upward spirals, descents like falling leaves and stop and go activity. He described the actions as antics and said they were generally performed in unison and close formation.

After around five minutes of this aerial display, the threesome formed a horizontal triangle. Later he said that it seemed like it was stalking them.

My sister and I may have experienced something like a display in our Massachusetts sighting also. For example, when our object circled the airport it may have been putting on a display, such as its circling and blinking pattern, as mentioned before. We left as it was circling and during this time, the truck driver chased us. When we returned it continued its circling.

Also during our bedroom sighting, the object changed its trajectory to circling the lamp. After a while it traveled in a precise, geometric spiral under the chandelier.

Many others have commented on the instructiveness of the UFO phenomenon and even its tendency to play games with people.

A number of others have studied psychic or poltergeist activity. My sister and I may have experienced some of this and received comments from several people who have had their own experiences of, or made an intensive study of such phenomenon.

For example in relation to poltergeist phenomenon and UFOs, Kathleen Marden told me, "Poltergeist activity is often reported in abduction cases hours after the event occurred. As you probably know, electromagnetic anomalies are also common." I had been really glad to find out that poltergeist activity might be related to UFO sightings, or I would still be worried about whether I had some kind of mental disorder. In an interview Marden had said, that "68% have experienced electromagnetic anomalies in their homes immediately after an incident."[123]

I wondered whether I might have experienced some sort of electromagnetic anomaly after the Massachusetts sighting because of my electrical alarm clock going off and possibly with the power failure after the OSU airport sighting.

Such information suggests that a UFO sighting psychic and UFO might be the tip of the iceberg for something else going on, for example a UFO event may last longer than the sighting.

In addition, the electromagnetic anomalies might make me wonder if any of these could relate to our unusual number of lightning events.

However in thinking about this technically, one would wonder exactly how to tell UFO from psychic phenomena. For example, if one sees an orb, it might be considered psychic. But if the orb is larger it might be viewed as a UFO.

Psychic and UFO phenomena might both have the same cause and just manifest differently.

Basically psychic and UFO events could even be defined as the same thing. Both are simply events that seem impossible in our normal experience, such as a levitating glowing fifteen-foot long object–Which would it be?

Also, our events did not seem tied to anything happening in our environment. They seemed random, completely unpredictable and occurred with no known stimuli.

Another example of possible poltergeist activity occurred when Whitley Strieber, interviewed me on May 16, 2017, on his Unknown country/Dreamland show.

He is the author of many bestselling books. Both the hardcover and paperback editions of *Communion* reached the number one position on The *New York Times* Best Seller list (non-fiction), with more than 2 million copies sold. He is also a bestselling author of: *The Wolfen* and *The Hunger,* an advocate of alternative concepts; has his Unknown Country Web site; and his Internet podcast, Dreamland.

During my interview, we kept receiving odd sounds during the recording. He commented on these and there were so many that he turned off the recording to re-record several times.

In his many books, he described meeting entities, which he called visitors and these became a large part of his life with their continuing presence, as described in his book, *Communion.* [124]

These visitors seem to show up in his life quite often. For example a posting in Paranormal UK Radio, said:

Strange Sounds Captured During Whitley Strieber Interview

Here at Unknown Origins Radio we are no strangers to having strange things happen during some of our interviews and this week was no exception.

During Wednesday's show with guest Whitley Strieber, we had two incidents where strange, unexplained sounds were heard during the broadcast that could not be accounted for at the time.

This first sound was captured right at the beginning of the broadcast while Mark was introducing the show.

This second sound was recorded later in the program while Whitley was talking about famed researcher Budd Hopkins. This unexplained growl was heard during the show and we do not know where it emanated from.

We are in no way claiming these sounds are paranormal, only that they are unusual and, so far, unexplained.[125]

Maybe they showed up in my life also, because this also happened during my interview with him. I made notes about it and may haves taped a sound:

Strieber says he sees beings often. In his interview and in the previous interview I had with someone else, there was a lot of noise in the connections. He and the other interviewers told me they thought it was from the government. During his interview with me there were sounds that sounded like something banging on the phone or something. He stopped taping the interview several times to get the sounds out. He sounded as if he thought it was from the government. I thought I was just moving the phone around and causing it, so I held the phone still and still heard it. At the end there were so many sounds they really interfered with things.

In my previous interview right before his, strange sounds had showed up also. I made notes about this.

The sounds seemed more intense whenever I mentioned the government. And when I said that maybe high people in the government might be controlled by UFO phenomena, the sounds seemed to go wild.

Could this have been some kind of poltergeist activity? Also there seemed to be some kind of trouble with the phone or the e-mail. In one instance, think I received an e-mail, but the interviewer did not send it. Then the e-mail sort of disappeared. Also, since my book came out several people have told me that they received e-mails from me, but they disappeared. In one case, I did not write an e-mail, so I do not know why the person saw one from me that disappeared. In another case, someone called to say that his message from me disappeared. I had sent a message, but had no idea why it would disappear. Probably these are just coincidences.

Although UFOs have been presented as spacecraft from other worlds looking us over, many scientific results would lead to a different conclusion. A careful scientific study by Dr. Harley Rutledge and others indicate that there exists some form of mental contact between the phenomena and people. Although some UFOs may be true spacecraft, it appears that the entire story is much more complex than this.

Several further comments about this include the subject of anthropomorphism. This is the attribution of human traits, emotions, or intentions to non-human entities. Its importance is drilled into those studying animal behavior. It is considered an innate tendency of human psychology. This would apply not only to animal behavior, but to UFO, poltergeist and other phenomena. Moreover, UFO phenomenon might be subject to a kind of Star Trek Prime Directive, allowing it to interact with us only according to specific regulations. Much UFO phenomena do not behave in what we would consider as reasonable ways and we tend to ignore it. But there is no reason to throw out the observations no matter how ridiculous they seem, because the phenomena may just not be us and its motives and behavior may be entirely different.

Many people have reported connections and even communication with UFO phenomena. Many years ago, people claimed to be in contact with space men, who took them on trips aboard their flying saucers. Although these are generally considered hoaxes by the reporters, one wonders if something or someone is sometimes feeding some of them these ideas.

Another comment is that since I cannot be hypnotized, several investigators have suggested other ways to explore this subject and one idea is to examine my dreams. The only dreams that I trust though are those I had before I knew anything about UFO phenomena. The media could have influenced the rest. Some of these dreams are listed in Appendix 1.

Much further study of UFO interactivity is needed and this may be possible through scientific methodology as shown by Rutledge's work.

What's in the story–mind control, telepathy:

In analyzing my own experience, it appeared to me that a UFO sighting might be just the tip of the iceberg for something else happening. For example, our Massachusetts event began around 10-11 pm on July the 13th with a UFO sighting. Strange things continued to happen after this, for on Sunday for some reason the men who traveled with me were unable to contact me. And even early on the 15th, I was still having a psychic experience. This made me think that something was happening, that can manifest as either a UFO sighting or a psychic event. It might have been going on for three days.

In the same way, in December 1983, I became terrified. I knew this fear was of UFOs, but I had no idea what caused it. It did not seem to be caused by something in my everyday life. Then in February, I had a sighting and this included other witnesses. But I continued to have sightings until August of 1984. And there seemed to be a sort of flap around my neighborhood and even in my family at that time.

Thus, I think that some type of undercurrent might have been occurring in my brain during those time periods. But I was not conscious of anything except the UFO sightings, the psychic events and the fear.

It also seemed that whatever it was, it could affect the emotions, without going through my conscious mind. Thus, it seemed to possibly be in some very deep center with little contact with the conscious part of my brain, but able to influence my emotions. And the emotions seemed to come from a deeper brain complex than my consciousness. Anyway, it seemed that something could turn on my emotions, without going through my consciousness, although one would think that consciousness of something would come before emotion.

Also this might be linked to my first feelings when I saw objects in the sky in my dreams and experienced a very diffuse terror, but had no idea of the cause. Later when I found out about and had a name for the objects, UFOs, I seemed to be able to sort of put these feelings into a bag, named UFO and seal them off a little. But possibly the initial diffuse feeling was related to some form of event that encompassed a lot more than just a sighting of an object.

Hence it seemed that something was going on that could affect me and this was quite powerful because it nearly resulted in my death.

And there exists the chilling possibility that it might be able to affect my behavior without, or to bypass, my consciousness.

Perhaps people who recall abduction and similar events are also affected by something underlying that is giving them the idea of abduction, for example, but something else might really be happening.

This, in a way, makes me think of biological phenomena, Zombie ants, where are supposedly simple organism, a fungus, can control the behavior of an intelligent organism, an ant, as described in the journal, *Public Library of Science (PLOS)*:

What's in the Story?

You wake up and stretch. You feel extra tired, but your sisters are already up. You follow them along a trail through the forest, but you fall behind.

Slowing, you look for a short cut. You walk off the trail and up the nearest plant stalk. You do not remember why you chose this plant, but you keep going until you crawl under a cool leaf. Suddenly, you find you are biting the leaf. That's when you realize you are not in control of your body.

Ant fungus

The leaf crunches in your mouth. You try to pull away, but can't. You are paralyzed. Not a muscle moves. Your vision blurs. A small pressure in your head is the last thing you feel before you black out.

This is not the plot of a new horror movie, but potential last moments of an ant infected with a deadly pathogen. In the *PLOS ONE* article, "Long-Term Disease Dynamics for a Specialized Parasite of Ant Societies: A Field Study," researchers explore the Ophiocordycep fungus and the 'zombifiying' threat it poses to its ant host. These researchers learn about how and when the fungus spreads and how ants might avoid turning into zombies.

The Spread of Spores

As you walk through the forest, you see many dead ant bodies. The bodies look twisted and a huge mushroom stalk shoots right out of each head. This is how the fungus spreads from ant to ant. It grows out of the ant, killing it in the process. The fungus then releases spores to infect the next wave of ants, turning them into zombies. How does this fungus infect ants? Let's take a look at the ants that carry the fungus. We call them the host.

The Host: Carpenter Ants

This species of carpenter ant (*Camponotus rufipes*) lives in South America and is primarily active at night. These ants build very distinctive nests on the forest floor.... The fungus starts life as a spore falling down onto an ant. The spore gets inside the ant's body and grows, gradually taking over its ant host. The ant stops doing normal tasks and starts to act for the benefit of the fungus.

One day the zombie ant leaves the nest in search of a place the fungus can grow. The ant will climb up above the forest floor and bite down on the underside of a leaf in just the right conditions. There, the ant dies. But that is not the end of this story. Firmly attached to the leaf through the ant's bite, the fungus again starts to grow. A long stalk bursts out of the ant's head and continues to develop until it forms an ascoma. This is the fungus fruit, which releases new spores to transform other ants into zombies.[126]

In other words, it is possible for a fungus to control such a complex organism as an ant, even to the point of having it select a leaf from a particular plant and then bite the leaf and die. Thus, although events such as UFO mental interactions are viewed as "supernatural," a form of it can be found in very prosaic biological organisms. In this case the ant made seemingly conscious decisions about where to go and what to do. However, they were not its decisions, but the ant would not know that.

The "supernatural" is not something that floats around affecting people, or just their imagination; it may actually just be everything that the brain does not understand, but something that can be explored, which then allows it to become natural.

UFO phenomena, of course, are much more complex than a fungus, but the ant information does show that something can control a being's conscious behavior even to the point of killing it.

In thinking about this as related to UFO phenomena, it may be even more terrifying than a physical invasion, because it may affect some deep centers of the brain. And possibly exert control over behavior in a way that bypasses consciousness.

Rutledge's examination through scientific instrumentation and through scientifically trained witnesses indicates also that mental interaction may exist between UFO phenomena and people.

John Keel also mentioned the mental aspects of the phenomena. From his perspective the UFO mystery is simply a modern version of the same "game" that he called the Ultra-terrestrials have been playing on humanity since time immemorial. As to what these entities are trying to achieve, he speculated that they might operate as part of a "subtle cosmological system of control that has been in effect since the beginning of humanity."[127]

This view mirrors that of the French computer scientist and UFO researcher Jacques Vallée, who had hypothesized that the UFO phenomenon is "a control system for human consciousness."

Perhaps I experienced something like this in having more unusual experiences than normal. For example, Leo Sprinkle mentioned that, "'invisible' UFOLK could create unusual events in the lives of UFO contactees, bringing attention to their experiences." Betty Andreasson expressed the same idea about her experiences, "A number of people afterwards described having some pretty interesting and unusual experiences, though the one who really stands out in my memory was Betty Andreasson Luca." She also gave an explanation for this, "Facing new and unusual experiences enhances our spiritual development. Why and what for, such contact takes place, may open a door to greater knowledge of the hidden world that surrounds us."[128]

Perhaps such seeming coincidences have some kind of a purpose, such as bringing attention to something going on in people's minds that they are not necessarily conscious of.

In my own experience, it appeared to me that there was possible interaction with UFO phenomenon, but this was subliminal. Something seemed to be happening somewhere in my brain that had very little contact with my consciousness. One trace of this seemed to be fear, but I really did not know what the fear was caused by. It seemed to affect my emotions–almost as if it could turn on or off whatever emotion it wanted to manipulate, as people do in brain electrode experiments in animals.

Although I was not directly conscious of it, it may have affected my motivation and drive. Such activity could have huge ramifications in all forms of human behavior and be especially dangerous when we can destroy most of our world with atomic and biological weapons. For example, why are we spending trillions of dollars developing our overkill, when each person can be killed only once? Why are "logical" scientists working on this? What if high people in the world's governments are under this influence? What did it mean when the man asked me what I was looking at, turned to the opposite direction twice and then gave me what appeared to be the crazy sign? Why did he then do something dangerous that could have killed us? Could this be some form of a warning about something or just happenstance? Why does the government debunk this phenomenon, when there is much evidence that could be examined?

By analyzing my own experience without reference to the many theories floating around, it appears that my conscious mind does not seem to have any (or very little) connection to UFO phenomena, because nothing seems to be fermenting to the surface. But this evidence suggests that something might be buried somewhere in parts of my mind that I am not in conscious contact with.

Thus on an intellectual level, all of this may be even more terrifying than a close encounter, abduction, or even invasion, because the phenomena may affect some buried centers of the brain, or even have control over one's behavior without the person knowing it.

For example, I have always been interested in astronomy ever since I could remember. I have no idea why–no one in my family has any even slightly similar interests. Could this have anything to do with such early experiences?

This, if it were possible, it would certainly cause one to have a lot of questions. For one, am I being controlled? How much of me is me and what part of my behavior is that of something else? Is my behavior under my will? Are other people being controlled? The media shows, such as "War of the Worlds," show aliens in a physical attack, but what if they could be doing something to us mentally? Could they be taking something from us that we do not even know about? Did this begin recently, such as in 1947 with Kenneth Arnold, or has it been going on for a long time? Does the government refuse to recognize UFO phenomena because it is being controlled? Is our reality real, or are we a part of a simulation? The best thinkers have tried to figure this out, unsuccessfully.

How many people could this affect? Would it just be those who report abductions, contacts and that kind of happening, or could it be highly-placed people in the government, or anyone, or even everyone?

What is the effect of this phenomenon on humanity in general? Could we be living in a Matrix/simulation kind of environment? Am I the ant in the ant/fungus relationship? These topics could be very important to us and should be examined.

******

CHAPTER NINE: "HARD EVIDENCE" AND WHAT IT MEANS

Astronomers and scientists do see and report UFOs–sometimes many

As mentioned, "No professional astronomer in his right mind would be caught dead stating publicly that he'd seen a UFO or been abducted by aliens..."[129]

However, this idea that astronomers disdain and do not "believe" in UFO phenomena is seriously incorrect and belongs to the Alt or Fake fact domain. The fact is that not only have astronomers stated publically that they have seen a UFO, but the world's top astronomer (who discovered a planet) has stated publicly that he has not one, but several sightings.

This astronomer is Clyde W. Tombaugh (1906-1977), who discovered the planet Pluto in February 1930 at Lowell Observatory, Flagstaff, Arizona. He holds the distinction of being the only man in the twentieth century, to have discovered a planet. Mr. Tombaugh has published many articles and was a professor of Astronomy at New Mexico State University Research Center. (Although Pluto is no longer considered a planet, this was an amazing discovery).[130]

Also through his careful observation and reliable reporting, he is probably the preeminent astronomer to have reported seeing UFOs. On August 20, 1949, Tombaugh reported seeing several UFOs near Las Cruces, New Mexico. He described them as six to eight rectangular lights and stated, "I doubt that the phenomenon was any terrestrial reflection, because... nothing of the kind has ever appeared before or since... I was so unprepared for such a strange sight that I was really petrified with astonishment." Tombaugh later reported having seen three of the mysterious Green Fireballs, which suddenly appeared over New Mexico in late 1948 and continued at least through the early 1950s. These have also been under scientific study. In 1956 Tombaugh said about his various sightings: "I have seen three objects in the last seven years which defied any explanation of known phenomenon, such as Venus, atmospheric optic, meteors or planes. I am a professional, highly skilled, professional astronomer. In addition I have seen three green fireballs which were unusual in behavior from normal green fireballs...I think that several reputable scientists are being unscientific in refusing to entertain the possibility of extraterrestrial origin and nature."[131]

His observation has been described as seeing "something with square, glowing windows."[132]

And, "On August 20, 1949, he observed a UFO that appeared as a geometrically arranged group of six to eight rectangles of light, window-like in appearance and yellowish-green in color, which moved from northwest to southeast over Las Cruces, New Mexico."[133]

This report of six to eight square, glowing windows, reminded me of the seven squares of our Massachusetts sighting.

The idea that astronomers do not see UFOs has been repeated many, many times. But no matter how often it is repeated, these general ideas are flat-out wrong. Astronomers do see UFOs, indeed they see more than the average. In his survey of members of the American Astronomical Society, Dr. Hynek reported that there is a higher percentage of sightings among astronomers than among the public at large. Dr. Peter Sturrock in his questionnaire targeting members of the American Astronomical Society, printed in the 1994 *Journal of Scientific Exploration*, found that the reporting rate was greater than assumed for the average population. A Soviet survey published by the Soviet Academy of Sciences, reported a highly significant percentage of astronomers among the observers: "The Soviet numbers are clear: astronomers report UFOs at astronomical rates." [134]

Scientists have stated publically that they have seen UFOs. For example physicist Dr. Harley Rutledge, who was mentioned previously.

This scientist may hold the world record for UFO sightings. In a letter to me, he said that he was sensitive to the skepticism of those researchers who thought that any sighting is suspect and that multiple sightings by the same person (called "repeater phenomena") may even indicate a mental disorder. He noted that a debunking article in *Omni Magazine* said Rutledge should be in the *Guinness Book of World Records* for his high number of UFO sightings. He called it an insensitive, inaccurate and insipid little piece of writing.

Rutledge stated, "To bring you and *Omni*, up-to-date, the total has crept to 160 sightings. Several of the sightings in that total, I have never reported." Rutledge had much confirming evidence of this, such as other witnesses and the results of scientific instrumentation.[135]

Dr. Rutledge in another letter also described this phenomenon to me and the ridicule he experienced:

In his second book, [Philip] Klass, one of three members of the UFO Subcommittee of CSICOP (Committee for the Scientific Investigation of Claims of the Paranormal), abandoned the ball lightning guess. I was especially interested in his statement: "Experienced UFO investigators, even those who believe in extraterrestrial spaceships, are very suspicious of reports that come from 'repeaters'…a term applied to any person claiming to have seen more than two UFOs in a lifetime"…wow and I claim to have seen 160 UFOs! Oh, well, I will never submit a manuscript to Klass's publisher, Random House.[136]

And even though it has been said that scientists say that UFO phenomena does not exist, scientists not only report sightings, but conduct experiments on the subject. A scientific study by physicist Dr. Harley Rutledge who was mentioned previously (and a study by Battelle, SR-14, to be described) may be the best scientific UFO research ever done.

His *Project Identification* was the first UFO scientific field study able to observe the phenomena in real time. This study is unique because the team of scientists using scientific instrumentation, observed UFOs during the events, rather than after the fact. They could determine a UFO's velocity, distance, course, position and size. UFO interactivity, a little-studied aspect of the UFO phenomena, could also be examined under controlled conditions.

He set up stations where trained observers using scientific instruments to study UFO activity including RF spectrum analyzers, electromagnetic frequency analyzer, cameras, Questar telescopes, low-high frequency audio detectors, a galvanometer to measure variations in the Earth's gravitational field and additional equipment.

The team investigated 178 anomalous objects, logged 158 viewing station set-ups, watched the sky for 427 hours and recorded 157 sightings, of which 34 UFOs were Class A (the best sightings—ones that had physical properties that defied conventional explanation).

The scientists discovered numerous reasons why studying UFO phenomena is difficult. They often were unable to photograph such subjects as Class A UFOs because the UFOs would disappear, would appear when cameras could not be brought to bear on them, or would not show up on film after being photographed.

One aspect of the UFOs' behavior was particularly puzzling: When certain UFOs came within the range of measurement, they would move, change course, or halt. They recorded 30 occasions when the movements of the objects synchronized with the actions of the observers. Objects sometimes responded to observers who switched lights off and on, to verbal or radio messages, pointing or aiming, flashlight beams, aiming of cameras or telescopes—and even the scientists' thoughts. Rutledge interpreted this behavior to mean the UFOs were detecting the investigators' intentions, voices, or thinking.

He speculated that the objects were able to react to thoughts, or show a form of consciousness and seemed to have capabilities beyond that period's prevailing technology.

The scientists' most astonishing discovery was that the intelligence controlling UFOs was aware of their presence and that the UFOs may have purposely attracted their attention. The UFOs reacted to the human presence by turning lights off and on, by moving away and by changing course or brightness. The scientists even wondered if the UFO events were being staged for their benefit.

In addition to the physical study of UFO phenomena, he also analyzed interactivity, which might also be called behavior. Some objects seemed to mimic the appearance of known aircraft, while many others violated the laws of physics. A most startling discovery was that on at least 32 recorded occasions, the movement of the lights synchronized with the actions of the observers. The phenomena appeared to respond to a light being switched on and off and to verbal or radio messages.

This study answered numerous questions about the phenomena, such as why it is so difficult to take photographs of it.

It is a study that was able to use good scientific methodology to demonstrate that UFO phenomena not only exists, but also has a psychic aspect.

Rutledge ultimately concluded that UFO phenomena result from a non-human intelligence and stated that a possibility exists that a great deal of UFO activity is subliminal. The final sentence in his book was, "Possibly a great deal of UFO activity is subliminal–which if true, could have serious ramifications."

However, the public never seems to be able to find out about such scientific study, thus, UFO phenomena are today generally considered supernatural. It is usually presented as belonging to the superstitious or religious realm, such as in "believers" vs. "non-believers." Such "believers" are often viewed as people not understanding the mechanical elements of the human concept of reality and thus trusting forms of the supernatural or as having an unreal religious experience.

Scientists are presented as "believers" that UFOs do not exist. However, such believers– either that UFOs can exist or that they cannot exist–are really just the same. Both sides are based upon belief, not on empirical evidence that can be examined.

As another example suggesting logical explanations, some of Rutledge's findings would be described as something only "believers" could see because what they report is impossible.

But such recounts could go along also with my observation that UFOs might use laser light. For example, Rutledge described an instance in which a man encountered a landed disc. When the man stepped back, two paces the disc was invisible and he could see the trees behind it, but when he stepped forward two paces it became visible again. In other cases, one observer could see an object but another nearby person would be unable to see it.

In general people would interpret this as magic or the supernatural–as something that is impossible and, thus, conclude that UFOs do not exist. In reality, it sounds quite possible–using holography. For example, "If you get too close to a hologram, it will temporarily disappear—just move away from it. Also, if you've placed a lot of holograms close together, some may disappear."[137] This can be done using laser light.

Laser light can also be used to create volumetric display images that float in mid-air and can be viewed from any angle. A recent paper published in *Nature*, described a free-space volumetric display platform that is based on photophoretic optical trapping and can produce full-color, aerial volumetric images with 10-micron image points.[138] They used a laser beam to trap a particle and then could steer it around to move the particle and create the image.

Some UFOs might be this type of images. However, even more amazingly, lasers can also produce physical effects–they can create matter. One such method is called the Breit-Wheeler theory or process, which indicates a way to turn light into matter (the opposite of Einstein's equation $E = mc^2$). For example, in the laser-modified Breit-Wheeler processes, the electron-positron pairs are created when a laser beam collides with non-laser photons.[139] "The Breit-Wheeler process is the simplest way matter can be made from light and one of the purest demonstrations of $E = mc^2$."[140]

This could explain how some traces left by UFO phenomenon are made. Thus, we have the science now to explain some of the "supernatural" effects of UFO phenomena.

And basically all the "Supernatural" really is anyway is everything we do not understand. It is not some mysterious place where people go to see ghosts or monsters. When examined scientifically and as our science develops, the supernatural becomes prosaic.

Scientific proof that the UFO phenomena is real so why don't people know about it?

However, excellent scientific studies have not only been conducted on UFO phenomena, but proven in completely acceptable scientific studies that it exists. Our studies today are in the same league as those of Ignaz Philip Semmelweis with childbed fever–we have empirical evidence, but no theory, thus we do not accept the facts.

Battelle Memorial Institute conducted one such study showing the reality of UFO phenomenon and this, with the Rutledge study, has provided the best UFO examination ever done.

Respected throughout the world for its scientific expertise and reputation, Battelle is the world's largest non-profit independent research and development organization. Accomplishments by Battelle scientists range from the development of projects such as the Xerox process– that has revolutionized the entire world, Snopake correction fluid, the Universal Product Code and compact disc digital storage. It includes the fabrication of the uranium fuel rods for the first full-nuclear scale reactor, to participation in the Manhattan Project. It has managed or co-managed many of the atomic age's top national laboratories on behalf of the US Department of Energy, including the Lawrence Livermore, Oak Ridge and Brookhaven National Laboratories. During the Cold War, Battelle personnel were a who's who of expertise in numerous scientific fields, including metallurgy, nuclear physics and chemical and mechanical engineering. Moreover, the institute is adjacent to the main campus of OSU, one of the nation's largest universities, which allows its scientists to work closely with their counterparts at OSU.

Under the government Project Blue Book, Battelle scientists conducted an extensive study of UFO phenomena. The results of this massive statistical analysis were presented in a report, *Project Blue Book Special Report No. 14 (Analysis of Reports of Unidentified Flying Objects)*, also known as *SR-14*. Even today, *SR-14* represents the largest such study ever undertaken and reigns as perhaps the most significant collection of evidence that UFO phenomena represent something real.

It investigated two of the most prominent theories that have been used to disprove UFO phenomena: (1) UFO reports result from a lack of reliable information and witnesses and (2) UFOs are known but misidentified objects. Blue Book scientists at Battelle tested these two theories by analyzing sighting reports and data using rigorous scientific statistical methods, as described by Bruce Maccabee, PhD, in his 1979 work, *Historical Introduction to Project Blue Book Special Report #14*.[141] [142]

The first theory, that unexplained UFO sightings are caused by a lack of information or by inaccurate perceptions, suggests that when reliable observers and a large amount of information are available, the number of unexplained sightings will decrease. The results of the Blue Book study by Battelle scientists were the exact opposite of those expected. Based on 3,201 of the most reliable sightings (selected from approximately 7,200), the most reliable report category ("excellent") had a higher percentage (33.3 percent) of unknowns than the least reliable report category (16.6 percent). In addition, 38 percent of the "excellent" sightings were by military personnel, compared to approximately one-quarter of the sightings in the "poor" category. This large study therefore refuted the idea that UFO sightings result from a lack of reliable information and observers.

The second theory is that UFOs are really known but misidentified objects. If this were true, one would expect characteristics of UFOs generally to match those of conventional objects. For example, a certain percentage of conventional flying objects are aircraft with predictable lighting arrangements and a certain percentage are meteors; therefore, the frequencies of such characteristics among UFOs should correspond to these percentages. In the Battelle study, the frequencies of certain characteristics of UFOs and Identified Flying Objects (IFOs) were evaluated according to a standard statistical procedure used in scientific studies–the widely used "chi-square." In five of six categories there were significance levels of ($P< 01$), which mathematically falsifies this hypothesis. Thus the hypothesis that UFOs are misidentifications of conventional objects was disproved. Battelle scientists determined that by every available criterion, the characteristics of the UFOs differed from those of the IFOs, that better qualified observers reported sightings of longer durations and that when more information was available, it was more likely that a report would defy explanation.

In other words, by the standard statistical methodology used in scientific studies, some UFO phenomena very likely represent something real, despite the government's representation that *SR-14* found nothing.

Characteristics of the scientists who made sound scientific studies of UFO phenomena: Theory vs. Observation

This excellent study might also show the influence of such events as a possible UFO experience on scientists. It appears that scientists who may have had UFO experiences of their own have headed the best ever scientific studies. This likely would make them curious about what is really going on, rather than thinking it is all nonsense and toeing the government line.

Thus, it also shows the distinction between theory (or the influence of scientific authority figures) and empirical data.

The empirical data is that a Howard Cross is thought to have reported viewing a UFO over Battelle. The information is that on October 2, 1951, in Columbus, Ohio, Cross reported viewing a UFO. It appeared as a bright oval with a clipped tail and it flew straight and level before fading into the distance after one minute.[143] After uncovering this information and after discussions with Battelle employees, I think that this Howard Cross is the H. C. Cross, the Battelle physicist.

This Howard Cross is thought to have headed the then-secret Project Stork, under which the *SR-14* study was done.

Harley Rutledge, as mentioned, is also a scientist who did an excellent study of UFO phenomenon and had experiences of his own.

Scientific method, empirical evidence and fatal flaws

Scientists, in general, are presented as viewing the phenomena as either mistaken observations of prosaic events, hoaxes and with similar concepts, rather than having the idea that something actually exists.

The reason behind this is that there is no "hard evidence"–a captured UFO. "Hard evidence" is considered the only means to ascertain an event's reality.

However, certain other happenings would convince people that hard evidence probably existed. For example, it could be accepted socially if a "flying saucer" landed on the White House lawn and an alien came out to greet the president. It could be accepted scientifically, if for example, after a landing, people found a completely new element or substance.

But science does have many resources to use in investigations of UFOs and it does not have to use hard evidence or even have a theory. The scientific method can be used for investigating the unknown. In order to be termed scientific, a method of inquiry is normally based on empirical or measurable evidence subject to specific principles of reasoning. It consists of systematic observation, measurement, experiment and then the formulation, testing and modification of hypotheses. Observation is what science is founded upon. Observations are called empirical evidence. Ways to gain scientific evidence vary according to the field of inquiry, but its strength is generally based on the results of statistical analysis and of comparison to controls.

As an example of hard evidence, consider the idea that the sun rises in the east each day. But suppose you are in northern Norway. Yesterday you saw the sun rise in the south, but today it did not rise at all. You have first-hand hard evidence against this theory. However the strength of this observation depends upon other measurements. For example, if many see this, it might be used as hard evidence, but if only one person reports it, it is likely considered soft evidence. However, one good observation is all that is needed to refute a theory.

Even though there is no "hard evidence" that we know of now, such subjects can be explored by science. An example given below is disease.

Scientific acceptance of disease:

Disease has a tremendous influence on human life. It very much is a life or death happening and has had enormous effects upon all spheres of human life

However during over 99 percent of human existence it has been ordained as belonging to the realm of the supernatural. This is because people have ignored hard evidence in the form of scientific study. For example, the germ theory has been operative in approximately the last 150 years, whereas humanity may have existed for 2-300,000 years; thus people have viewed disease as scientific phenomena for only about .05 percent of humanity's lifespan.

Disease used to be understood under the category of "Supernatural," people did not understand it. The explanations generally were that the Gods caused it; people burned women on stakes when disease broke out. But it existed and affected people regardless of their religion, feelings, theories, etc. People understood it better after microscopes were invented and this provided "hard evidence" that organisms existed that were too small to see–this not only saved women from burning on stakes but helped to prevent disease.

However, disease is highly important in both individual lives and in all of humanity's existence and it is somewhat amazing that people had no understanding of such a highly important phenomenon.

Moreover, it would have been possible to examine disease, if science had been properly used, a long time before "Hard Evidence," such as the germ theory of disease. One method is by statistical examination.

However even if microscopes had never been invented and thus no hard evidence such as seeing microorganisms ever existed, we could still understand disease.

For example, one of many diseases, childbed (puerperal) fever, killed and sickened many women. This disease was common in mid-19th-century hospitals. The Gods and similar ideas were offered as explanation for it and people thought nothing could be done about it.

Despite this view, a doctor Ignaz Philip Semmelweis, through scientific method, was able to drastically cut its incidence. This was through the use of hand disinfection in obstetrical clinics. He published a book describing his findings and methods, *Etiology, Concept and Prophylaxis of Childbeds Fever.*

Despite actual experiments and publications, of the results showing that hand washing reduced mortality to below 1%, Semmelweis's observations conflicted with the established scientific and medical opinions of the time. Thus his ideas were rejected by the medical community.

This was because there was no "hard evidence" to explain the results. Semmelweis offered no acceptable scientific explanation for his findings. Indeed some doctors were even offended by the very suggestion that they should wash their hands.

Thus even without seeing such "hard evidence," as microorganisms, disease could easily be explored by science. This was not done because of the prejudice of scientists for popular theory over actual facts.

Today UFO phenomena are viewed as disease was 150 years ago. Although science has the methods to explore this subject and could use numerous scientific experimental designs in experiments, it generally does not. One reason is that scientists who go along with the idea that UFO phenomena do not exist, are successful and respected. Another, of course, is the government (which is not a body of scientists) would not allocate the funding. And scientists, although they present themselves as being logical, generally prefer theory to empirical data (which can differ from their theories).

Scientific acceptance of meteors and the scientist's ego:

Still another example of scientists sticking to their theories, even though they are refuted by empirical evidence can be found in the history of meteors.

The idea that scientists are scientific (logically and unemotionally basing their opinions on facts) is strongly contradicted by the history of meteors. Before the Industrial Revolution, the skies were clear and people might have been able to see a meteor many times in a year/even a week. But in Western culture there are very few reports of this. This is because the theories of the authority structure claimed that anything falling from the sky, except rain, could not exist. Reports of something falling from the sky were simply considered as superstitious/supernatural ideas among uneducated peasants.

Although there is evidence that more ancient people understood these rocks came from the sky and treasured meteorites, it appears that several thousand years ago as patriarchy began, it was extremely antagonistic to the idea that anything like a rock could be in the sky. Many were influenced by religious ideas and viewed the heavens as "pure" and inhabited only by their male deity, thus the sky could not contain common rocks. Perhaps this is related also to the competitive nature of men. They viewed the earth as the center of the universe and they were the supreme rulers of this universe, thus any evidence to the contrary was not only debunked, but met with such emotional responses as burning people on stakes.

But this antagonism continued for much longer than this symbolism and extends into today's world. The idea that the skies could contain anything but the deity and rain and snow has always drawn intense emotional reaction.

In ancient times, objects in the night sky conjured superstition and were associated with gods and religion. But misunderstandings about meteors lasted longer than they did about most other celestial objects.[144]

Occasional meteorites have been found throughout history, but their extraterrestrial origin was not accepted by scientists until the beginning of the nineteenth century. Before that, these strange stones were either ignored or considered to have a supernatural origin.[145]

The modern scientific history of meteorites begins in the late eighteenth century, when a few scientists suggested that some strange-looking stones had such peculiar composition and structure that they were probably not of terrestrial origin. The idea that indeed "stones fall from the sky" was generally accepted only after a scientific team led by French physicist Jean-Baptiste Biot investigated a well-observed fall in 1803.

Perhaps such egotistical ideas that we are the only intelligent life in the universe, still inhibits the study of UFOs today.

Scientific acceptance of ball lightning and strange forms of matter

As mentioned the idea of ball lightning has been accepted by science only recently and by only some scientists. Even today ball lighting is not something that scientists understand. It has outlandish properties–it can levitate, go through walls, show intelligent behavior and have many other properties not explained by, accepted by, or even acknowledged by science. (And one could wonder whether some objects presented as normal lightning balls are really UFO-related, or whether UFO phenomena can sometimes use this form of matter.) There is a fuzzy area here:

...The theory put forward by the Spanish investigators cannot explain why lightning balls can float horizontally and are capable of passing through glass windows or even walls.

The ball lightning phenomenon was very large and estimated to be about the size of a bus. It was described as a brilliant yellow-green transparent ball with a fuzzy outline, which descended from the base of a towering cumulus...and appeared to float down the hillside.[146]

A perhaps related mystery is spontaneous human combustion.

Could ball lightning represent some strange form of matter in our environment that is massively different than our normal ideas of matter?

But are even our theories correct–a thought experiment involving a new Q-field hypothesis

As discussed in depth in *UFOs Today*, many mechanisms now exist to explain UFO behavior. Research into quantum mechanics presents such concepts as observer-dependent phenomena, the observer-created universe, Schrödinger's equation, wormholes, nonlocality, coincidence and the questioning the idea of cause and effect. Such ideas could be highly relevant to UFO phenomena with its reports of objects going through walls, balls of light that appear to transform into humanoid shapes and many other accounts that contradict our common sense ideas of reality. The results of some of these experiments suggest that our ideas of time and space and even the framework of what we view as reality should be questioned.

For example, observer-dependent phenomena are characteristic representations of the weird world of quantum relationships. Thus, today's physics could allow one to postulate ways for such mechanisms to occur. In older views of the universe, it would be impossible for anything to pass through walls. Thus, such observations were ridiculed. However, such processes as quantum tunneling, when a particle passes through a barrier that it seemingly should not be able to, would allow this. And having something appear when we stare at open space might be some aspect of the quantum idea of "consciousness creates reality," such as shown in double-slit optical system experiments and still under study.

Moreover, the chief known way for information to be transferred by faster-than-light mechanisms is through quantum interactions, such as those shown in "entangled pair" studies.

For example, the fundamentals of physics are based on conservation laws, such as the conservation of momentum. One might hypothesize a new fundamental law of physics: that everything is composed of a field of potential values, a quantum field, or Q-Field. Under this law, what is conserved is not actual properties, such as momentum or particles, but the quantum values of which our universe is composed. One might further propose that these quantum values to which humans are sensitive are points in a range of values and that any specific point, such as the energy of an electron, is dependent on everything else in its Q-Field (as I proposed in *UFOs and the Millennium*). This theory would allow one to exchange the billiard-ball concept of today's physics with the idea of a Q-Field potential. And perhaps a quantum is actually a form of gateway into a more complex physics than we understand.

This might provide an explanation the idea of the expanding universe, which is normally conveyed as dark matter pushing the universe apart. However the idea of a Q–Field would make it easy to understand. Our universe is expanding because the amount of energy in it contains is decreasing. This to our very limited view would make it appear that the Q-Field values are further apart.

Additional phenomenon studied by scientific methods–repeaters

From the beginning, it was assumed that a UFO sighting is a very rare and extraordinary event–"a UFO witness was simply in the "right place at the right time" and that observing another UFO sometime in their life would be like being stuck by lightning more than once."[147] Indeed, the skeptics say "UFOlogy rule of thumb: Repeaters (people who say they film a lot of UFOs or have lots of encounters) are ALWAYS hoaxers or deluded. There has never been a Repeater who presented any real evidence of anomalies that pass muster and most of them have been exposed as hoaxers or crazy. It would be incredibly unlikely for just one person out of billions to keep encountering something as spectacularly rare and brief as a truly anomalous UFO event with such regularity. It is just not credible."

However, in regard to repeat sightings, as mentioned previously, astronomers do see UFOs and they see more than the average.[148]

These events happen to top scientists, such as Clyde Tombaugh, as mentioned and to Dr. Harley Rutledge, who as mentioned previously has had over a hundred sightings and these were with other witnesses, with instrumentation and under scientific study.

Some of these results can be explained scientifically–by the fact that astronomers spend more time looking at the sky. This provides one very logical explanation for why some people see more UFOs than others, "Section 3.2 of the paper titled "Comparison of Witnesses and Non-Witnesses" contains a table showing that UFO witnesses were actually more likely to be night sky observers (professional or amateur) while non-witnesses are more likely to not even be observing the skies at all!" [149]

Many other prosaic explanations may be found in studying the repeater phenomena–it can definitely be examined by science. The amount of time spent watching the sky, whether someone normally carries a camera and other factors offer some prosaic explanation for repeater phenomena. There may be ways to examine additional aspects of the repeater phenomena such as that of people who begin with the bedroom type of sightings and continue with other sightings and even abduction.

There is something about repeaters that should be studied in more detail, especially since they appear to have more contact with the cause of UFO sightings than the rest of us.

Accepted through scientific peer review–wave phenomena

A similar example is the UFO wave or flap phenomena, where there will be a sudden increase in UFO reports. I made a rough statistical study of this myself that was accepted by scientific peer review of the AAAS, "Examination of Social and Environmental Factors in Relation to Unidentified Aerial Phenomena" (Figure 1).[150]

This study related UFO phenomena to social, economic and environmental factors. I used correlation and regression procedures such as Analysis of Variance, curve-fitting and Chi Square tests. One unique aspect of the UFO phenomenon is the wave, or an unexplained increase in the frequency of sighting reports over a certain period of time. Among the theories advanced to explain these waves are "war nerves"; publicity or media exposure; societal stress; hysterical contagion; physical factors such as electromagnetic activity, geological faults and earthquake lights and fixed intervals such as conjunctions with the relative positions of Mars or Venus. But most of these hypothesized correlations have failed. UFO data used in the study included those on worldwide waves reported in the UFO literature, as well as those collected at Wright-Patterson AFB between 1947 and 1969, when the Air Force's public UFO project was functioning. I also drew on a variety of other sources, such as the U.S. Bureau of the Census' Statistical Abstracts of the United States.

I found significant relationships between UFO activity and (a) sunspot activity (P< 01), (b) power failures (P<.O2) and (c) Israeli military activity (P<.001). Nonsignificant relationships included war nerves, studied as years of American wars and as years of American nuclear-bomb testing; societal stress, hysterical contamination and other psychological factors studied as (a) frequency of visits to American physicians, (b) yearly number of American murder victims, (c) yearly number of American murder victims by unusual causes, (d) yearly number of American patent applications, (e) SAT scores and (f) physical relationships studied as yearly earthquake activity.

Additional comments: UFO wave phenomena were used rather than continuous data because of the possible confounding effects of different collection agencies and differences in investigative techniques over the years. I thought it might be possible to investigate abductions in this manner; for example, if some people are abducted, perhaps not all are returned. Thus, I wanted to examine whether UFO waves were associated with increases in missing-person reports. I discovered, however, that no central agency collects information about missing persons. I examined the relationship with Israeli military activity because of a friend's claim that UFO activity increases when Israel is at war. The friend speculated that "signs" and fighting were associated with biblical prophecies about the end time. Although this significant relationship does not prove or disprove this or any other idea, it suggests that relationships between such factors as military and solar activity could merit additional examination, of the three significant relationships studied, two were natural. These relationships indicate that electrical phenomena, or the types of physical forces associated with sunspot activity, may be involved in some portion of UFO events.

Roswell

But good reports are another form of this is empirical data. This can be physical data as measured by scientific instrumentation, but it can also consist of the descriptions of observation such as those by Clyde Tombaugh.

Another form of such empirical data can come from interviews. Because of a lack of government interest or funding, most such research is done by groups of dedicated volunteers that finance themselves and their methods would be called "Leg work."

An example is something that I recently found out from relatives who know him. This is about a dermatologist who was sent to Roswell, New Mexico, to take tissue samples and analyze the outer covering of an alien body that had been kept in cryogenic storage. This doctor has until recently been in practice. He is a retired MD and was a US Air Force Flight Surgeon, who retired as a colonel. He had told people about this when he was younger, but no one believed him, so he has not talked about it recently.

I have been able to contact him and he told me that he had never been to Roswell and did not know what I was talking about. He said he did have several quite interesting UFO sightings though. I again contacted the person who told me this and she said he was lying. She said he was in his house, he told her and several other people about this and they were drinking some. She had worked in his office and knew for sure that he was a doctor.

She thought that he might still be in the military and that he might have come under security. She is trying to remember the other people he told the story to. This story is still under investigation.

He told me about several events he knew about that the government had covered up. He had experienced several UFO sightings. One was at Ellsworth AFB. He saw a UFO on the ground near the base and said police, firefighters and other emergency crews surrounded it. It kept trying to lift off from the ground but was not successful. Then it very rapidly flew away. He saw something about it for one day only in the newspaper.

He also said he saw one over Lake Charles in Louisiana. It flew over a group of people quite low and had a multi-colored exhaust. He said the newspapers said it had come in from the Pacific Ocean and passed over California, Arizona, New Mexico, Texas and Louisiana. It exploded over Lake Charles.

I am still looking into these sightings. He also said that he had copies of an AF bulletin about how to investigate UFO crashes, that was official. He is looking for this.

He wondered how the government could so completely cover up these events. I should have asked him if he was part of the Roswell cover-up.

Although it is said that an event such as Roswell cannot be covered up, it is quite possible that it can be.

This account is still under investigation.

An example of this is the further research that Philip Mantle and I conducted on an additional Roswell witness that we had first mentioned in *UFOs Today* and published in openminds.tv/update.[151] Although this obviously does not prove that UFOs, exist it can add to the data that has already been collected.

In this research we obtained information suggesting that the alleged witness to the Roswell crash, could have actually been there, although when we reported it, we though that he likely had not been. The following article was published in 2017.10.22 *Ufologist* Vol.21 No4 November-December 2017 and versions of it were also published in other places:

ALLEGED ROSWELL WITNESS UPDATE
By Irena Scott PhD & Philip Mantle

Philip Mantle and I released the testimony of a new Roswell witness, the late Deputy Sheriff Charles Forgus, in the new book, *UFOs TODAY, 70 Years of Lies, Misinformation and Government Cover-Up*, in June 2017. Mr. Forgus thought that he had witnessed the UFO crash at Roswell in 1947. He had been the Deputy Sheriff in Big Springs, Texas, after serving in the military during WWII.

He was en-route to Roswell with the Sheriff to pick up a prisoner. When they approached the Roswell area, they heard about the crash on the police radio and were able to find the roads to this area. When they arrived, they observed the recovery of a 100-foot diameter round craft and four strange-looking dead bodies before being told to leave the area. This testimony was given to a US private investigator by the name of Deanna Short in 1999. Unfortunately she has also passed away. There is a video interview of Mr. Forgus where he details these events.

Philip Mantle and I investigated this testimony as did the Mutual UFO Network and our full information at that time was revealed in *UFOs TODAY, 70 Years of Lies, Misinformation and*

Government Cover-Up. Philip Mantle then published it in a number of UFO publications and it was also featured in the online editions of several of the UK's national newspapers.

At that time, MUFON and we had researched Deputy Sheriff Forgus's claims and speculated that he might have been witness to an event in 1953 and not 1947. It was said that Forgus travelled with Sheriff Jess Slaughter, although many times in the video Mr. Forgus simply said the word sheriff, rather than Slaughter, which might give one the impression that he may not have remembered for sure who he went with.

Thus, we had speculated that he might have been witness to an event in 1953. One thing that is certain is that the Sheriff he thought he was likely with at the time, Jess Slaughter, was not the Sheriff in 1947. He was a Sheriff in the 1930s and the 1950s but not the 1940s. In addition we found articles in the local paper, the Big Springs Weekly Herald, about sheriff Slaughter and deputy Forgus in 1953. However, Scott called the sheriff's department and they did not have records of who had been deputies that far back.

One of the reasons we released this testimony was in the hope that either a family member or a friend might come forward with some further information. We assumed this was a long shot but we gave it a try.

To our surprise, on July 17th a nephew of the late Deputy Sheriff Forgus contacted Philip Mantle. He did not want his name used in public but we have it on file.

He said: "Hello, I just discovered the video you posted of the interview with CH Forgus. He was my uncle. Interestingly, he never spoke to us about this incident when I was young and I only recently found out about the story from an east coast MUFON investigator. I can tell you, he is not a person who would have fabricated this story. He was very straight laced and no nonsense type of person...that's why he was in law enforcement. I have the full transcript of the interview if you would like to read and post it. One thing I will mention; my uncles' sighting was not at Roswell. He was a deputy in 1953. I have a very good MUFON report I will forward to you on the event." Mantle replied that he already had the transcript–as it was him who had released it.

On July 19th, he talked with Mantle again and said that Forgus had a son, Glen Lee Forgus and a daughter, Toma Forgus, but he has not kept in touch with them. The nephew had found a phone listing a few months ago and called Glen Lee and left a message, but never got a response. He said the only other person that might know the story is his nephew, Charles Buzzbee in Big Spring, Texas. He also believed that Forgus could have mentioned it to his brother but added that "if you knew the Forgus family and west Texans in particular, Uncle CH would have been roundly made fun of for sharing his experience. That's what assures me even more that he is telling the truth. He was ex-military and ex-law enforcement and was not the type of a person to make up a story like this. I knew him well and can tell you his personality was not one that liked or sought the spotlight. He was also not an imaginative person to create such a story."

The nephew added that Forgus "was very straight laced like all of the Forgus men and women for that matter. It was certainly a very different time when they grew up and my father's family grew up very poor. So, they were extremely pragmatic and not ones for hyperbole. They believed only what they could see and hold."

I hope this is of some help."

On September 6 and 23, Irena Scott talked to Mr. Forgus' son, Glen Lee Forgus and this conversation helped to answer several questions, such as the time frame of Forgus' sighting and whether he had talked about it previously.

Glen provided the new information that Charles had talked about seeing the crash previously. Glen said that he had mentioned this observation maybe 4-5 times over the years, but not in a long drawn out discussion. He spoke about it to Glen when Glen was young. It was Glen's opinion that Charles thought it was the Roswell crash. He did not talk about seeing bodies. At first, he did not necessarily think it was a UFO, Glen said that at that time he may have had no idea what it was. Charles might have not thought about UFOs when he first saw the crash, because he hadn't been exposed to much or even any information about UFOs. Later when he heard in the media about UFOs and Roswell, he thought this might have been what it was.

Glen said that the family moved to California around 1951, so his observation might have happened before that. The family moved because of illness in the family, but moved back and forth several times. There were not any good doctors in Big Springs at that time.

Glen also said that he thought that when Charles made the trip to Roswell that he did not go with Sheriff Slaughter but with a different person, who might have been another deputy. He could not recall the name of the person that Charles had travelled with or who was sheriff at that time.

Thus, the crash might have happened in 1947, which was the time that Mr. Forgus recalled that it was.

Glen said that Charles was very straight arrow and not impressed by false knowledge. He was a no-nonsense type of person, having been in law enforcement. He had been a police officer and in the military. Glen looked up to his father as a John Wayne kind of hero. During the war, Charles was in the army but on loan to the Navy and was a deep-sea diver. Charles and his crew would dive down, weld patches on the sunken ships so they could refloat them and get them out of the harbor. When MacArthur made his reappearance to the Philippians, there had been a lot of fighting and there were many ships sunk in the harbor. One of the ships settled on a reef and the wave action would rock it. The ship slipped off the reef, squashed Charles in the mud and it took three days to get him out.

One main thing Glen emphasized was that his father was very honest and ethical. He was definitely not the kind of person who would make up a lie. Glen gave the same impression–he was very knowledgeable about current news and events and very civic minded. He had an electric car and powered it using a wind turbine power generator.

Thus the possibility exists that Charles Forgus did see the crash in the period that he reported. Charles had said that neither he nor the person he was with talked about it much and this was likely because no one had heard of UFOs or Roswell at that time, which might help to further date the event. In addition, he did not recognize the uniforms of the attendant soldiers as Air Force, which did not did not become a separate military service until September 1947.

When we released the original information regarding the late Deputy Charles Forgus we were criticized far and wide despite the fact that we also pointed out the number of discrepancies in the testimony on tape. One well-known Roswell researcher simply labeled the testimony from Deputy Forgus as a lie. Now, we have information from a nephew and the son of this witness the latter of whom supports his late father's story. No doubt we will still be criticized but I think it is fair to say that we have now been vindicated in releasing this information and to continue to look for more.

This type of anecdotal evidence is what is generally used in UFO study and it can provide very good information that includes more material than just physical measurement. However, although such information as interviews and sighting descriptions, do not prove that UFO phenomenon is real, in combination with additional information it can be used to refine the ideas of what is going on.

Summary and conclusions

Scientists do see UFOs. They have reported complex, involved sightings. They even do excellent studies of the subject, such as ones that have proven under standard scientific paradigms that UFO phenomenon is real. Results of UFO study such as presented here are acceptable to science and can include elements that constitute hard evidence. And not only have several examinations shown the reality of UFO phenomena, but some characteristics have been delineated.

Although UFOs generally have been presented as spacecraft from other worlds looking us over, these scientific results could lead to several conclusions. Some UFOs may be true spacecraft, but it appears that the entire story is much more complex than this. Such results can lead to a number of possible theories. Many UFOs show characteristics that are very difficult to explain and that do not fit into our standard paradigms of reality.

Characteristics of the phenomena include its mysterious power source. There was no evidence of a power source in many observations. For example, in our 1984 sighting over the airport, the object flew toward the wind. This takes power. Moreover it was able to continuously rotate in a controlled fashion and may have had a light. All this would take power, but there was no evidence of what it was.

In the 1968 Massachusetts sighting, we saw a large object making all kinds of maneuvers. It was lit and could travel at tremendous speeds, but there was no evidence of a power source.

In the 2016 sighting, the objects could emit light, travel against the wind and switch their lighting off and on, but there was no evidence of a power source.

The object in our bedroom could rise in altitude and speed up, but there were no wind currents in the room to account for this.

In all the sightings the objects were suspended and not supported by the ground. It would take power to do this and also to cause their luminescence, but there was no evidence of what the power was.

Perhaps this ability to be levitated does not require a power source. One assumes that it takes some form of energy for this, but what this ability basically shows is that the object is not experiencing the usual effects of gravity. Thus as mentioned above, it might be a different form of matter than our normal experience encompasses, or as I discussed in *UFOs Today* there may be physics principles involved. This would not be the memory metal associated with Roswell because this metal is subject to gravity. However some familiar forms can also show this non-reaction to gravity, such as ball lightning. This suggests that some UFOs might be formed of material that is completely new to science, be based upon quantum principles that we do not yet understand and/or use completely unknown power sources. Both UFO phenomena and ball lightning, which show characteristics such as traveling through walls, should be examined much more intensively to even develop a theoretical view of how they are composed and operate.

And as mentioned, much amazing physics, such as quantum phenomena, nuclear reactions, self-organization, positrons, antimatter, mini black hole, cosmic string phenomena, intelligence, etc., is theorized as involved in the formation of ball lightning. Because of their similarity, UFOs phenomena might encompass such strange physics.

In addition in all of the sightings, the objects were soundless. For example, in the Massachusetts sighting, we watched the close object when it was lower than the airplanes, but we heard no sounds from it, even though we could hear the airplanes. We checked this by asking each other what we heard. In the Buff Ledge sightings, the UFO was accompanied by sound, but this did not correlate with what the observer saw. For example when the object plunged into the water one or two miles away, the witness said, "Instantaneously…a steady gale buffeted the dock and three-foot white capped waves sprang up out of nowhere all over the calm lake surface. A the same time, dogs and cats reportedly howled and screamed up and down the lake as if the animals were in pain. The wild scene was unreal and unearthly." These sounds did not correlate with the events. This also appeared to happen to us, when the object circled the airport, there were sounds like a booming that did not seem to be in synchrony with the object's movement. This suggests that the objects might be images or a simulation.

The Massachusetts object had amazing speed. It could be one place and then another so quickly that one could not see it move. This was the first thing that attracted my sister's attention when we were watching it from a distance. When we were close, she said that it could be right over you and then be somewhere else. I noticed the speed when it was circling. It could make a semicircle so quickly that you could not see it and it must have traveled over a mile. Nothing known to be manufactured by humans could travel that quickly. Although in several instances it seemed to travel much faster than the speed of sound, there appeared to be no sonic boom accompanying it. This suggests that it was either an image or a different form of matter. The Buff Ledge account mentioned a number of incidences where the sound did not match the sighting. Thus again it may have been made of a new kind of material, or the whole scene was simulated and included some incongruous elements. (Although it would appear someplace and then someplace else, we did not lose track of it; it always looked the same from a distance–a low, white, blinking light and we had no trouble identifying it and could easily tell it from anything else.)

The UFO phenomenon also appears to have the ability to actually manifest into our material universe. Perhaps it has the ability the convert energy into mass, $E = mc^2$, which we have little ability to do. And it would take a tremendous amount of energy to create even the tiniest amount of matter.

However, this actually can be done using laser light:

While modern technology finally makes it possible to conduct the Breit-Wheeler process for the first time, Pike says they'll have only just begun to scratch the surface of its capabilities; as lasers become more powerful over time, scientists will be able to produce more and different particles than just positron-electron pairs. He says their initial discovery, though accidental, was ultimately an inevitable scientific advance.[152]

This shows that laser light can actually produce effects in our material world. Such information could explain much about the UFO phenomena that has not been understood today, such as how the phenomena can affect matter in our world. For example, it might cause radiation effects in people and provide an explanation for some physical traces.

Some scientific explanation may exist to help elucidate some of these mystery characteristics. Many of them, such as levitation, speed and soundlessness, can be created by laser technology, such as through holographic and volumetric display. It has been shown that UFO phenomenon has lighting that is out of the human visibility range and this can include laser technology. In regard to levitation, for example, at first the volumetric display researchers thought gravity would make the small particles composing the image fall and, thus, make it impossible to sustain an image, but the laser light energy can change air pressure in a way to keep them aloft. Some UFOs could be such images and perhaps advanced technology could endow such images with complex behavior. For example, perhaps volumetric displays could be made using atoms, rather than larger particles.

In addition, there may be ways to scientifically determine whether an object is real or some type of hologram/volumetric display. Such knowledge could be used to help bring UFO phenomena into our understanding and, thus, reality.

I photographed and observed events suggesting laser or some type of similar technology in three instances: the 1968 photography showing light and the 2016 photography showing objects that I did not see visually and our observing of lighting inside the car. From these observations one could hypothesize that laser or similar phenomenon could have been employed.

We both saw the inside of our car light up in different colors. Sue thought the light came from the larger object and I saw it twice when we passed the rotating object. It is possible that laser technology could produce these effects. For example, laser technology might provide an explanation for why I did not see a light beam, when the inside of the car lit up.

It is uncertain what happened here, but others have reported strange effects when exposed to such lighting, such as the Coyne helicopter event. In this case, the object shined a green light into the helicopter cockpit. The pilot's description of the effects resembled the green that we saw in our car: "It was a bright green light. And all of the red night lights that we utilize for night navigation were dissolved in this green light — the whole cabin turned green. It hit all of us directly in the face."[153] This light also seemed to have tractor beam characteristics:

We were at 1,700 feet...Then this craft began to move slowly to the west away from us. At this time, I was worried we were going to hit the ground and I looked at my altimeter and our helicopter was at 3,500 feet, climbing 1,000 feet a minute with no changes in the control. We went from 1,700 feet to 3,500 feet in a matter of seconds and never knew it! The helicopter topped out at 3,800 feet and the four men felt a bump, like turbulence, at which time we had control of the aircraft again...[154]

Magnetic anomalies also occurred in the helicopter. After the object had broken off its hovering, the pilots noted that the magnetic compass disk was rotating approximately four times per minute and the altimeter read approximately 3,500 feet,–a 1,000 foot-per-minute climb was in progress. Coyne insists that the collective was still bottomed from his evasive dive.[155] Lasers might produce such an effect. In addition, the ground witnesses saw a ground area light up in green, which suggests that it may have been quite powerful as some lasers might be.

It is possible that laser light could also be used to create mental effects, such as when Walter Webb mentioned that beams of light focused on UFO witnesses often precede impressions of missing time and abduction scenarios.[156]

In another case, that of the Soviet Aeroflot airliner flying over Minsk, the UFO shot out a blob-like body that cast a greenish tint over the landscape. When one of the beams projected into the cabin, it caused weird effects including multiple lights of different colors and fiery zigzags.

The beams outside, changed shape to mimic the plane. A laser might be able to cause the different colors, such as we saw inside our car and to produce a shape to mimic an airplane by such means as holographic or volumetric display.

Perhaps there was a similar relationship between my sister's observation of the blue light and my observation of the meteor and then the sudden close appearance of the object over the treetops at the same time.

Such events could involve highly advanced technology such as in the Schirmer abduction case, when a green light seemed to be a sort of tractor beam also.

But lasers can actually be used to create tractor beams. This can be done by using a hollow laser beam to surround the particle, then heat from the beam manipulates the air and thus can move the particle forward, hold it still, or even pull it in reverse.[157] So far this works only for small particles but scientists can manipulate them from a distance of 20 cm and researchers think it is possible to use such a technique over longer ranges. A *New Scientist* article tells of another way this might be used and that NASA is interested.[158] Thus, even this is something that can be understood scientifically.

Such displays as green lights might also be a tracer to show that something more involved is taking place. Perhaps the beam just shows the path or existence of a force. The CIA in ways that suggested they were studying abduction/mental/psychic phenomenon, questioned Coyne about such matters as his dreams later.

These reports might provide additional hard evidence of UFO existence, such as the trace of vegetation burned to a cinder found in a farmer's field that was investigated through mass spectrometry, agricultural and chemical techniques and similar methods, but could not be explained scientifically.

In another instance, a sound was heard over a wide area of the country. It was audible over a much larger area than an airplane sonic boom would encompass. It was investigated through seismographic and similar methods, but has remained unexplained. It was associated with a large international UFO wave.

In other studies, several unusual commonalities have been discovered in some related UFO events, such as the Massachusetts one. These include components that have never been reported such as the rotating objects flashing a spectrum of light, or in our case flashing a partial spectrum of light in individual colors and an accompanying green color inside the car, or the unblinking lights seen on both sides of the object's lighted windows, as noted in some of these reports.

This information in conjunction with other studies suggests that some form of mental interaction could exist between UFO phenomena and people. This phenomenon also has been reported and examined scientifically by researchers. Although, abduction and similar elements are the most publicized, it is unknown exactly what is happening. It is possible that this linkage can even bypass the conscious mind and exist in brain areas that are not directly in contact with consciousness. A portion of, or even most of, these experiences may be subliminal. The person may have little awareness of this linkage. In addition, for unknown reasons some individuals seem to have an unusual number of experiences. In fact, some people seem to be a part of a general pattern in that they begin these experiences in early childhood and continue to have additional experiences during the rest of our lives. These people may also experience more unusual events in their life than just UFO experiences. This phenomenon should also be investigated in terms of studying the characteristics of people whose experience follows certain directions such as this, rather than just a study of the shapes of UFOs.

Thus a UFO experience may entail much more than simply a sighting. Although a sighting/poltergeist/abduction event appears as a physical observation or activity, it may be the tip of an iceberg for something that involves the experiencers' brain or even soul. The whole experience could be both mental and physical. It can happen to an individual or a group of people.

It also appears that that people cannot hide from the phenomenon and it does not necessarily hide. In the several times when I experienced unexplainable fear, I kept hiding under trees and was afraid to go to the farm fields. However many of my sightings were somewhat in public. The first one was with my sister. In our Massachusetts one, we were by a freeway most of the time. If abduction did occur, it was in a public place. Also my sighting at OSU was in a very public place. After the OSU sighting, I wondered if something were telling me that one cannot really hide–they could appear at any time. But this also had advantages, because I had other witnesses.

One way the phenomena seemed to communicate or disguise itself was through coincidence. One would wonder if a particular occurrence was real, or just coincidence. This for example, happened when I saw a UFO at OSU at the time I began to fill out the CUFOS forms. Rutledge mentioned it numerous times in his book. Leo Sprinkle mentioned that, "'invisible' UFOLK could create unusual events in the lives of UFO contactees, bringing attention to their experiences."

Andreasson mentioned new and unusual experiences. All she consciously remembered at first was just a small fraction of her encounters; such as, the power failure, the colored light flashing through the window and the beings entering the house, which may have seemed like small coincidences. But later she was able to tie these events together. For example her only conscious memories of unusual events was of getting stung by a bee, seeing the moon growing larger in size and an animal trap that was missing from where she had set it up. But many years later, her subconscious UFO memories were recovered through hypnosis.[159] She had no idea that these small, insignificant experiences were connected to these phenomena.

One could hypothesize from all this that we are living in a simulation, rather than a real world. Science needs to explore ways to discern coincidence and devise theories to explore simulation.

Such ideas about how to identify reality are very old and date to some of our first writing. "I think, therefore I am" was stated by René Descartes, who is dubbed the father of modern western philosophy and credited as the father of analytical geometry—used in the discovery of infinitesimal calculus and analysis. These ideas are still valid and correlate with such theories as simulated reality as a quite logical explanation for UFO phenomena, maybe even foretelling the future, even today.

Her only conscious memory of something unusual was getting bitten by a bee, seeing the moon growing larger in size and an animal trap that was missing from where she had set it up. Many years later, her subconscious UFO memories were recovered through hypnosis.[160] She had no idea that such little; insignificant experiences were connected to this phenomena.

Some people report unusual beings during UFO experiences. We did also. This was a truck driver who looked normal, but acted in a very unusual manner—he might have attempted to kill us, he prevented me from possibly taking a photograph of the inside of a UFO and he caused my sister and I to split apart. What did it mean when he appeared to call me crazy? Was this some kind of message? These actions occurred while the object was in sight, but their meaning is unknown.

Also this occurred while I was working for the DIA with high security clearances and right after my section had reported a UFO on their satellite photography. I wondered if some connection might exist between these events, but do not know.

I definitely think there is a government cover-up. I had firsthand experience with this when I worked for the DIA. The DIA and other intelligence agencies have been heavily involved in investigations and in debunking. They are doing this in the recent December 2017 reports. It is unknown why this happens, but my experience suggests that a cover-up is so deep in the organization such that even people with the clearances who should be aware of the phenomenon are not. This has a crucial importance because, for example, it has been reported that the UFO phenomena is capable of changing the targeting coordinates of our nuclear missiles. This and many other abilities associated with this phenomenon could destroy our world.

Important discoveries can be made using photographic data, such as this. Photographs are hard evidence. One photograph was taken by a Polaroid camera in 1968 and I still have the original and the original camera also. This photograph was taken before today's digital mechanisms and it would not be possible to manipulate it digitally.

And photography can provide hard data to support descriptions of UFO phenomena. My photography provides evidence that UFOs may carry lighting that is not in the visible range for people. The photography showed wavelengths that were out of the human visual range. For example, I very definitely saw only one light source when I photographed the object during our Massachusetts sighting, but two traces show on the photography. In my 2016 photography, I saw nothing when I took the iPhone photographs, but the camera definitely photographed some objects.

My photography suggests that some UFOs may be equipped with an energy source, such as laser light. This can project images into the human visible range. These images such as holograms and volumetric displays are not real themselves but maybe this is how they can take many forms, such as when "orbs" change into UFOs, aliens, monsters, or poltergeists. But the "objects" cannot be examined or captured (like a cat chasing a laser reflection on a wall). Perhaps some UFOs themselves are made of new forms of matter, such that they can appear to people when they want to, but do not have to be seen. In addition many forms of matter are invisible to humans as discussed earlier.

Thus several conclusions could be drawn from this photography and because photographs are hard evidence, there is actual data to support these inferences–they are not just conjectures:

    1.1 UFO phenomena may carry lighting that is not in the visual range of humans.

    2.2 Some of this lighting might come from lasers, because they can emit different and varying wavelengths of radiation.

    3.Lasers can be used to make holographic and volumetric display images. This might explain much UFO data that at first seems impossible. People may be seeing images. In addition, lasers can set up such images so that only some people can see them, or different people can see different things–which could also explain much of UFO phenomena.

4.*Some UFO phenomena may be composed of a different form of matter than we are normally conscious of encountering. It could also be alive and have intelligence, as has been postulated by physicists for Dark Matter.*

5.*Something composed of this matter may be able to choose what wavelength it emits, or it can be invisible to us. It can go through walls.*

6.*The selective emission of wavelengths could explain many UFO characteristics such as the ability of objects to disappear and reappear. It could also help to explain some poltergeist phenomena.*

7.*In addition, we have the ability to create matter using lasers, although it is in a very primitive level today. Such ability could explain some of the hard evidence left by UFO phenomena.*

8.*Although UFO phenomena seems mysterious and seems to belong to the supernatural, it appears that scientific method and modern technology might be used to explore some mysterious aspects of the phenomena. For example, ways to distinguish an image from a real object would help to explore different forms of the phenomena.*

This with additional data provide strong evidence that UFO phenomenon may actually exist and be used to help understand some of its elements that have so far been inexplicable. It is not only possible, but needed, for the UFO phenomena to be studied by science.

I have much experience in the field of science, including training in scientific methodology, statistics, data analysis, experimental design, photo analysis and publication in peer-reviewed journals. I have tried to use the material as I would in writing any scientific paper for peer review and publication. And I have remembered the words of my thesis advisor–to draw both as much general information as possible from the material, but to also hypothesize unique new theories.

Many people report abductions, communication with other beings, trips into space and other such concrete and dramatic adventures. These are of high interest because they could reveal the secrets of the universe, our future, what the aliens think of us, what amazing gifts they will give us and much else.

But most often the general summaries of these events simply are that we do not understand what is going on. The findings here agree with those other common summaries, but they differ in offering pathways to scientifically explore the events. Our finding of invisible radiation–of possible laser or volumetric display–could explain many properties of the phenomena and thus offer an opening to explore it in terms of what is possible in our science. Perhaps because a UFO sighting might represent a tip of an iceberg phenomena, it might be possible to study this by such means as electroencephalogram or similar measure of brain activity. These findings also suggest that forms of matter and even intelligence may exist in our world that we need to explore with an open mind.

This book is unique–it contains first-hand accounts from scientists of complex and bizarre UFO events, not just sightings. These events include electrical and radiation effects, abduction phenomena and mind control. Other reports include strange sounds, close encounters, missing time, photography, children's interactions, possible attempted murder, weird incidents, possible "Men in Black," peculiar activities by representatives of government agencies, psychic effects and much more.

It also includes new Roswell information including more about a witness that we had reported earlier and information about a new professional Roswell witness.

New information can come from this research, such as hard evidence that UFO phenomenon can employ light that is not in the visible human range. This has enormous implications as does the idea expressed in Rutledge's final sentence, "Possibly a great deal of UFO activity is subliminal–which if true, could have serious ramifications."

What constitutes proof? Maybe some of this is compatible with the normal paradigms of scientific proof because it may be the only UFO book in which the research was submitted to and accepted after peer review by established scientific societies.

We hope these prospectives may help people to be curious about aspects of their environment that are puzzling today, but might help also to construct the human destiny.

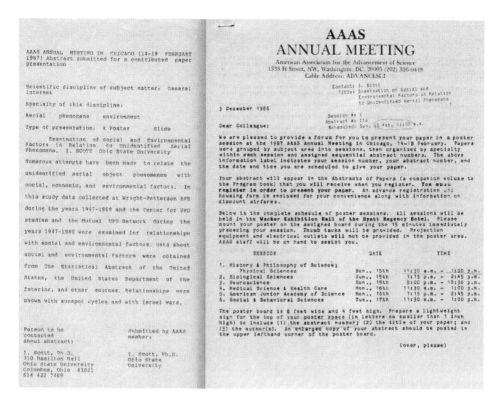

Figure 1: Wave or flap phenomena, when there is a sudden increase in UFO reports, remains an unexplained aspect of UFO phenomena. I made a rough statistical study of this element that was accepted by the scientific peer review of the AAAS. I found significant relationships between UFO activity and (a) sunspot activity (P< 01), (b) power failures (P.O2) and (c) Israeli military activity (P.001). The association with sunspot activity and power failures might suggest that some types of UFO activity could have some relationship with electrical phenomenon.

* * * * * *

APPENDIX 1 DISCOVERIES IN A SPOOKY, BUT BEAUTIFUL, OLD FARMHOUSE

Because a number of these sightings occurred on our family farm along with some additional somewhat strange events, I should describe it.

Its location has about everything often associated with UFO phenomena: ancient Indian campgrounds and mounds, many Indian artifacts, a possible effigy mound, power lines, water, rivers, graveyards and much else. Among other items, there once had been a large crater in the area–that was taken down when this portion was developed into a water treatment plant. A form of iron ore-swamp iron surrounded this crater. The area was once glaciated. Limestone can be found underground at certain depths. There are underground caverns, which were discovered during oil drilling.

This farm began in around 1803, when our great-great-grandfather with his father entered Ohio's wilderness. [161] [162] They spotted a squatter's clearing and an abandoned cabin and moved in. We grew up in a newer house there. This was so long ago that people generally married their next door neighbors, so that a daughter married the son of the family to the south and their daughter married the son of the family to the north and all became our ancestors. The farm became larger because it included the farms of several families. It remained very rural with relative's homes on all sides and houses about one fourth of a mile apart. We were quite poor–at first we farmed with horses and had no telephone, TV, or indoor plumbing. We were very familiar with the territory and with what our neighbors were doing. This is the house where I had my first two sightings.

There are at least two Indian mounds on the farm, much Indian activity must have taken place here because we have found many artifacts and the house is in a wide valley overlooking a waterway, Alum Creek.

It also has a large variety of aircraft with which we are familiar. It is close to Columbus, Ohio and within about 100 miles of a number of airports. These include Wright-Patterson AFB (WPAFB around 80-miles away), the John Glenn Columbus International Airport in Columbus, Bolton Field, Rickenbacker International Airport, the Ohio State University Airport (Don Scott Airport), Delaware Municipal Airport and others, so we have much experience seeing all kinds of aircraft and I have photographed many (as shown in my YouTube site). Thus, we are very familiar with a variety of normal and unusual aircraft–such as ultra-lights, hot air balloons, helicopters, blimps with lighted sides and even TV shows on their sides, military aircraft, Chinese lanterns, all kinds of advertising airplanes–including ones towing signs and ones with lighted signs under the wings, etc. and I have videotaped many. Some have landed on the farm. We live by an interstate freeway that blimps often follow from city to city and are very familiar with blimps by a freeway. I have had flying lessons and have flown in helicopters, large and small aircraft, balloons and gliders.

Today, the farm is notable for several reasons. For one, it was chosen as a site for two universities. Bishop Philander Chase chose it as one of the first sites for what later became Kenyon College. John Purdue helped to purchase the farm to the north. He was the founder of Purdue University and many other institutes, as described in my book *Uncle: My Journey with John Purdue*. We are descended from both the Purdue and the Chase family. Neither university was built there.

It is also somewhat well known today because The Ohio Bicentennial Commission to celebrate Ohio's birthday chose our barn to represent Delaware County and painted an Ohio logo on its side to commemorate it. There were articles about this in *The Wall Street Journal, USA Today, Ripley's Believe It Or Not, Ohio Magazine, Country Magazine* and many more.[163] The barn was then used as the cover photograph on *Ohio's Bicentennial Barns,* [164] and many Internet sites still feature it.

There are plans to develop the farm into a large park–Preservation Park's new McCammon Park that may soon be one of Ohio's largest parks.

Today the farm has large power lines on both sides with tall metal towers, an Interstate freeway cutting through it and it is near the Alum Creek State Park that contains the largest inland beach in Ohio's state park system. Such features are sometimes linked with UFO activity and we have plenty of them.

Also the house where I saw the lightning ball and the purple object above my head is also on our family farm. It belonged to relatives, the Crippen family.

It was also a house where I found out about John Purdue. And I once had a strange experience that later made me aware of him and even later I published the book about him and his founding of Purdue University, which became the first of the Founder's Series published by the Purdue University Press.

In this house, my relatives always had a large oil painting of a man in their living room. It seemed as if his eyes looked at you wherever you were. When young, I used to hide from him behind chairs and other things. I thought it was just a nice painting someone had bought in an antique shop.

Although no one could predict when someone was to die in those days, my great aunt was gravely ill. One night my parents and I were visiting them, they all were in her bedroom and I was in the living room alone with the painting. But it had disappeared. Although no one had ever moved the painting, it was missing. I could not believe this and felt the wall behind it to make sure it was not there. Then I looked all over the house for the big painting. My aunt died that night. Later we returned from the funeral home and the painting was back up. This seemed very strange, because it disappeared before she died. I asked people about this, but everyone said no one had moved it.

Later I found out that this was a portrait of John Purdue and later I found out that it appeared to have been painted by the same artist as one in the Purdue Room at Purdue University. But this happening drew my attention to him; although it was several years before I found out who he was and it may have had something to do with my writing the book (we also discovered that we had his effects in the attic).

Also my mother and I used to have the same dream that the house contained a treasure. Because of the dreams, we viewed it as somewhat haunted. My mother and I pictured the treasure we dreamed about as maybe a big treasure chest filled with money and jewelry, but we never found anything. After my father's cousin's death, my mother was going through things and found boxes of old documents, letters, photographs, etc. Although many would just use this for fireplace fodder, Mom began to carefully read each document. It turned out that these materials contained a whole lot of information about our family, including who John Purdue was.

For one, we found letters and other material about a Hannah Chase. She was interesting because many of these documents told about a huge Chase fortune that existed in England described in several books. [165] [166] [167] So, of course, I wondered if this Hannah Chase were connected with the fortune.

I searched several libraries but was unable to find anything. However, one day I found out about her entirely by accident. I happened to be in the local library during a community celebration. When everyone left for the festivities, I browsed and found an open book on a table. [168] It was open to a page that told the story of Hannah Chase.

To my utter astonishment, I not only discovered who this Hannah Chase was, but that she was my own great-great-great-grandmother. The attic letters also gave Hannah's ancestry. She was descended from many of the first pilgrim families in the country, such as the father of one of the Mayflower leaders, William Brewster.

I later took the Ancestry.com DNA test and found that the results agreed with the family information from this material. The DNA test was so accurate that it showed direct ancestors back into the 1600s and related people into the dawn of European history. For example, one early direct ancestor was Ruth Stratton White (1650-1740). She was descended from the Bancroft family and her sister was an ancestor of Cornelius Vanderbilt. Some lines went into the royal families of Europe and had lineages that could be traced as far back as such lines go.

The family tree I made from this material contains over 16,000 people–whose lines went back about as far as any of Europe's genetic lines. Such a family tree is interesting because a number of researchers have reported that UFO experiences may run in families. This could be helpful, because it might be used with similar information from other families to look for commonalities among the ancestry of UFO experiencers.

Because many people have an interest in genealogy and with modern-day computers can trace their ancestors far back, a comparison of such information might provide insight into why some families have more UFO experiences than usual.

Thus, the house did contain a real treasure–we can go back even into early European ancestors and actually read their writings and find out what they were doing. So our dreams were right.

******

APPENDIX 2 DREAMS

The earliest dream about objects in the sky that I recall was of having two stars come down from the sky and chase me. They were bright red objects. I believe I was 3-5 years old.

Another early dream (around 7 years old) was of having a friend phone me at my grandparent's (we did not have a phone) to tell me about a bad storm approaching. To calm her I told her not to worry about it. I ran home and on the way saw the storm cloud and then looked above it to see a large purple sphere. I woke up terrified. I. did not know anything about UFOs and assumed that I my terror was due to conscience because I had lied to my friend.

Other dreams that I recall are of nightmares about the windows in my parent's house, especially at night and around north windows. I had were a number of dreams about things coming in through the north windows. Once I dreamed a huge eagle was outside. I knew it was going to reach in with its talons and kill me. In the same dream, I dreamt that there was a traffic jam all over the eastern US. I used to have a lot of dreams about a horse staring at me through the windows with hatred that plans to kill me.

I also dreamed of flying objects that changed shape Sometimes I would dream of a large object, such as an airplane, which would become smaller as it moved toward me–the opposite of parallax.

Also all through my childhood and high school years, I had a fear of the dark, of open spaces–I would hide under trees when in open fields, electrical appliances near my bed–such as clocks and fans, of ceiling lights and lamps hanging from the ceiling, of being crushed by something coming down from above, of swallowing, choking, having things placed inside my body and of medical examinations. I also recall dreaming that I was to prophesize, but that I did not believe in religion. (These may be normal fears that do not relate to UFOs, however I don't recall any specific incidents that would produce the fears and I remember my childhood well).

The following dreams may have been influenced by the media, because I had heard UFOs by then. In one dream from the 1950's, I was in a long narrow house about 500 ft. long and 20 ft. wide. There was a hallway down the middle and rooms off from it. The doors to the rooms had small windows. People in the rooms had to learn or perform routines. Mentally retarded people learned how to stuff Kleenexes into purses and a little gypsy girl practiced how to walk on water. She could do this very well, but she couldn't walk on kerosene. Her teacher told her that kerosene was the same as water. Further down the hall, the tasks became more specialized. A man ate sugar coated pennies, phonograph needles, crystals, erasures, hypodermic syringes, buttons, transistors and bolts. Sometimes he didn't eat them, instead he jabbed then under his fingernails and sucked the blood or stuck them into his eyes, nose and ear openings.

Through one hole I could see a man looking at the sky. Next I became him. I stood in a yard at dusk. The yard was growing larger with a labyrinth of passageways between and around it. The ground was cement and the plants were artificial but had slime dripping from the leaves. The leaves and petals were very fragile, dropping at the slightest movement, but they felt real. The air was cool and damp and everything smelled like plastic. An airplane flew over. Then it made a second much lower pass. It was a jet and I was afraid it would crash in the yard. It made several more passes but each time it looked different. It sometimes flashed on a white light that illuminated the yard. Sometimes I could only see its windows, sometimes it had rows of windows and sometimes it was streamlined with long swept—back wings. Other times it resembled a fish or a snake and had a yellow stripe and fins instead of wings. A man said there would be a plane crash. I said I didn't know if I could fly, yet. The plants began to look magenta; then I saw a fire coming toward me from the west.

Next, I was me and watched the man. His floor was covered with broken nails. I asked a priest if the man knew what he saw and the priest said he didn't. A man beside me said they let people have dominion over the fowl of the air because the jet could fly higher than the birds.

I had walked nearly 1/3 of the way through the house and came to a window facing the east. Beside it was a mirror; I opened it and picked up a hand pistol. It was shiny stainless steel, so neatly polished that the light reflected a blue line along its barrel and it had a marble handle covered with western designs. As I gazed at it became larger and more beautiful I looked down the muzzle and started to pull the trigger to find our whether it was loaded. There was a sign in the window that said, "Don't pull triggers." Then I could see the revolver part and decided it was loaded.

It had been daylight outside the house–a driveway led up to the window. A ford drove up and parked under the window. It did not have a driver. As it began getting darker outside, bright lights came on inside the house, which gradually became extremely brilliant. I thought I should move away from the window so no one could see me. I kept looking at the gun. It was even shinier in the bright light. When I looked outside, I could see the car parked right below the window. Inside the car under the front seat were two round glowing spheres. Terrified, I screamed, "Those aren't anyone's eyes."

Once in the 50's, I dreamed I was in a UFO. It was dome shaped and the only other personality in it was a rectangular computer, which talked. It had a very human personality and conversation, but was in control all the time. After a while it dumped me on top of an ice jam on a river. I managed to get off it and then climbed to the top of a hill. There was a woman hanging white sheets on her (laundry line in the snow. I thought I was supposed to look for someone named Meredith. In several similar dreams I would be awakened, as if I were a mummy and find out that I was expected to do something. I never had any idea what. In another dream about a UFO, I dreamed that my sister and I were in a field. We saw a big purple UFO that came toward us and then started to land on us. I was frightened but then discovered I was inside it. There was a small purple UFO inside of it and a balcony. After a while I discovered that I would just be anywhere in it I thought about and did not have to walk.

In 1965, I dreamed about visiting my parents. I parked in their yard and noticed that everything was burned to charcoal. Small intricately detailed statues of people made of clay, silver, wood, plastic and marble were scattered around. I wondered what caused all this. My father gave me a book titled, "Places to go in Ohio," and I read about a cave under Lake Erie. Suddenly, I was in the cave walking down a very long flight of beautiful well-worn marble stairs that had a blue-grey tone. The stairways were well lit but I couldn't see the source of the light. There were small people, with large heads and bright costumes that did not have openings, working in caves along the stairs. Then I began to see people my own size that I thought were regular people. I would look at them and think, "People at last." Then I would look at their eyes, which looked normal, but I would think that they looked strange. They I would think, "Those aren't people." After a while, I came to an arena-shaped area with a raised platform like a boxing area in its center. I went in and sat down among the strange people. A ballet was taking place. A lovely woman with strange eyes danced with a big brown hamburger colored glob in the shape of a person. He had arms legs and a body, but his skin looked like sausage and he didn't have joints, but he was amorphous and just bent anyplace (his body was brownish and reminded me of the object I saw Feb. 29, 1987 on the OSU campus). I became very nauseous when I watched this. The music stopped and everyone left. I continued up the steps, began to see people I knew and thought they were real people.

I climbed to the top of the steps and noticed that I was back home. I dreamed that I awakened lying flat on my back on my parent's kitchen table under a ceiling lamp. I went to the porch, saw my father flat on his back on a couch under a ceiling lamp and looked out a window. From behind the trees a brilliant orange sphere shot up and traveled rapidly across the sky (which looked like the object in my 1950's possible UFO sighting). It was the moon. I could dimly see craters on it. I ran into the house after a telescope (as I think I did during the 1950s observation) and discovered my mother flat on her back on the dining room table under a ceiling lamp. She sat straight up bending at a right angle, like a robot and told me she would knock my head off if I didn't get out of the dining room. I ran back and looked for the object, but was gone.

In another dream many years ago, I was in my grandparents' corncrib–a long, narrow, wooden building with windows to shovel corn in. I looked out the door and saw an elk coming toward me. Then its eyes flew out and became glowing objects that were flying around me like two balls. I was terrified.

I used to dream that I could fly. I just flapped my arms in any position and could fly around.

Some more recent dreams I have had include one in which my sister and I were in my house. We heard an odd sound and went outside. There was a large heavy gravel truck cavorting and doing acrobatics in the sky. It looked as if it were having fun. Then it went behind the garage and landed. We saw people of various ages in the green-brown shade of old military garb, with military pockets, but no insignia. We sort of wrestled to keep them out of the house, but they came in anyway. Then I began screaming at Sue, "Don't look at their eyes," This was because they could take your will (whatever that meant). I shouted so loud that I woke myself up.

In another one, I dreamed I was aboard a UFO. I entered a room that looked military–the doorway was curved and everything was the green-brown of old army uniforms. They put me on a gurney-type thing they use in operating rooms. Then they burned my face off. All I had was this horrible looking thing, burned, with flesh falling off. Then they dumped me on an ice jam and I knew I had to find a job, even though I looked so terrible that no one could look at me and I needed medical attention but had no money–I may have been blind also.

I dreamt some others and I were looking at a big full moon. After a while, it seemed translucent and seemed to be rapidly floating across the countryside. Later I saw it close up and it looked like the big round concretion rock Dad had hauled to his front yard. Then some others and I saw it very close. In spite of weighing many tons, it floated up to me and I went out to it. Part of it was missing, but it still looked just like Dad's big rock and it stretched out a rocky hand to me. It appeared somewhat pearly translucent and light colored. Then I was in with a group of people following it into a large brick building. They seemed to have somewhat euphoric expressions as if they were experiencing some form of religious ecstasy. The building seemed like a church or government building. Then I dreamed I left the building, but I could not for the life of me remember what happened in the building. I left by a back door and was alone. I did not know where the other people were. When I finally woke up, I still could not remember anything about being inside the building. I've had many dreams that the rock is the moon, but do not know why.

My sister and I had exactly the same dream. It was a dream about our grandparents' house, where I live now. We dreamed that there were a number of stories in it (it has only two and a big attic). We would enter this one closet and somehow get up to this high room. In the room were all these fancy, sort of Victorian pieces of beautiful furniture, but everything was covered with white sheets. I have no idea why we would have the same dream because such a room does not exist. I also sometimes dream there are many more rooms in the house. I will almost get lost going through all the rooms. Sometimes I dreamed that the house looked like the Russian Kremlin. For some reason I used to dream about that closet-as if there were something in it that I seemed to want to know about. This place was purchased by John Purdue for his sister, our great-grandmother and it was where he first thought about founding Purdue University.

Another dream began with my seeing a man walking up the driveway to my house. For some reason, I was terrified of him. Then the electricity went off. I thought he might be able to turn it off some way and was even more terrified, but then woke up.

I dreamed about a purple thing. I was viewing a purple spot as my essence or as something that controlled me. Then I realized that there was a much smaller purple spot that seemed to represent me.

I dreamed that our universe was created when two universes collided. I dreamed that if it were made of one universe, physics would be simple. There would be no time and no space. Interactions would be instantaneous. Our universe is more complex because physics interactions are translated through the quantum framework of two universes or through two different types of physics frameworks. This makes us think that time and space exists, because our interactions cannot be converted from one set to another instantaneously.

I dreamed about the question of how light could be both particle and wave at same time. So what I dreamed was that it has something to do with time. Then the dream added that particles have some type of marker that tells them how long they can last and this has an influence on their power, size and other elements. Then the dream went on and on, for what seemed like hours about markers and how they could exist, but I forget that part. When I woke up, I thought this dream is stupid; it did not say a word about the question. Then I wondered why particles do have a particular time span.

I dreamed that I wanted to find out about reality. I dreamed that the material world doesn't exist. Something puts these ideas in the mind, but not real. Something controls not only the government but each person's mind. It is all over every neuron. This causes people to think the world is what it looks like. This could be changed easily in a fraction of a second into another world. People would not know it, because it could block the information. The dream said that people are not judged on faith, but on their works. It also said that the quantum is the real world, but people's brains are not wired to understand it.

I dreamed I was in a lab that was about to be hit with a nuclear bomb. Everyone was trying to 1 preserve the people and 2 preserve the data. Someone found a real old thing of mine, about the size of a sugar cube that contained many, many GB of data. Then they also discovered that it could project holograms, so that a person near it would think they were someplace else. People were trying to figure out its range and asking me where I got it. I did not remember but it seemed very cool that you could stand near it and see an entirely different world.

Once I had sleep paralysis. I realized what it was, but was paralyzed and terrified during it anyway. I heard an explosive sound outside. Then a number of other explosive sounds and then sounds like something moving around in the yard. For some reason, I was terrified (although this would be a normal nighttime). I finally went out of the house with my camcorder posting live video to the Internet, got in the car and drove around. When I came back home, I was still terrified.

Then I had some weird dreams. I woke up somewhat paralyzed. My muscles wouldn't move, I had to really work to get them to move and sometimes the wrong muscles did. I was terrified of something in the house but could not move around. I woke up like this several times. The lights in the house seemed to go on and off on their own.

I realized that it was sleep paralysis, but I never had it before, was terrified during it and thought something was in the house. I could barely move and my muscles did not seem to work. I thought I had something in my hand but could not feel what it was. I saw my house light timer light go off at the regular time, got scared and thought I should turn a light on. But none of the lights would turn on. Then when I finally actually woke up, a light was on at the wrong time. Then it went out on its own.

******

REFERENCES

Andrus, Walter and Irena Scott, eds. *The Fiftieth Anniversary of UFOlogy*. MUFON 1997 International UFO Symposium Proceedings: Mutual UFO Network Inc., 1997.

___. *UFOs in the New Millennium*. MUFON 2000 International UFO Symposium Proceedings: Mutual UFO Network Inc., 2000.

Arnold, Kenneth and Ray Palmer. *The Coming of the Saucers*. Boise, ID and Amherst, WI: Kenneth Arnold and Ray Palmer, 1952.

Bragalia, Anthony. "The Final Secrets of Roswell's Memory Metal Revealed." *The UFO Iconoclast(s)*. June 7, 2009. <http://ufocon.blogspot.com/2009/06/final-secrets-of-roswells-memory-metal.html>.

___. "Roswell Alcoholics: The Alien Anguish." *The UFO Iconoclast(s)*. March 14, 2010. <http://ufocon.blogspot.com/2010/03/roswell-alcoholics-alien-anguish-by.html>.

___. "Roswell, Battelle & Memory Metal: The New Revelations." Posted by Maria Luisa de Vasconcellos. *Light Eye: Tribute to an UFO Watcher*. August 8, 2010. <http://fgportugal.blogspot.com/2010_08_01_archive.html>.

___. "Roswell Debris Confirmed as Extraterrestrial: Lab Located, Scientists Named." *The UFO Iconoclast(s)*. May 26, 2009. <http://ufocon.blogspot.com/2009/05/roswell-debris-confirmed-as.html>.

___. "Roswell Debris Inspired Memory Metal Nitinol; Lab Located. Scientists Named." *MUFON UFO Journal* (July, 2009): 3-10.

___. "Roswell Metal Scientist: The Curious Dr. Cross." *The UFO Iconoclast(s)*. May 21, 2009. <http://ufocon.blogspot.com/2009/05/roswell-metal-scientist-curious-dr.html>.

___. "Scientist Admits to Study of Roswell Crash Debris." *The UFO Iconoclast(s)*. August 16, 2009. <http://ufocon.blogspot.com/2009/08/scientist-admits-to-study-of-roswell.html>.

Burrell, Paul and Paul Althouse. "Ross and Pike Counties, Ohio April/May 1996." *Ohio UFO Notebook* 12 (1996): 8-10.

Burrell, Paul, Delbert Anderson, William E. Jones and Irena Scott. "Dancing Red Lights, Logan, Ohio, October/November, 1995." *MUFON of Ohio Newsletter* (November, 2009): 4-5.

Carey, Thomas J. and Donald R. Schmitt. *Witness to Roswell: Unmasking the Government's Biggest Cover-Up*. Franklin Lakes, NJ: New Page Books, 2009.

Clark, Jerome. *The UFO Book*. Detroit: Visible Ink Press, 1998.

___. *Unexplained! 347 Strange Sightings, Incredible Occurrences and Puzzling Physical Phenomena. Detroit: Visible Ink Press, 1993.*

Collins, Robert M., Richard C. Doty and Timothy S. Cooper. *Exempt from Disclosure.* Vandalia, OH: Peregrine Communications, 2005.

Condon, Edward U. Scientific Study of Unidentified Flying Objects. Boston: E.P. Dutton, 1969.

Denzler, Brenda. The Lure of the Edge: Scientific Passions, Religious Beliefs and the Pursuit of UFOs. Berkeley: University of California Press, 2003.

___. "Who Are We?" *MUFON UFO Journal* (May, 1977): 9-14.

Dolan, Richard. UFOs and the National Security State: An Unclassified History, Volume 1: 1941-1973. New York: Keyhole Publishing, 2000.

Fawcett, Lawrence and Barry J. Greenwood. *Clear Intent: The Government Cover-Up of the UFO Experience*. Englewood Cliffs, NJ: Prentice-Hall, 1984.

___. The UFO Cover-Up: What the Government Won't Say. Old Tappan, NJ: Fireside, 1990.

Fowler, Raymond E. *UFOs: Interplanetary Visitors*. Bloomington, IN: iUniverse, 2001.

___. The Watchers: The Secret Design behind UFO Abduction. New York: Bantam, 1991.

Friedman, Stanton. "Arsenic and (the Same) Old Story: Media Fascination with Aliens Is Misguided." *MUFON UFO Journal* (January, 2011): 8-9.

___. *"More 'why'questions." MUFON UFO Journal (October, 2016): 6-7.*

___. "A Scientific Approach to Flying Saucer Behavior." In *Thesis Antithesis: Proceedings of a Symposium Sponsored by A IAA and World Future Society* (Los Angeles, CA, September, 1975): 22-36.

Fuller, John. Interrupted Journey: Two Lost Hours aboard a Flying Saucer. New York: Dial Press, 1966.

Good, Timothy. *Above Top Secret: The Worldwide UFO Cover-Up*. New York: Quill Publishing, 1989.

___. Need to Know: UFOs, the Military and Intelligence. New York: Pegasus Books, 2007.

Hall, Richard. *The UFO Evidence*. New York: Barnes & Noble, 1997.

___. Uninvited Guests: A Documented History of UFO Sightings, Alien Encounters and Cover-Ups. Santa Fe, NM: Aurora Press, 1988.

Hesemann, Michael and Philip Mantle. Beyond Roswell: The Alien Autopsy Film, Area 51, & the U.S. Government Cover-Up of UFOs. New York: Marlowe & Company, 1998.

Hilkevitch, Jon. "In the Sky! A Bird? A Plane? A . . . UFO?," *Chicago Tribune* January 1, 2007: 1.1.

Hopkins, Budd. Intruders: The Incredible Visitations at Copley Woods. New York: Random House, 1987.

___. *Missing Time*. New York: Berkley, 1983.

Hynek, J. Allen. *The UFO Experience: A Scientific Inquiry*. Chicago: Henry Regnery Company, 1972.

Jacobs, David. *UFOs and Abductions: Challenging the Borders of Knowledge*. Lawrence, KS: University Press of Kansas, 2000.

___. *The UFO Controversy in America*. Bloomington, IN: Indiana University Press, 1975.

Jones, William E. "Another MJ-12 Document." *Ohio UFO Notebook* 11 (1996): 11-14.

___. "Books and Articles of Note." *Ohio UFO Notebook* 10 (1995): 14-18.

___. "Confirmation of UFOlogy's Darker Side." *Ohio UFO Notebook* (July, 1993): 4-7.

___. "Confirmation That J. Allen Hynek Communicated with Neil Armstrong." *MUFON of Ohio Newsletter* (Spring, 2008): 7-8.

___. "Darlington, Ohio, October, 1953: A Case That Can't Be Documented." *Ohio UFO Notebook* 1 (August, 1991): 15-17.

___. "Historical Notes: Thomas Mantell." *MUFON UFO Journal* (April, 1990): 18-19.

___. "Human Mutilations Again." *Ohio UFO Notebook* 6 and 7 (July, 1993): 13-14.

___. "Information, Disinformation, Hints, or Lies?" *Ohio UFO Notebook* 11 (1996): 24-25.

___. "Neil Armstrong and Len Stringfield." *Ohio UFO Notebook* 9 (1995): 20-21.

___. "Point Pleasant, West Virginia Moth Man Follow Up." *Ohio UFO Notebook* 1 (August, 1991): 12.

___. "Project Grudge/Bluebook Special Report 13." *Ohio UFO Notebook* 15 (1997): 1-2.

Jones, William E. and Irena Scott. "June 20-23, 1985, Columbus." *Ohio UFO Notebook* 12 (1996): 19-22.

___. "Laurie, Missouri." *Ohio UFO Notebook* 12 (1996): 26-27.

___. "North American Aviation, Columbus, Ohio, Test Site for UFO Materials?" *Ohio UFO Notebook* 12 (1996): 35-37.

___. "The Spaur Case—Reporting a UFO Can Be Hazardous to Your Health." *Ohio UFO Notebook* 14 (1997): 36-40.

___. "U.S. Navy Support of UFO Research." *Ohio UFO Notebook* 11 (1996): 5-6.

Jones, William E. and Eloise G. Watson. "Pre-World War II 'Creature' Retrieval?" *International UFO Reporter* (Winter, 2001-2002): 6-30.

Keel, John. *The Mothman Prophecies*. New York: Saturday Review Press, 1975.

Kelleher, Colm A. and George Knapp. Hunt for the Skinwalker: Science Confronts the Unexplained at a Remote Ranch in Utah. New York: Paraview Pocket Books, 2005.

Keyhoe, Donald. *The Flying Saucers Are Real* (reprint). New York: Cosimo Classics, 2004.

Klass, Philip J. "CIA Mission." *MUFON UFO Journal* (February, 1993): 20.

Lang, Richard. "The SIP Project—Star Team Report." *MUFON UFO Journal* (July, 2009): 7.

___. "Woman and Dog Observe Multiple Lights, Orbs." *MUFON UFO Journal* (August, 2009): 9-10.

Maccabee, Bruce S. *Historical Introduction to* Project Blue Book Special Report No. 14. Evanston, IL: Center for UFO Studies, 1979.

Maccabee, Bruce S. *The FBI CIA UFO Connection*. New York: Richard Dolan Press, 2014.

Oberg, James. "French 'Flap' a Flop?" *MUFON UFO Journal* (September, 1992): 21.

Project Blue Book Special Report No. 14 (Analysis of Reports of Unidentified Flying Objects). Wright-Patterson Air Force Base, OH: Air Technical Intelligence Center, 1955.

Project-1947 – Air Intelligence Report 100-203-79, "Analysis of Flying Object Incidents in the U.S." Headquarters United States Air Force Directorate of Intelligence, Washington, D.C., 1949.

"RAAF Captures Flying Saucer on Ranch in Roswell Region," *Roswell Daily Record* July 8, 1947: 1.

Randle, Kevin D. *A History of UFO Crashes*. New York: Avon Books, 1995.

___. *The UFO Casebook*. New York: Warner Books, 1989.

Randle, Kevin D. and Donald R. Schmitt. "Roswell and the Flying Wing." *International UFO Reporter* (July/August, 1995): 10-12.

___. *The Truth about the UFO Crash at Roswell*. New York: M. Evans and Company, Inc., 1994.

___. *The UFO Dossier: 100 Years of Government Secrets, Conspiracies and Cover-Ups*. Detroit: *Visible Ink Press, 2015.*

___. *UFO Crash at Roswell*. New York: Avon, 1991.

Randles, Jenny. *The Truth Behind Men in Black: Government Agents—or Visitors from Beyond.* New York: St. Martin's Paperbacks; St. Martin's, 1997.

___. Star Children: The True Story Of Alien Offspring Among Us. New York: Sterling Publishing Co., Inc., 1995.

___.The UFO Conspiracy: The First Forty Years. New York: Barnes & Noble, 1987.

___. UFO Retrievals: The Recovery of Alien Spacecraft. London: Blandford Press, 1995.

Reddit UFOs/CaerBannog. "Kevin Randle Distances Himself from Schmitt, Carey, Bragalia & Dew's "Roswell Slides."

https://www.reddit.com/r/UFOs/comments/2xntee/kevin_randle_distances_himself_from_s chmitt_carey/

Richelson, Jeffrey T. America's Secret Eyes in Space: The U.S. Keyhole Satellite Program. New York: HarperCollins, 1990.

Ring, Kenneth. The Omega Project: Near-Death Experiences, UFO Encounters and Mind at Large. New York: William Morrow & Co., 1992.

Rondinone, Peter. "Antimatter." *OMNI Magazine* May, 1982: 114.

Ruppelt, Edward J. *The Report on Unidentified Flying Objects*. New York: Doubleday, 1956.

Rutledge, Harley D. Project Identification: The First Scientific Field Study of UFO Phenomena. Englewood Cliffs, NJ: Prentice-Hall, 1981.

Schuessler, John F. *The Cash-Landrum UFO Incident*. La Porte, TX: Geo Graphics, 1998.

Scott, Irena. "A Photograph and its aftermath" *International UFO Reporter* (September/October, 1990): 12-14.

___."Additional Information Wright-Patterson AFB (WPAFB)." *Ohio UFO Notebook* (January, 1994): 23-24.

___. "Bedroom Light" *International UFO Reporter* (March/April, 1988): 14-15.

___. "CIA, UFO Photography and Tunnels." *Ohio UFO Notebook* (July, 1993): 34-40.

___. "Crisman, Military Intelligence and Roswell." *Ohio UFO Notebook* (May, 1992): 27-32.

___. "Description of an Aerial Anomaly Viewed over Columbus, Ohio." *Ohio Journal of Science* 88.2 (1988): 23.

___. "Examination of Social and Environmental Factors in Relation to Unidentified Aerial Phenomena." In *American Association for the Advancement of Science Abstracts of Papers 153rd National Meeting* (Chicago, IL, February 14-18, 1987): 93.

___. "Fear and ambiguity in Massachusetts" *International UFO Reporter* (July/August, 1988): 14-17.

___. "Informants." *Ohio UFO Notebook* (January, 1994): 24.

___. "Interview with Budd Hopkins." *Ohio UFO Notebook* (January, 1994): 23.

___. "Interview with an Informant." *Ohio UFO Notebook* (July, 1993): 19-23.

___. "Investigation of a Sound Heard over a Wide Area." *Ohio Journal of Science* 87.2 (1987): 11.

___. "Is MORA under Surveillance?" *Ohio UFO Notebook* (July, 1993): 32-34.

___. "More Cattle Mutilation Information." *Ohio UFO Notebook* (January, 1994): 35.

___. "Observation of an Alien Figure." *International UFO Reporter* (January/February, 1987): 20-25.

___. "Ohio UFOlogists." *Ohio UFO Notebook* (January, 1994): 27.

___. *Ohio UFOs (and Many Others)*. Columbus, OH: Greyden Press, 1997.

___. "Ohioans in Aerospace Exploration." *Ohio UFO Notebook* (January, 1994): 31.

___. "Photogrammetric Analysis of a Photograph of an Aerial Anomaly." In *American Association for the Advancement of Science Abstracts of Papers 154th National Meeting* (Boston, MA, February 11-15, 1988): 86.

___. "A Power Failure." *Ohio UFO Notebook* (January, 1994): 34.

___. "Rectangular UFOs." *Ohio UFO Notebook* 12 (1996): 14-18.

___. "Scientists should look closely at the Big Bang, 1973's great wave of UFOs," *MUFON UFO Journal* (March, 2011): 6-7.

___. "SR-71 explanation for the Big Bang of 1973 poses some thorny problems," *MUFON UFO Journal* (May, 2011): 8-9.

___. "Survey of Unidentified Aerial Phenomenon Reports in Delaware County, Ohio." *Ohio Journal of Science* 87.1 (1987): 24-26.

___. "The Ohio UFO Crash Connection and Other Stories." *Ohio UFO Notebook* (Summer, 1994): 19-20.

___. "Tracking Traces." *MUFON UFO Journal* (September, 1991): 8-9.

___. "UFO Activity over Ohio." *MUFON UFO Journal* (May, 1986): 4-5.

___. "UFO Reports from the North Columbus Area, Report 1." *Ohio UFO Notebook* (July, 1993): 24.

___. "UFO Reports from the North Columbus Area, Report 2." *Ohio UFO Notebook* (July, 1993): 24-25.

___. *UFOs and the Millennium.* Columbus, OH: Greyden Press, 1999.

___. *UFOs Today: 70 Years of Lies, Misinformation and Government Cover-up,* UK: Flying Disk Press, 2017.

___. "Wright Patterson Air Force Base." *Ohio UFO Notebook* 6 and 7 (July, 1993): 35-40.

Scott, Irena and William Jones. "Aircraft Missing, South Dakota, Summer 1957." *Ohio UFO Notebook* 13 (1997): 10-11.

___. "Bruce Ashcroft." *Ohio UFO Notebook* 10 (1995): 2-4.

___. "The Ohio UFO Crash Connection and Other Stories." *Ohio UFO Notebook* (Summer, 1994): 19-20.

___. "An Original Crash Story Remembered." *Ohio UFO Notebook* 9 (1995): 1-6.

___. "Roswell, the B-29 and the FUGO Balloons." *Ohio UFO Notebook* 6 and 7 (July, 1993): 30.

___. "Telephone Conversation with Len Stringfield." *Ohio UFO Notebook* (Summer, 1994): 31.

___. "UFO Sighted over Missile Base in Southern Indiana." *MUFON UFO Journal* (December, 1999): 10-11

___. "Wright-Patterson Air Force Base Historian Investigates the Roswell, New Mexico Flying Saucer Crash Story." *Ohio UFO Notebook* 9 (1995): 1-3.

Shawcross, Tim. *The Roswell Files.* Osceola, FL: Motorbooks International, 1997.

Sider, Jean. "Results and Reasons for the Roswell Crash." *Ohio UFO Notebook* (1995): 7-11.

Sider, Jean and Irena Scott. "French Flap Goes Largely Unnoticed." *MUFON UFO Journal* (May, 1992): 6-7.

___. "Roswell and Its Possible Consequences on American Policy." *MUFON UFO Journal* (December, 1992): 10-11.

Simmons, C. W., C.T. Greenidge, C.M. Craighead and others. "Second Progress Report Covering the Period September 1 to October 21, 1949 on Research and Development on Titanium Alloys Contract No. 33 (038)-3736." Columbus, OH: Battelle Memorial Institute, 1949.

Story, Ronald D. *The Encyclopedia of UFOs*. Garden City, NY: Doubleday, 1980.

Stringfield, Leonard H. *Situation Red. The UFO Siege!* Garden City, NY: Doubleday, 1977.

Swords, Michael D. "The Portage County (Ravenna), Ohio, Police Car Chase, April 17, 1966." Historical Document Series No. 4. Chicago: The J. Allen Hynek Center for UFO Studies, October, 1992.

___. Swords, Michael D. "Project Sign and the Estimate of the Situation," *Journal of UFO Studies, New Series*, Vol. 7, (2000): 27-64.

Tester, Joseph. "Efidence shows SR-71 Blackbird may have caused the Big Bang of 1973." *MUFON UFO Journal* (April, 2011): 4-5.

"Technical Report No. F-TR-2274-IA Unidentified Aerial Objects Project 'Sign' AMC Wright-Patterson Air Force Base. (B1 UFO 1947)." Wright-Patterson Air Force Base, OH: Air Mobility Command, 1947.

UFO Cover-Up?: Live! By Barry Taff and Tracy Tormé. Dir. Martin Pasetta. Host Mick Farrell. LBS and Seligman Productions. KTLA, Los Angeles. October 14, 1988.

"UFOs A to Z: Cooke, Charles, Lt. Col." *UFOS at Close Sight*. November 17, 2010. <http://wiki.razing.net/ufologie.net/htm/c.htm#cooke>.

Vallée, Jacques. *Forbidden Science*. Berkeley, CA: North Atlantic Books, 1992.

Von Keviczky, Colman. "The 1973 UFO Invasion, Parts I-IV." *Official UFO* (Collector's Edition) Fall, 1976: 10-20.

Webb, Walter, *Encounter at Buff Ledge*, Chicago, Il: CUFOS, 1994.

Weitzel, William B. "The Portage County Sighting." *National Investigations Committee on Aerial Phenomena (NICAP) Report*. Washington, DC: NICAP, April 8, 1967.

Zeidman, Jennie. *Helicopter-UFO Encounter over Ohio*. Evanston, IL: Center for UFO Studies, 1979.

WPAFB. "National Air And Space Intelligence Center History." http://www.wpafb.af.mil/library/factsheets/factsheet.asp?id=21928

___. "I Remember Blue Book." *International UFO Reporter* (March/April, 1991): 7-23.

___. "Internal Lighting." *International UFO Reporter* (July/August, 1988): 21.

___. "Investigating UFOs—Lessons from a Teacher and Mentor." *Ohio UFO Notebook* 21 (Summer, 2000): 1-7.

___. "J. Allen Hynek—A 'Rocket Man.'" *Ohio UFO Notebook* (Summer, 1999): 2-5.

******

NOTES

[1] http://www.bigear.org/guide.htm

[2] https://www.huffingtonpost.com/dan-mack/astronomers-ufo_b_1901480.html

[3] Randles, Jenny. *Star Children: The True Story Of Alien Offspring Among Us*. New York: Sterling Publishing Co., Inc., 1995.

[4] Hopkins, Budd. *Intruders: The Incredible Visitations at Copley Woods*. New York: Random House, 1987.

[5] Hynek's credentials as a scientist are impeccable. He received his Ph.D. in astrophysics from Yerkes Observatory. As an astronomer with the Smithsonian Astrophysical Observatory, he was responsible for tracking the earth's first artificial satellite, Sputnik. At Ohio State University, he was Professor of Astronomy, Director of McMillin Observatory and Assistant Dean of the Graduate School. At Johns Hopkins Applied Physics Laboratory, he helped to develop the US Navy's radio proximity fuse.

He was Chairman of the Northwestern University Astronomy Department, Director of its Lindheimer Astronomical Research Center and Visiting Lecturer at Harvard University. He conducted pioneering work on image orthicon astronomy, which the National Science Foundation proposed as the most significant astronomical advance since photography and on rocket research for such projects as the V-2, where he was considered one of the nation's leading rocket researchers.

As an author, he wrote an astronomy textbook and his articles appeared in numerous periodicals, including an astronomy column for *Science Digest* and a column called "Scanning the Skies" for the *Columbus Dispatch*. He is also a top UFOlogist. He wrote five enormously successful books and many articles published in popular magazines. He went against the establishment and founded the Center for UFO Studies (CUFOS). In his *The UFO Experience: A Scientific Inquiry*, he famously presented three classes of "close encounters." Director Stephen Spielberg used *Close Encounters of the Third Kind* as the title of his film about UFOs. was involved in all aspects of UFO study and was scientific adviser to UFO studies undertaken by the U.S. Air Force under three consecutive names: Project Sign (1947-1949), Project Grudge (1949-1952) and Project Blue Book (1952-1969). He worked on these projects at Battelle, WPAFB and Ohio State University. He founded the concept of scientific analysis of UFO evidence.

[6] Scott, Irena. *UFOs Today: 70 Years of Lies, Misinformation and Government Cover-up*, UK: Flying Disk Press, 2017.

[7] "Survey of Unidentified Aerial Phenomenon Reports in Delaware County, Ohio." *Ohio Journal of Science* 87.1 (1987): 24-26.

[8] Bajak, Ivan "A Discussion On A Physical Model Of Ball Lightning And UFO," *International Journal of Scientific & Technology Research*.Vol.6: No. 7 (2017). "It is proposed that the ball lightning and UFO are analogous objects....It is proposed on a uniform basis using a hypothesis that the ball lightning and UFO are created like a spherical capacitor filled by polar molecules mainly and in some cases by various chemicals which influence the final manifest of the object....A peculiar behavior like e.g. sudden change of direction of motion shape of disc and possible penetration through wall is explained as a consequence of internal structure of the object.

[9] Klass, Philip J. (1968). UFOs—Identified. Random House. ISBN 9780394450032. OCLC 1200561.

[10] https://en.wikipedia.org/wiki/Ball_lightning

[11] https://www.sciencedirect.com/science/article/pii/037015739390121S

[12] https://physics.aps.org/articles/v7/5

[13] Oreshko, A. G. "An investigation of the generation and properties of laboratory-produced ball lightning." *J. Plasma Physics*: Cambridge University Press 2015 (https://www.researchgate.net/profile/Alexander_Oreshko/publication/276912866_An_investigation_of_the_generation_and_properties_of_laboratory-produced_ball_lightning/links/57148f1008aeebe07c06462a/An-investigation-of-the-generation-and-properties-of-laboratory-produced-ball-lightning.pdf).

[14] Wu, H. "Relativistic-microwave theory of ball lightning," (https://www.ncbi.nlm.nih.gov/pmc/articles/PMC4916449/).

[15] Newman Steve, Earthweek: A diary of the planet, Antimatter bolt," the *Columbus Dispatch*, December 3, 2017, A 20.

[16] http://theconversation.com/ball-lightning-exists-but-what-on-earth-is-it-10419

[17] http://rspa.royalsocietypublishing.org/content/467/2129/1427

[18] https://en.wikipedia.org/wiki/Ball_lightning

[19] Devereux, Paul, Earth Lights Revelation, Blandford Press, UK, 1989, 15.(http://mysteriousuniverse.org/2014/11/strange-electromagnetic-dimensions-the-science-of-the-unexplainable-2/

[20] https://youtu.be/2MWhAUo9lJQ

[21] https://electronics.stackexchange.com/questions/15597/why-do-smoke-detectors-go-off-when-lightning-strikes

[22] https://www.doityourself.com/forum/electrical-ac-dc/496780-strange-smoke-detector-problem.html

[23] https://www.thoughtco.com/the-mystery-of-ball-lightning-2596519.

[24] http://www.paulaurand.com/near-death-experience/

[25] https://www.accuweather.com/en/weather-news/what-happens-when-the-body-is-struck-by-lightning/70002047.

[26] https://www.npr.org/sections/krulwich/2012/07/16/156851175/five-men-agree-to-stand-directly-under-an-exploding-nuclear-bomb

[27] A paper in *Physical Review Letters* described Ball lightning as observed with two slitless spectrographs at a distance of 0.9 km. This spectral analysis indicates that the radiation from soil elements is present for the entire lifetime of the ball lightning, which indicated that this one certainly was made of dirt and thus debris from the strike, but not the nature of ball lightning. In our case, it appeared that the whiteout was instantaneous and not debris. (https://journals.aps.org/prl/abstract/10.1103/PhysRevLett.112.035001) (https://physics.aps.org/articles/v7/5)

[28] http://www.astronomycafe.net/weird/lights/marfa13.htm

[29] http://www.pauldevereux.co.uk/v5/html/body_earthlights.html

[30] shttps://books.google.com/books?id=YdxEDwAAQBAJ&pg=PT200&lpg=PT200&dq=%22Marfa,+Texas%22+%22earthquake%22&source=bl&ots=VykGCzr1UH&sig=yrw4A8FgdK2pD8kUCrWlAyDNycY&hl=en&sa=X&ved=0ahUKEwjljuid2cHZAhVN2VMKHW5tCJsQ6AEISDAE#v=onepage&q=%22Marfa%2C%20Texas%22%20%22earthquake%22&f=falses

[31] Irena Scott e-mail from Dottie Schaaf March 15, 2018.

[32] Irena Scott, e-mail from Dottie Schaaf, March 15, 2018.

[33] Fully adjustable c. 1930's factory green enameled antique American industrial bench top factory task lamp with goose neck arm and rolled rim parabolic steel shade, https://www.urbanremainschicago.com/products/lighting/vintage-table-lamps.html

[34] https://weather.com/news/news/ball-lightning-seen-first-time-20140120.

[35] http://amasci.com/weird/unusual/bl.html and https://search.aps.org/?collection=aps&q=lightning&x=0&y=0

[36] http://amasci.com/weird/unusual/bl.html

[37] Joel K <kllgg2 a cs com>va USA - Thursday, February 08, 2001 at 02:40:27 (PST)

[38] https://arxiv.org/pdf/0708.4064.pdf

[39] https://arxiv.org/pdf/0708.4064.pdf

[40] https://news.nationalgeographic.com/news/2006/05/060531-ball-lightning_2.html

[41] https://www.scientificamerican.com/article/periodically-i-hear-stori/

[42] Scott, Irena. Bedroom Light" *International UFO Reporter* (March/April, 1988): 14-15

[43] Stenhoff, Mark. Ball Lightning: An Unsolved Problem in Atmospheric Physics (Berlin/Heidelberg, Germany: Springer Science & Business Media, 1999). https://books.google.com/books?id=f5wSBwAAQBAJ&pg=PA294&lpg=PA294&dq=A.I.+%22Grigoriev%22,+%22Statistical+Analysis+of+the+Ball+Lightning+Properties%22+in+Science+of+Ball+Lightning&source=bl&ots=yUHjxAu5Xm&sig=cIAHsRB6n45gEDfjubwpxdQQ5-Q&hl=en&sa=X&ved=0ahUKEwjI17KVuYfYAhXFE7wKHTTIA5kQ6AEINDAC#v=snippet&q=lifetime&f=false

[44] Randles, Jenny. *Star Children: The True Story Of Alien Offspring Among Us*. New York: Sterling Publishing Co., Inc., 1995.

[45] Irena Scott, e-mail from David Amacher March 15, 2018.

[46] Randles, Jenny. *Star Children: The True Story Of Alien Offspring Among Us*. New York: Sterling Publishing Co., Inc., 1995.

[47] Fowler, Raymond. *The Andreasson Affair: The Documented Investigation of a Woman's Abduction Aboard a Ufo.* (Wild Flower Pr. (September 1, 1994) and similar publications.

[48] http://www.ufodigest.com/news/0107/andresasson.html

[49] I have also been somewhat nervous about sleeping with electrical appliances by my bed, but do not know why this would be. I used to be unable to stand medical examinations and would fight back by reflex even though I did not want to, have trouble swallowing and even now cannot look at enlarged views of eyes–I still have to look away.

[50] Ball Lightning: An Unsolved Problem in Atmospheric Physics (Germany: Berlin/Heidelberg, 1999): 20.

[51] https://www.scientificamerican.com/article/periodically-i-hear-stori/

[52] https://www.ncbi.nlm.nih.gov/pmc/articles/PMC4916449/

[53] http://www.phschool.com/science/science_news/articles/anatomy_of_lightning.html

[54] Wu, H.-C. Relativistic-microwave theory of ball lightning. *Sci. Rep.* **6**, 28263; doi: 10.1038/srep28263 (2016).

[55] https://www.ncbi.nlm.nih.gov/pmc/articles/PMC4916449/

[56] Fowler, Raymond. *The Andreasson Affair: The Documented Investigation of a Woman's Abduction Aboard a Ufo.*

(Wild Flower Pr. (September 1, 1994).

[57] "Photogrammetric Analysis of a Photograph of an Aerial Anomaly," in *American Association for the Advancement of Science Abstracts of Papers 154th National Meeting*. Boston, February, 1988.

[58] Scott, Irena. "Fear and ambiguity in Massachusetts" *International UFO Reporter* (July/August, 1988): 14-17

[59] Scott, Irena. "A Photograph and its aftermath" *International UFO Reporter* (September/October, 1990): 12-14.

[60] http://www.ufo-hunters.com/sightings/search/553ce932ee28c4778c9df15d/UFO%20Sighting%20in%20Boston,%20Massachusetts%20(United%20States)%20on%20Saturday%2013%20July%201968

[61] Scott, Irena. Message from Deb White Kauble on November 19, 2017.

[62] Hopkins, Budd. *Intruders: The Incredible Visitations at Copley Woods*. New York: Random House, 1987.

[63] ___. *Missing Time*. New York: Berkley, 1983.

[64] https://allaboutnan.wordpress.com/2013/03/06/i-know-all-about-st-elmos-fire/

[65] https://www.sciencefacts.net/st-elmos-fire.html

[66] http://rspa.royalsocietypublishing.org/content/467/2129/1427

[67] Baumjohann, Wolfgang and Rudolf A Treumann. *Basic Space Plasma Physics. World Scientific Publishing Company*, Singapore. 2012. (https://books.google.com/books?id=Ss42DwAAQBAJ&pg=PA87&lpg=PA87&dq=green+aurora+owing+to+557.7%E2%80%89nm+emission+from+metastable+neutral+oxygen&source=bl&ots=RdqjreAkEh&sig=shmsEODUpIIxc54G6VtN7xb0eqE&hl=en&sa=X&ved=0ahUKEwj1zvvZ_4zZAhXNwFMKHf7aA8MQ6AEIOjAD#v=onepage&q=green%20aurora%20owing%20to%20557.7%E2%80%89nm%20emission%20from%20metastable%20neutral%20oxygen&f=false).

[68] https://books.google.com/books?id=CYE_AAAAQBAJ&pg=PA530&lpg=PA530&dq=can+you+send+a+beam+to+excite+electrons&source=bl&ots=vP3zHEDJjn&sig=56bWGghevcXV6LBTiZ-BbNAGX6k&hl=en&sa=X&ved=0ahUKEwij85S1i43ZAhVWwWMKHX3-CSIQ6AEISDAF#v=onepage&q=can%20you%20send%20a%20beam%20to%20excite%20electrons&f=false

[69] http://www.webexhibits.org/causesofcolor/4D.html.

[70] http://www.ufo-hunters.com/sightings/search/553ce932ee28c4778c9df15d/UFO%20Sighting%20in%20Boston,%20Massachusetts%20(United%20States)%20on%20Saturday%2013%20July%201968

[71] Zeidman, Jennie. *Helicopter-UFO Encounter over Ohio*. Evanston, IL: Center for UFO Studies, 1979.

[72] Webb, Walter, *Encounter at Buff Ledge*, Chicago, Il: CUFOS, 1994.

[73] https://www.google.com/search?num=100&safe=active&ei=iYoLWoazMouz8QWq56a4CQ&q=distance+between+madison+nj+and+boston+ma&oq=distance+between+madison+nj+and+boston+ma&gs_l=psy-ab.3..33i160k1l2.22167.25462.0.25853.9.9.0.0.0.0.116.850.6j3.9.0....0...1.1.64.psy-ab..0.9.849...33i22i29i30k1.0.pIHInrYR3ho

[74] https://en.wikipedia.org/wiki/Budd_Hopkins

[75] http://apmagazine.info/index.php?option=com_content&view=article&id=731&Itemid=194

[76] Scott, Irena and Phyllis Budinger. *MUFON of Ohio Newsletter*, "Uncommon Commonalities: A Personal Experience Comparison to Buff Ledge and Other Events," July, 2016, p. 6-9.

[77] Webb, Walter, *Encounter at Buff Ledge*, Chicago, Il: CUFOS, 1994.

[78] http://www.ufoevidence.org/cases/case548.htm)

[79] E-mails from Kathlene Marden to Irena Scott from January 21, 2014 to the present.

[80] Scott, Irena, Message from Betty Andreasson Luca on November 11, 2017.

[81] http://www.ufodigest.com/news/0107/andreasson.html

[82] https://www.bibliotecapleyades.net/vida_alien/alien_andreasson.htm#The Trigger of Alien Abduction

[83] https://www.bibliotecapleyades.net/vida_alien/alien_andreasson.htm

[84] E-mails from Kathlene Marden to Irena Scott from January 21, 2014 to the present.

[85] https://www.defensenews.com/air/2017/11/07/coming-in-2021-a-laser-weapon-for-fighter-jets/

[86] Scott, Irena, UFOs Today: 70 Years of Lies, Misinformation and Government Cover-up (UK: Flying Disc Press

[87] http://www.thedailybeast.com/articles/2015/08/12/the-spy-satellite-secrets-in-hillary-s-emails.html

[88] I recall seeing at least three pictures—probably two pictures from one mission and one from another.

[89] https://www.cia.gov/library/readingroom/document/cia-rdp79b00752a000300100005-0

[90] "Description of an Aerial Anomaly Viewed over Columbus, Ohio." *Ohio Journal of Science* 88.2 (1988): 23. (https://kb.osu.edu/dspace/bitstream/handle/1811/23248/V088N2_001.pdf?sequence=1).

[91] Scott, Irena. "UFO activity over Ohio" *MUFON UFO JR* May 1986

[92] Scott, Irena., "UFO-Poltergeist Connection." FATE 38 (April 1985):114-15. (in http://www.cufos.org/books/Ufos_And_The_Extraterrestrial_Contact_Movement_v1.pdf)

[93] Scott, Irena, "An Improbable Airport Sighting Could this be mind control?," *MUFON of Ohio Newsletter*, October 2016, p. 10–12

[94] http://www.wunderground.com/history/airport/KCMH/1984/2/23/DailyHistory.html?MR=1

[95] http://www.wral.com/what-does-a-nw-wind-mean-/1986859/

[96] http://www.cufon.org/cufon/pentacle.htm

[97] A letter from Dr. Rutledge to Irena Scott, June 17, 1986.

[98] Anonymous, *Delaware Gazette* "Flying object seen in Galena." August, 08,1984, pg. 2.

[99] Scott, Irena. *Ohio Journal of Science* ,Vol. 87. No 1. 1987

[100] Scott, Irena. "Tracking Traces." *MUFON UFO Journal* (September, 1991): 8-9.

[101] http://www.ufocasebook.com/copelywoods.html

[102] http://channel.nationalgeographic.com/chasing-ufos/articles/five-good-reasons-to-believe-in-ufos/

[103] https://en.wikipedia.org/wiki/Lonnie_Zamora_incident

[104] https://www.newscientist.com/article/dn11443-france-opens-up-its-ufo-files/

[105] http://www.theblackvault.com/casefiles/bright-red-white-flying-flashing-objects-lewis-center-ohio-november-4-2016/

[106] Burrell, Paul, Delbert Anderson, William E. Jones and Irena Scott. "Dancing Red Lights, Logan, Ohio, October/November, 1995." MUFON of Ohio Newsletter (November, 2009): 4-5.

[107] On Nov 2, 2017, at 9:27 PM, from <EtheMage@SBCGlobal.net> wrote

[108] A letter from Dr. Rutledge to Irena Scott, June 17, 1986.

[109] Rutledge, Harley D. *Project Identification: The First Scientific Field Study of UFO Phenomena.* Englewood Cliffs, NJ: Prentice-Hall, 1981.

[110] http://www.pbs.org/wgbh/nova/next/physics/interacting-dark-matter/

[111] https://www.quora.com/Why-are-most-forms-of-energy-invisible-to-the-naked-eyes-while-we-can-see-heat-as-fire-for-example-What-make-some-forms-seen-and-other-not

[112] https://iainthegreat.wordpress.com/page/15/?pages-list

[113] https://www.zillow.com/homedetails/9650-Copley-Dr-Indianapolis-IN-46290/73239967_zpid/

[114] https://www.newspapers.com/newspage/159579678/

[115] Scott, Irena. "Investigation of a Sound Heard over a Wide Area." *Ohio Journal of Science* 87.2 (1987): 11. (https://kb.osu.edu/dspace/bitstream/handle/1811/23189/V087N2_001.pdf?sequence=1).

[116] Scott, Irena. "Scientists should look closely at the Big Bang, 1973's great wave of UFOs," *MUFON UFO Journal* (March, 2011): 6-7.

[117] Tester, Joseph. "Evidence shows SR-71 Blackbird may have caused the Big Bang of 1973." *MUFON UFO Journal* (April, 2011): 4-5.

[118] Scott, Irena. "SR-71 explanation for the Big Bang of 1973 poses some thorny problems," *MUFON UFO Journal* (May, 2011): 8-9.

[119] A letter from Dr. Rutledge to Irena Scott, June 17, 1986.

[120] Rutledge, Harley D. *Project Identification: The First Scientific Field Study of UFO Phenomena.* Englewood Cliffs, NJ: Prentice-Hall, 1981.

[121] A letter from Dr. Rutledge to Irena Scott, June 17, 1986.

[122] A letter from Dr. Rutledge to Irena Scott, June 17, 1986.

[123] http://www.morethanpassingstrange.com/beyond-the-abduction-experience-an-interview-with-kathleen-marden/

[124] Strieber, Whitley. *Communion: A True Story* (New York: William Morrow, 1987. 299pp).

[125] http://www.paukradio.com/strange-sounds-captured-during-whitley-strieber-interview/

[126] https://askabiologist.asu.edu/zombie-ants

[127] http://mysteriousuniverse.org/2016/08/a-brief-look-at-the-life-and-ideas-of-john-a-keel-part-two/

[128] https://www.bibliotecapleyades.net/vida_alien/alien_andreasson.htm

[129] http://www.bigear.org/guide.htm

[130] https://www.amazon.com/Out-Darkness-Planet-Clyde-Tombaugh/dp/0451619978

[131] http://www.ufosightingsdaily.com/2015/07/lets-celebrate-clyde-tombaugh-who.html

[132] http://www.ufosightingsdaily.com/2011/02/

[133] http://www.bibliotecapleyades.net/ciencia/ufo_briefingdocument/quosci.htm

[134] https://www.huffingtonpost.com/dan-mack/astronomers-ufo_b_1901480.html

[135] A letter from Dr. Rutledge to Irena Scott, June 17, 1986.

[136] A letter from Dr. Rutledge to Irena Scott, June 17, 1986.

[137] https://support.microsoft.com/en-us/help/13456/hololens-and-holograms-faq

[138] Smalley, D. E. et al., A photophoretic-trap volumetric display. *Nature* V 553: 486–490 (25 January 2018) and https://www.theengineer.co.uk/volumetric-display-3d-images/.

[139] G. Breit and J. A. Wheeler, Phys. Rev. 46, 1087 (1934).

[140] https://www.theatlantic.com/technology/archive/2014/05/how-to-create-matter-from-light/371155/

[141] Maccabee, Bruce, *Historical Introduction to Project Blue Book Special Report #14* (J.Allen Hynek Center for UFO Studies, 1994)

[142] Maccabee, who is listed in *Who's Who in Technology Today* and in *American Men and Women of Science*, has worked on optical data processing, lasers and the Ballistic Missile Defense (BMD).

[143] This information comes from a list of Project Blue Book UFOs that have never been identified. Don Berliner of the Fund for UFO Research posted this list on the Internet for UFO research.

[144] https://www.space.com/15353-meteor-showers-facts-shooting-stars-skywatching-sdcmp.html

[145] https://courses.lumenlearning.com/suny-astronomy/chapter/meteorites-stones-from-heaven/

[146] https://books.google.com/books?id=PmuqCHDC3pwC&pg=PA811&lpg=PA811&dq=why+do+%22lightning+balls%22+%22float%22&source=bl&ots=odGDbeYvUg&sig=0i112RchKG_eZzmHYHr0OmTpKFY&hl=en&sa=X&ved=0ahUKEwiRjr3hjNrYAhVPt1MKHU1cDC8Q6AEIUTAH#v=onepage&q=why%20do%20%22lightning%20balls%22%20%22float%22&f=false (History of Shock Waves, Explosions and Impact: A Chronological By Peter O. K. Krehl

[147] http://uforeview.tripod.com/conspiracyjournal816.html

[148] https://www.huffingtonpost.com/dan-mack/astronomers-ufo_b_1901480.html

[149] https://www.huffingtonpost.com/dan-mack/astronomers-ufo_b_1901480.html

[150] Scott, Irena. "Examination of Social and Environmental Factors in Relation to Unidentified Aerial Phenomena." In *American Association for the Advancement of Science Abstracts of Papers* 153rd National Meeting (Chicago, IL, February 14-18, 1987): 93.

[151] http://www.openminds.tv/update-on-former-deputy-sheriffs-roswell-ufo-sighting-claims/41082.

[152] https://www.popsci.com/article/science/how-prove-light-can-be-converted-matter.

[153] https://www.huffingtonpost.com/2013/10/18/ufo-nearcollision-with-army-helicopter-40-years-ago_n_4119987.html

[154] https://www.huffingtonpost.com/2013/10/18/ufo-nearcollision-with-army-helicopter-40-years-ago_n_4119987.html

[155] Zeidman, Jennie. *Helicopter-UFO Encounter over Ohio*. Evanston, IL: Center for UFO Studies, 1979.

[156] Webb, Walter, *Encounter at Buff Ledge*, Chicago, Il: CUFOS, 1994.

[157] http://www.iflscience.com/physics/physicists-develop-reversible-laser-tractor-beam-functional-over-long-distances/

[158] https://www.newscientist.com/article/dn22406-tractor-beam-built-from-rings-of-laser-light/

[159] http://www.ufodigest.com/news/0107/andreasson.html

[160] http://www.ufodigest.com/news/0107/andreasson.html

[161] Newton Bateman, Paul Selby and H. C. Bell, *Historical Encyclopedia of Illinois and History of Clark County*

(Chicago: Middle West Publishing Company, 1907), 771.

[162] *History of Delaware County and Ohio* (Chicago: O. L. Baskin & Co., 1880), 195.

[163] Scott Hagan, "The Barn Artist," http://barnartist.com/about-the-barn-artist/

[164] Beth Gorczyca and B. Miller (photographer), *Ohio's Bicentennial Barns, A collection of the Historic Barns Celebrating Ohio's Bicentennial* (Wooster, Ohio: The Wooster Book Company, 2003).s

[165] James Usher, *History of the Lawrence-Townley and Chase-Townley estates in England: With copious historical and genealogical notes of the Lawrence-Chase and Townley families and much other valuable information* (New York: James Usher 1883), 32-36, 49-50.

[166] *The Chase Chronicle*, (Haverhill, MA: The Chase-Chace Family Association Chase Press, 1910).

[167] Frank Alden Hill, *The Mystery Solved* (Boston: Rand Avery Company, 1888).

[168] *Memorial Record of the Counties of Delaware, Union and Morrow, Ohio* (Chicago: The Lewis Publishing Company, 1895).

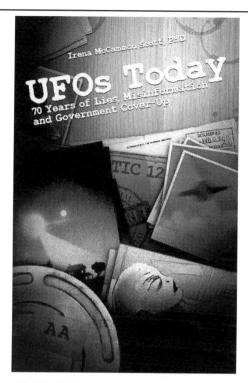

ALSO FROM IRENA SCOTT PhD

Available on Amazon

MORE BOOKS FROM FLYING DISK PRESS

http://flyingdiskpress.blogspot.co.uk/

UFO MEMORABILIA AND T-SHIRTS

Printed in Great Britain
by Amazon